SEE!
HEAR!
CUT!
KILL!

SEE! HEAR! CUT! KILL!

EXPERIENCING FRIDAY THE 13TH

Wickham Clayton

University Press of Mississippi / Jackson

The University Press of Mississippi is the scholarly publishing agency of
the Mississippi Institutions of Higher Learning: Alcorn State University,
Delta State University, Jackson State University, Mississippi State University,
Mississippi University for Women, Mississippi Valley State University,
University of Mississippi, and University of Southern Mississippi.

www.upress.state.ms.us

The University Press of Mississippi is a member
of the Association of University Presses.

Copyright © 2020 by Wickham Clayton
All rights reserved

First printing 2020
∞

Library of Congress Control Number: 2020944301
Hardback: 978-1-4968-3031-9
Trade Paperback: 978-1-4968-3032-6
Epub Single: 978-1-4968-3033-3
Epub Insitutional: 978-1-4968-3030-2
PDF Single: 978-1-4968-3034-0
PDF Institutional: 978-1-4968-3035-7

British Library Cataloging-in-Publication Data available

I dedicate this to my son George,
who continues to terrify me,
despite being younger
than the research
in this book.

Contents

Preface: This book could be for you, depending on how you read it ix

Acknowledgments xiii

Chapter 1   Meet Jason Voorhees: An Autopsy 3

Chapter 2   Jason's Mechanical Eye... 45

Chapter 3   Hearing Cutting 83

Chapter 4   Have You Met Jason? 119

Chapter 5   The Importance of Being Jason 153

Appendix 1   Plot Summaries for the *Friday the 13th* Films 179

Appendix 2   List and Description of Characters in the *Friday the 13th* Films............ 185

Works Cited 199

Index 217

Preface

This book could be for you, depending on how you read it

Happy fortieth anniversary! On May 9, 1980, the first *Friday the 13th* film premiered in cinemas to rather surprising success. This purely profit-driven, moneymaking enterprise manifested into a franchise still viewed and loved by a significant fan base, and remains relevant in popular culture.

This book, though, was not written as a crude effort to capitalize on this particular anniversary (but I won't complain if it is successful). I began research on this in 2007, in preparation for writing my PhD thesis. At that point, I was a decade-long fan of the films, and I really wanted to continue my academic career by focusing on the series intensively.

This book began with that thesis. After thirteen years of researching, writing, reworking, and revising, I present to you all of this in its final form. While I will continue to study and write about the *Friday the 13th* films, I will be sorry to see the end of this particular project as it means a lot to me.

The original thesis, entitled "Bearing Witness to a Whole Bunch of Murders: The Aesthetics of Perspective in the *Friday the 13th* Films," is available online. However, theses often end up deeply focused and jargoned. The editors and reviewers at the University Press of Mississippi were generous and encouraging enough to suggest that a wider audience than the academic research community (which I do have a great fondness for) might be interested in this material too. What you are reading is the result of a few years' work to make this particular project more readable and accessible, while still useful to the academic community.

On the surface, this book might sound like a list of descriptions of scenes and sequences, but these descriptions help support an understanding of how the style of these films work to provide us with story information and how the elements of style develop over time. This is also a very ground-level, straightforward form of analysis (one which a particular friend of mine finds very annoying), but it is the sort of analysis from which more complex forms of critique can build. However, I would like to take a moment here at the start to advise readers about the best ways of approaching what I've written, based on the level of your approach or preferred engagement.

For general, casual, and fan readers—welcome! I hope I have made this as accessible and readable as possible for you. While you may find some of the points a bit labored and over-described or -supported, you will hopefully see that there is enough evidence to back up my discussion. Furthermore, I have tried to write a book that gives you the pleasure of revisiting these films in detail, and possibly even give you some close insight into movies that have been traditionally considered trashy. I'm arguing in this book that the small details reveal why we love these movies, while most other writers tend to just look at the "big picture." Perhaps you can even use some of these points to defend them to your friends. Furthermore, in my career I have been very keen on showing the general public the kind of work that film studies academics *actually do*. And I hope you find it as fun as I do in some ways. At the very least, I have tried to define key words and ideas, provide a useful history, and address some of the central discussions around these movies. Hopefully this will give you a handle on the jargon and concepts we use in the field.

If you're an **undergraduate or an early film studies student**, there's useful material here for you, too. Pay particular attention in chapter 1, where I outline a history of the way first-person camera has appeared in film going back to the early days of primitive shorts. While this history focuses on movies within the orbit of horror, it can still give you an idea of the way a simple filmic device is seeded in the early days of film language and grows into a common trope we see today. You will also discover some of the work that is going on in academia around how we think about sound, editing, and sequels. Furthermore, as with general readers, I have defined key terms for you throughout, referenced a number of useful significant research sources and theorists, and provided a strong example of how formalist analysis works. While David Bordwell and Kristin Thompson have explained (neo)formalism to undergraduates far better than I ever could, this can be a useful supplement to their work, and you can see how these ideas can apply to examples within a specific popular genre.

Preface   xi

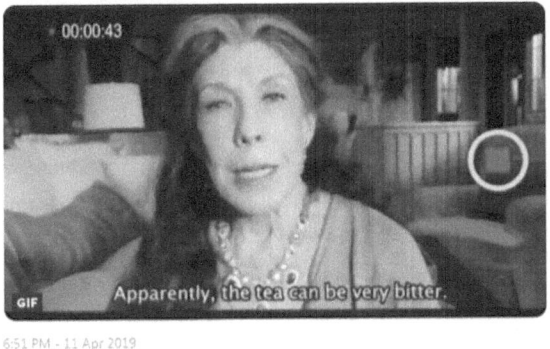

Figure 0.1. Twitter post by Daniel Sheppard, featuring Lily Tomlin from *Grace and Frankie* (Netflix, 2015–present). (Twitter / Daniel Sheppard, 2019) (Netflix, 2015). Used with the permission of Daniel Sheppard.

And for my original audience, **postgraduate students and professional academic researchers**: the heart and the structure of this book was created with you in mind. While I hope the language and writing is not as dense as much of the material you usually encounter, this is based entirely on a PhD thesis aiming to create an original argument. I have developed concepts and ideas, such as a device I call the "eye/camera," which have subtle, precise distinctions from theoretical concepts and models that exist to date. To make clear the points I wish to make, the book is organized thematically rather than using a more casual chronological overview of the series; there are books that have already taken this approach, so I am going deeper.

This is a researched, evidenced argument on a segment of popular cinema that has important historical implications that has been subjected to very little close observation and analysis. Furthermore, the writing that exists on these films tend to circumvent the close formalist and aesthetic analysis I have done here. I am making an argument for the influential function of, and aesthetic pleasures of, films with an unseemly reputation in academic circles.

I'd like to say, finally, that I know most if not all of these films are socially and politically troubling in some ways—perhaps even in many ways. Gender, race, sexuality, and class are just four areas the *Friday the 13th* films egregiously stumble over, to put it generously. To be less generous, I could say they gleefully uphold biases and power imbalances in society. It is important for all readers to be aware of this, and it is also important to be able to reconcile what you love and why you love it with real issues you may have with its content. That said, Daniel Sheppard, in figure 0.1, has provided a fun account of gay fandom.

It is really okay to love these movies (and games, which I also address) while remaining conscientious. And I wrote this book with a lot of love. I hope this comes across, and I hope you enjoy revisiting all of these movies with me.

Acknowledgments

Without the following people, this book would probably be considerably different, if it would even exist at all.

I would first like to thank Emily Bandy, Craig Gill, Laura Strong, Todd Lape, and the fantastic editorial and production staff at the University Press of Mississippi. Their interest in (and patience with) this project since I proposed it has been deeply appreciated. The anonymous reviewers who gave me extensive feedback on this manuscript only served to make this book more accessible, conscientious, and generally better, and I'd like to say thank you to whoever you may be. I'd also like to thank Peter Tonguette, who was an encouraging and fastidious copy editor: thank you for your time and hard work.

My mentors, Dr. Stacey Abbott, Dr. Michael Chanan, and Dr. Paul Sutton, have all given valuable advice, tireless effort, and extraordinary commitment. They also shared a fair chunk of their knowledge with me, for which I am greatly indebted to them. Thank you to my family, the source of lots of moral (and financial) support. Lots. The Clough family and the Humphreys family also supported me through much of this.

Many thanks to Jaymes Fox, Bethan Jones, and Zalfa Feghali, who have provided valuable editorial comments, encouragement, and support. Jaymes and Zalfa also had the incredible good humor to field late-night panicky texts from me. For various pieces of information and moral support, I would like to thank Todd Berliner, Evan Hayles Gledhill, Kate Egan, Ian Conrich, Johnny Walker, Tom Watson, Laura Mee, Sarah Wharton, Jarkko Toikkanen, Karra

Shimabukuro, Paul Booth, Nick Hall, Emma James, Emma Grylls, Chiara Mestieri, Alex Pearson, Michael Ahmed, and Gareth James. For tireless encouragement from the moment I conceived this idea, through the initial application process, and consistently throughout my research, I'd like to thank Jerry DeMario, Jason Russell, and Joe Ketchum. I would like to thank Brean Cunningham for an incredibly polite email in which he declined, in lieu of Sean S. Cunningham, participating in an interview. If the Cunninghams continue making films, I will harbor no resentment.

I'd like to tip my (green John Deere) hat to Edward Gibbon, who turned 283 this year. *The History of the Decline and Fall of the Roman Empire* (1776–88) taught me the correct way to use footnotes.

Tes and Isaac, though coming into my life near the end of this project, certainly helped give me the final push to rewrite. Thank you very much to them.

There are numerous others to thank, and all of them are wonderful.

Finally, to my son, who has kept my spirits up while I persevered through this project, I owe a lot, and I will probably end up paying back every bit of it.

SEE!
HEAR!
CUT!
KILL!

Chapter 1

Meet Jason Voorhees: An Autopsy

Sometimes the weirdest movies strike you in unexpected ways. In the winter of 1997, I attended a late-night screening of *Friday the 13th* (1980) at the campus theater at James Madison University in Harrisonburg, Virginia. I'd never seen the film before, but I was aware of its cultural significance. I expected a generic slasher film with extensive violence and nudity. I expected something ultimately forgettable. Having watched it seventeen years after its initial release, I found it generic; it did have violence and nudity, and was entertaining. However, I did not find it forgettable. Walking home with the first flecks of a winter snow weaving around me in the dark, I found myself thinking over it. I continually recalled images, sounds, and narrative moments that were vivid in my mind. *Friday the 13th* wormed into my brain, with its haunting and atmospheric style.

After watching the original film several more times, I started in on the sequels, preparing myself for disappointment each time. To my surprise, each one thoroughly entertained me. I watched them all multiple times. As I began studying film four years later, I would frequently admit to liking them with a touch of embarrassment, dismissing them as a guilty pleasure. After taking a class with film theorist Todd Berliner, I began to ask myself why I felt the need to dismiss my enjoyment of them. If I find them entertaining, I thought, there must be a reason why. This stayed with me until I began to consider ideas for a doctoral research project.

Wherefore art thou writing about *Friday the 13th*?

The *Friday the 13th* series found success according to Hollywood's preferred metric: money. However, the bulk of critical and academic writing on the films deride them. I could almost excuse someone who has never seen them for assuming they are meritless. However, we can't ignore how important the series is to the slasher subgenre.

The "slasher" film is a subgenre of horror with a story focusing on the detailed actions of a serial murderer and their victims. Slasher films mostly tell stories of an aggressor, sometimes working in tandem with supernatural forces, stalking and killing victims, and leading to a climactic confrontation with the killer. Plot and character develop in a minimal fashion, with the focus mainly directed toward the final or surviving victim and the killer. Although fear and suspense traditionally characterize horror, slasher films focus mostly on the cause of death, with particular attention to details of bodily mutilation.

I write this book to shine a light on this subgenre, and especially the films in my chosen franchise, with three aims. First, I explore the way in which "perspective" is established and communicated within the *Friday the 13th* films, which is central to the way we experience and respond emotionally to these movies. Second, I outline the way that this perspective is created through the stylistic choices of the filmmakers over time. The style of these films develop and evolve as the series progresses, and this particular series provides us a unique opportunity to explore these changes over a thirty-year period. Finally, I argue that the series doesn't develop all alone. What we see in these films relates to contemporary slasher films and critically successful Hollywood films. What is happening in these films either reflects popular trends of film style or sometimes act as key examples that their generic contemporaries respond to. Such an analysis holds implications for our understanding of film texts outside of the genre as well.

Duck!

Theorist Steven Shaviro writes of the visceral effect of watching cinema: "Images confront the viewer directly, without mediation. What we see is what we see; the figures that unroll before us cannot be regarded merely as arbitrary representations or conventional signs. We respond viscerally to visual forms, before having the leisure to read or interpret them as symbols" (26). Perhaps not many but a fair number of scholars write about horror, and slashers particularly, through a position of social, cultural, or political analysis. Typically (and not at all unfairly), they conclude that they often interact with our subconscious fears, play with contemporary concerns, and hold very backward views of society and culture. I'll explore some of these arguments later, but it's fair to say that, true or not, it's been done before. I'm interested in what Shaviro points out: before we "read" or "interpret" movies, we respond to them. While filmmakers design all kinds of movies with the viewer's response in mind, slashers are created specifically for this impact. We "jump" out of our seat. We "cringe" at the cutting of a victim. We instinctively cover our eyes when we know something is coming, but are not quite sure when. We feel scared or tense. And there's a method of analysis that is great for considering this response we have to movies.

Viktor Shklovsky, a Russian literary critic and theorist, says, "Compositions are made, they are developed; the author creates in them semantic knots that are correlated, intensifying the perceptibility of the composition. New structures emerge" (20). Shklovsky's view foregrounds the construction of these works of art. He is more interested in the choices made in their creation and how they impact us, which is a radical (and politically subversive) approach in Russia post-revolution. Shklovsky worked in an area called "formalism" which has since been applied to other art forms, including movies.

Some of the foremost scholars in Film Studies wield formalism to chop up movies into little pieces and see what those pieces do. Unlike Jason's victims, these films still work the same as before when put back intact, but what is done with these pieces varies. One of these significant theorists, Kristin Thompson, has written about a concept known as *Historical Poetics*. Thompson writes that every viewing of a film "occurs in a specific situation, and the spectator cannot engage with the film except by using viewing skills learned in encounters with other artworks and in everyday experience" (21). Formalist critics see viewers as active participants in the puzzle-game of film viewing rather than passive receivers of messages, as other analytical forms seem to suggest. But how do we interact? We know what we have seen in other movies, so we expect what we are watching to be like them. And either they are or they aren't. Thus, based on what happens in *this* movie, we decide what we think will happen next—again, based on other movies we have seen. We can look at the history of films, what came before a movie we analyze and what came after, and see how this context influences what we, or even audiences from the past, expect to happen based on what they *would have seen*. Then we consider how this movie, depending on its stylistic choices, may influence later filmmakers, or at least influence the way in which viewers interact with other movies after having seen it.

During the very long process of writing this book, I've tried to remind myself of something Susan Sontag once wrote: "The aim of all commentary on art now should be to make works of art—and, by analogy, our own experience—more, rather than less, real to us. The function of criticism should be to show *how it is what it is*, even *that it is what it is*, rather than to show *what it means*" (14) [emphasis in original]. Sontag, as brilliant and provocative as she was, broke this aim often. Maybe it's my fault for taking it so seriously.

Look the way you feel

Imagine the following film sequence: Tom Cruise plays a character arriving home to his lavish upscale New York apartment very late at night. He closes the door and goes into the kitchen, has a beer, and sits at the kitchen table. After a while, he goes to sleep next to his wife in their bedroom, and finds a mask on his pillow.

That is exactly what happens in the sequence. What I did not tell you is that when Tom Cruise enters the house, it is very dark, bathed in deep blue light and run through with even darker shadows. As he walks toward the kitchen, we see the background punctuated with startling red and white pinpoints emanating from the Christmas lights used to decorate the home for the holiday season. Meanwhile, we hear the rustle and flutter of his clothes as he removes his coat and slowly moves through the house, as two notes from a piano repeatedly trudge back and forth, which is the musical score to the sequence. In the kitchen, harsh white light fills the room from the overhead fluorescent fixtures. Up to this point, the camera has steadily followed Cruise's movements, not swaying or distracted and keeping him central to the composition without cutting away. However, as he sits at the table, the image slowly dissolves (or fades from one image into another) to him entering the doorway to his bedroom. The entire room is blue with intense shadows playing against the interiors, and a whip pan reveals his wife in their marital bed with a mask—a physical remnant of his attempted, and failed, infidelity.

This sequence in Stanley Kubrick's *Eyes Wide Shut* (1999) takes a simple scenario and makes it startling. His home is unpleasant. The shadowed area becomes frightening, the Christmas lights make this familiar location feel alien, and the pleasantry of the kitchen has become cold and clinical. The slow dissolve shows the inevitable reluctance with which he joins his wife in their bedroom. Even without the context of this situation, the viewer understands that Cruise's house, although familiar, now seems unhomely and unwelcoming, fostering a feeling of claustrophobia. The sequence climaxes with the greatest terror in the entire house: his marital bed and his mask from the orgy he attended—a physical sign of his infidelity. While the events themselves are relatively banal, the sequence becomes suspenseful and frightening.[1] Kubrick uses lighting, camerawork, editing, and sound to show the viewer how Cruise's character feels and experiences these events and locations.

In his book about the film, Michel Chion addresses the function of point-of-view in *Eyes Wide Shut*, and cinema in general. He states:

> In the cinema, "point of view" is only suggested. It is linked, in particular, to the question of "in whose presence" the scene takes place. If a character is in almost all the scenes—as Bill is—with two or three "exceptions," the film will be regarded as being told from his point of view, although we see him just as we see the other characters, from the outside. Another important question is that of knowledge: do we know less than the character, or more, or as much? Do we share his "secrets?" In the case of Bill we do, since we alone follow him through different situations whose connections are in principle known only to him (and us). (52) [parentheses in original]

Furthermore, Chion later addresses the viewer's relationship to an established point-of-view. Speaking specifically of *Eyes Wide Shut*, he states:

> The cinema audience is in an ambiguous position: they know both more and less than each of the characters in isolation, but this knowledge is all logical speculation, which they know the film can overturn like a set of skittles from one moment to the next. Through cross-cutting they know that Alice does not have a lover she sees while her husband is at work; but the ellipses in this cross-cutting enable them to imagine that there are things they have not been shown, and will not discover until the end.
>
> The question is not what we know, but the form in which we learn it. (53)

Chion suggests two significant concepts here: the importance of the viewer's positioning in relation to the film text, and the importance of style in creating point-of-view.

Perspective establishes and reinforces the relationship of the viewer to a film text. *Eyes Wide Shut* allows the spectator to, figuratively, see the world through the eyes of Bill Harford. Bill's experiences guide us through this universe, and the action we see is shown because it is significant to this character. While we don't witness an accurate presentation of reality, we are given a clearer understanding of the people, places, and events in the story because of the stylistic choices being made. And these choices indicate that we are seeing what Bill feels.

---

1. Some critics and "friends" of mine have suggested it's still boring. These people are wrong.

Related to this dynamic created between the viewer, the character, and the film (the viewer-character-film dynamic, if you will), the point-of-view adopted by a film creates an understanding and empathy within the viewer. Bill Harford may not be likable as his failed attempts at infidelity[2] are generally unappealing. The suspense and the way the film impacts us and engages us emotionally, however, depends entirely on the fact that the viewer experiences the events of the film as they relate to Bill. The sensations of fear, excitement, arousal, sadness, and so forth depend on the expressionistic use of the elements of style like sound, lighting, camerawork, and editing, to create the relevant character's perspective.

Theorist Edward Branigan writes that the idea of subjectivity "may be conceived as a specific instance or level of narration where the telling is *attributed* to a character in the narrative and received by us *as if* we were in the situation of a character" (73) [emphasis in original]. So subjectivity and perspective share a lot of similar ideas to the point of being synonymous.

I mention Branigan as he discusses two theoretical approaches to point-of-view: one approach aligns point-of-view with perception, the other with attitude. In reference to the argument for perception, Branigan writes:

> The approach seeks to expand, in a literal fashion, the "we see" into a set of spatial and temporal *constraints* on our vision—what the film presents to us. These constraints are to be interpreted as modelling the activity of a unique perceiver: we see "through a singular mind." For example, it is claimed that our perception of pictorial space is related to some person's monocular vision. The lines of linear perspective are used to define a hypothetical point of vision from which the space is ordered and made intelligent (perceived). This viewing position lies outside the represented space and corresponds to that place where a hypothetical observer of the scene, present at the scene, would have to stand in order to give us the space as pictured. (5–6) [emphasis in original]

Branigan certainly explained this in quite a dense way. However, this quote helps me identify three points which I will use to define "perspective" for my purposes here:

a) Perspective is a stylistic design, using the most basic elements of filmmaking, created in order to house (contain) and convey the point-of-view *of a specific character, whether the character is identified or not*;

---

2. I do love the nice touch of the word "fidelio" being used as the password to the orgy.

b) Perspective also indicates the elements of style which communicate a point-of-view which *connects or changes between multiple characters*;

c) Perspective relates to the point-of-view *of the spectator* in terms of both advance expectation (what we think will happen next) and immediate experiential viewing (how we are thinking about and processing what we are seeing) of the film.

My definition of perspective acknowledges both perception and attitude. But how can we identify perspective? First, perspective shows us what the viewer witnesses or experiences. Secondly, perspective affects how the events and information are communicated to the spectator.

Daniel Frampton writes of film as a thinking entity, a notion I find to be quite absurd. However, Frampton provides useful information in considering movies in this way: "In thinking 'for' a character the film can give an impression of their mental state, perhaps, without aligning itself point-of-view-style. We may in fact be looking at the character while seeing what they are feeling" (86). It sounds a bit inside-out, but the observation is sound: we don't need to be inside a character's head to see what they see and feel what they feel.

Experiencing fear: Horrors and Slashers

German expressionist cinema and its frequent depiction of horror stories provides the earliest and most significant examples of the close link between perspective and horror in film. The strange sets of *The Cabinet of Dr. Caligari* (1920), and the exaggerated movement and performances as well as the disorienting editing in Fritz Lang's *M* (1931), prove this point. The sets of *The Cabinet of Dr. Caligari* consist almost wholly of painted backdrops, which exaggerate the angles and features of the surroundings. These sets even include painted shadows, which can directly oppose the lighting of the characters in the foreground. Peter Lorre's performance in *M* changes from a mysterious sinister figure to a panicked man chased to, in the final sequences, a manically gesticulating madman of monstrous proportions. The editing disorients us, making sudden, jolting movements between similar conversations in different locations. One such sequence juxtaposes the police with the mob discussing how to handle the killer, making the viewer unsure of the specific location and thematically connecting the two seemingly disparate organizations.

Slasher films are no exception to the strong usage of perspective. Since slasher films usually have sparse, streamlined plots, filmmakers often use perspective not only to provide the appropriate emotional response but also to fling the film through the flimsy fiction. While most movies tend to establish both a protagonist and an antagonist as soon as possible, slasher films often show us the antagonist first (even if their identity is a mystery), and slowly develop the protagonist, as secondary characters fall by the wayside. This makes sense when one considers the issue of perspective. We might not sense the immediate terror of the victim of a violent act if a slasher film adopted the perspective of a singular protagonist that meets the antagonist in the climax. This is why a film such as *Terror Train* (1980) benefits from slowly developing the characters, as the perspective can move fluidly between them, depending on who is experiencing a violent act. Sometimes—rarely, in fact—slashers jettison characters from the development of perspective. Impartial omniscience appears more often in other genres, but horror as a whole depends largely upon the effect provided by showing the viewer the experience of a character.

The choice of character perspective limits the scope of a story, dictating how the viewer is to respond to the events portrayed. For instance, a movie showing the perspective of a killer would look very different from a movie showing the perspective of a victim. Significantly, horror's tendency to change fluidly between perspectives allows for either added simplicity or complexity in how the story itself is presented.

For an example of simpler structure, we can look at most mainstream slasher films. *The Slumber Party Massacre* (1982), though thematically complex, employs changing perspectives to create a more straightforward episodic narrative. We see the events through a progressing series of victims. The escalation of violence and the deaths of increasingly more significant characters drives the film from sequence to sequence, as opposed to a cause-and-effect plot structure. *Psycho* (1960) also uses this episodic structure, but the changes in perspective discomfort the viewer more, and the transitions between perspectives must work more rigidly and intricately. After the infamous shower scene,[3] in which the seeming protagonist, Marion Crane, is brutally done away with, the camera is left to wander the hotel room, focusing on certain potentially significant details. Norman Bates then enters the scene, and after a seemingly protracted absence of any character for the film to use to dictate perspective, the film immediately assumes his point-of-view. The film experiences locations and events through Norman until the car containing Marion's body sinks into the swamp.

After a dissolve to black, the story resumes in a very jolting manner, immediately assuming the perspective of Marion's sister, Lila. At one point,

---

3. If you are sufficiently familiar with *Friday the 13th* and all of its sequels to be reading this book without having seen *Psycho*, you honestly deserve to have this spoiled for you.

the film's perspective moves to Detective Arbogast fairly seamlessly, but his death creates a jolt, making the transition back to Lila still uncomfortable. *Psycho* provides an interesting case due to the fact that the episodic nature of the plot is also driven by a cause-and-effect structure. This is unique as episodic films generally hinge on similar concepts or interrelated characters. However, Hitchcock builds *Psycho* on the seemingly unrelated set pieces, which are all connected by progressive developments in the search for Marion Crane and/or the money she has stolen. These changes in perspective affect the events seen and the film's structure as a whole.

Horror films also create perspective through the distortion of space. A sense of a character's perceived relationship to an object, or specifically a threat can heighten a viewer's emotional response. In an early scene in *A Nightmare on Elm Street* (1985), the menacing Freddy Krueger approaches the character of Tina from a distance. As he slowly moves towards her, he stretches his arms out, but his arms have grown to be several yards long. While his arms may not actually be that long, the film communicates Tina's feeling that his arms are overwhelming and inescapable. Tina's perception distorts space within the dream and the viewer experiences Tina's perspective. Slasher films frequently employ stylistic devices like wide-angle lenses that enhance swift movement towards the camera, low-angle shots that make the subject look big, high-angle shots that make the subject look small, and disproportionate relationships between subject and sound that create an unsettling and indeterminate sense of distance.

Finally, horror films accentuate and distort time through perspective. Filmmakers use devices like slow-motion, rapid editing, and crosscutting between simultaneous events to distort time. Within horror, these devices communicate the perspective of a particular character. Slow-motion provides a feel of a slowly moving but impending and inevitable action. Fast editing creates a sense of swift unexpected movement. Crosscutting between simultaneous events can create tension by protracting the time before an anticipated event.

We can understand a film's aesthetic design through perspective, which proves a valuable tool, and an appropriate starting point for beginning a formalist analysis of any film, particularly slashers. However, slashers do not stand alone in a vacuum with no history. The slasher, as a subgenre of horror, holds stylistic similarities to the genre dating back to early cinema. The slasher draws on stylistic elements outside horror, going as far back as the primitive silent film shorts. Theorists, historians, critics, and novelists have written many books about the history of moving images, and I imagine many more will be written for years to come. I won't recap all of this, as it would result in a much larger book, but it is important to understand where the stylistic elements that have informed the way perspective is communicated in the slasher film originated.

The Eye/Camera: Looking like somebody else

The first-person camera, a very popular trope, shows a moving image from the point-of-view of a character. This camera position replicates movement and positioning that would connect the audience to the experience of seeing out of a person's eyes. Writers have grappled with ideas around this device, particularly in regards to horror. Academics and critics have theorized and interpreted the first-person shot in a variety of ways in terms of how it works, what it means, and whether it's a good or bad thing.

A critical book on slasher movies is never quite complete if it fails to acknowledge the work of Carol J. Clover. Her book *Men, Women, and Chainsaws: Gender in the Modern Horror Film* broke assumptions about slashers in academia wide open, making them seem serious and legitimate subjects for study.[4] In this book, Clover brought the term "I"-camera to academic prominence, and critics regularly use it in relation to the slasher. Clover's model focuses on the relationship between the camera and the self, hence the use of "I."[5] However, this use of "I" creates a Gordian knot between the image and you. Ignoring yourself for a moment, as I clearly have trouble doing, this type of shot compresses three visual planes so that they inhabit the same space. The eye of the viewer, the lens of the camera, and the eye of the character within the film all exist within the same place and time (figure 1.1). These two sets of eyes, one real, one imagined, conjoined by the camera expresses something more akin to an "eye/camera" than an "I"-camera, and sometimes, a "mind's eye/camera." This term also bypasses those pesky debates about the link between first-person images and "identification," which we won't see the end of anytime soon.

Viewers should not put too much trust in the character eye; it is not always reliable and is subject to variety and change. Although viewers live different lives, and we change and grow as people (hopefully), we rarely change during the course of watching a movie. Furthermore, the movie itself never changes, unless Michael Mann, Ridley Scott, or heaven forbid, George Lucas should

---

4. She was by no means the first—Vera Dika wrote about them in her 1990 book *Games of Terror: Halloween, Friday the 13th, and the films of the Stalker Cycle*. And, prior to that, Robin Wood in 1986 addressed them in his book *Hollywood from Vietnam to Reagan*, which was updated in 2003.

5. This connection resembles Dziga Vertov's idea of the "kino eye" (1922).

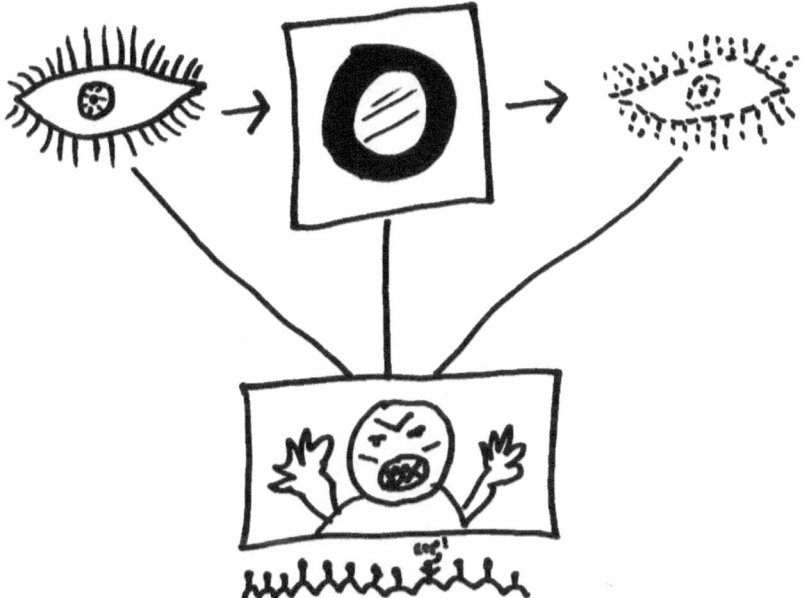

Figure 1.1. Author's drawing of how the eye/camera works. Viewer eye → camera lens → Character eye.

slip in silently and tinker with your DVDs. The camera codes the eye/camera composition, and the viewer decodes these elements to perceive a first-person point-of-view.[6] The character eye influences the image's design, and each character presumably has different qualities. This creates distinctive differences in eye/camera coding from film to film, and visual representations of the eye/camera have evolved since the origins of cinema.

The eye/camera contains very specific elements, which make the audience aware that it is witnessing a first-person point-of-view. The shaky image of a handheld camera creates an unsteadiness that is usually associated with personal eye, head, and body movement. Viewers may recognize the swish pan/tilt, which also results from filming with a handheld camera. A swift movement of the camera upwards, downwards, or from side to side mimics human head and eye movement. We may also detect an eye/camera shot from an image filmed at a relatable or understandable height. The camera

---

6. Keep in mind that I don't mean "coding" and "decoding" as in creating hidden messages in the manner of "the killer is a symbol for Trump's attitude to climate change." I refer more about creating an image with certain narrative meanings, such as an image where the characters are around trees, but it is very dark around them, so they are likely in a forest and it's probably nighttime.

typically shoots the action from a height of about six feet with a variation of approximately six inches. This height variant reflects the perceived height of an adult human.[7] These basic elements reflect median human experiential vision. While variations on these elements occur, the variants tend to be exceptions that prove the rule.

The genealogy of Jason's eyeballs

The eye/camera appeared quite early in the history of cinema, although the elements I have outlined do not firmly appear until the early 1940s, and the device itself evolves along with cinematic technology. Two films from George Albert Smith provide the opportunity to examine the early history of the eye/camera as they both house the camera within the theoretical position of a character's eye. *Grandma's Reading Glass* (1900) assumes the point-of-view of a child looking through a reading glass, highlighting this eye/camera shot through a wide black iris. This also helped develop early film language, particularly concerning editing. A shot of somebody looking followed by a cut to their point-of-view makes visual representation seem consistent and guides the flow of the narrative, which is also demonstrated in *As Seen Through a Telescope* (1900).

Although it's not the first horror film, nor the first German expressionist film, F. W. Murnau's movie *Nosferatu* (1922) contains an instructive example of the way the horror genre uses the eye/camera, while also using strange variations of the device. Let us consider one of the most recognizable sequences in the movie: Hutter's first night in the castle of Count Orlock. When the clock chimes midnight, Hutter moves to the bedroom door, opens it a crack and peers out. At this point, we see the shots shown in figures 1.2 through 1.4, with the first two shots connected by a dissolve.

Hutter runs to the window to look for a way out, but the climb down is impossible. Hutter gets in his bed and watches as the door to the room opens on its own. Figures 1.5 through 1.8 show the next series of shots: Hutter looks away, Orlock approaches toward the camera, Hutter covers his head with a sheet, and Orlock enters the room, looking from the camera to the bed.

While this sequence seems to engage the audience without drawing the viewer into the first-person, I would argue that Murnau uses the eye/camera in a way that plays with perspective and subverts typical spatial relationships.

---

7. People, of course, come in all sizes, but where Hollywood is concerned, hegemony is the *ordre des affaires*.

Figures 1.2, 1.3, and 1.4. *Nosferatu* (1922)—Hutter's view of Count Orlock—first visually, then emotionally. (Jofa-Atelier Berlin-Johannisthal / Prana-Film GmbH, 1922)

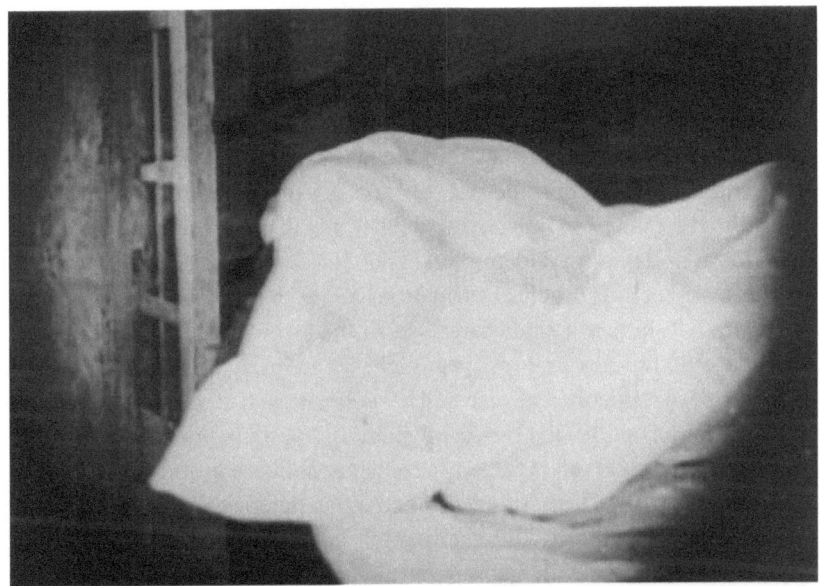

Figures 1.5, 1.6, 1.7, and 1.8. *Nosferatu* (1921)—Hutter's perspective—seeing the approach of Orlock in spite of looking away, then covering his head. (Jofa-Atelier Berlin-Johannisthal / Prana-Film GmbH, 1922)

This type of perspective development clearly serves the purposes of the genre. While expressionism specifically employs a style that distorts perspective to show the monstrousness of the modern world, people make horror films to scare and frighten, so it helps to ask how the eye/camera aids in this sense of fear. The dissolve that occurs between the two shots of Count Orlock standing at the end of the corridor is the first set of images that seems to take the viewer out of the eye/camera. However, it actually works in much the same way as the snap-zoom in modern eye/camera shots does.

The snap-zoom is a quick, unexpected zoom that takes place within the camera, usually indicating sudden realization and focus within an image or scene with a larger scope. For example, you might see an image of a crowd of people, and the image suddenly and very quickly enlarges so that we see a large focal character in the middle of a crowd. My point is that sometimes the snap-zoom technique is meant to reflect the way a character notices something small out of a bigger image or suddenly realizes something is significant about this picture.

This dissolve captures Hutter's mental realization not only that Count Orlock is at the end of the hallway but that Count Orlock is a vampire that is looking at and waiting for him. This realization is a horrifying moment for Hutter, and as a result of the use of the eye/camera, coupled with the dissolve, this becomes a horrifying moment for the viewer.

When Hutter shuts the door, he runs to the left of the image to check the window and then moves forward to the bed, still keeping him to the left of the doorway. When the doorway opens and Count Orlock approaches, however, it is shot straight on, making a direct eye/camera shot impossible. However, this is how Murnau distorts and subverts the relationships between objects and people within the space of the movie. As Count Orlock approaches, he looks into the camera and seems to be coming for the viewer. We know within the context of the scene that he is coming for Hutter. However, before the first shot of the doorway, Hutter looks away, and before the second shot of the doorway, Hutter covers his head with a sheet. There is no possible way for these to be direct eye/camera shots, but we become aware of perspective. We are seeing this from Hutter's point-of-view, albeit indirectly.

Although Hutter may not be looking, he knows Count Orlock is coming for him slowly and steadily. The striking image is made more powerful because we see what Hutter feels. He is terrified of this unavoidable encounter and by filming this as an eye/camera shot, the viewer fears it as well. So while we can't claim this sequence is shot from a character's literal eye, or as I call it, a direct eye/camera shot, we witness a first-person perspective. The viewer's eye shares a space with the camera lens along with the character's "mind's eye." The character eye, as we see it, changes, shifts, and morphs. It is a volatile fictional eye.

German expressionism influenced many of the later horror films in classical Hollywood, and movies both in Hollywood and abroad approached eye/camera shots in different ways stylistically. The monster movies produced by Universal Studios such as *The Wolf Man* (1941) and *Dracula* (1931) contain eye/camera shots conspicuously rooted to the tripod. *The Last Laugh* (1924), made in Germany also by Murnau, helped the development of moving eye/camera shots through the introduction of wire-guided cameras. An innovative example can be seen in *Dr. Jekyll and Mr. Hyde* (1931) and *Lady in the Lake* (1947). These films use extensive and intricate eye/camera shots. In fact, director Robert Montgomery shot *Lady in the Lake* entirely from a first-person point-of-view. These different methods of creating perspective show efforts to tell stories in ways unique to cinema, setting themselves apart from the theatricality of early cinema, particularly early American cinema. Filmmaker Brian De Palma discusses this idea in an interview:

> Film is one of the only art forms where you can give the audience the same visual information the character has. I learned it from Hitchcock. It's unique to cinema and it connects the audience directly to the experience—unlike the fourth wall approach, which belongs to the Xerox school of filmmaking. (quoted in Pally 1984, 100)

De Palma nicely points to Alfred Hitchcock as a mentor here. Hitchcock provides consistent examples of the eye/camera as it changes throughout early and classical cinema. While maintaining the expressionistic sense of experiential perception—in other words, the way expressionism aims to make us feel and experience the way a character perceives their situation and surrounding—Hitchcock manipulated elements internal and external to the camera.

In doing this, Hitchcock creates a greater sense of movement more closely acquainted with the modern eye/camera. In *Vertigo* (1958), Hitchcock used the zoom-out/push-in camera technique to enhance spatial differences between foreground and background elements of the composition, or the parts of the image and their relationship to each other. Jimmy Stewart's character, Scotty, has a fear of heights, and in a key scene, he climbs an open spiral (if squares can be made spiral) staircase and intermittently looks downward. When he does so, the stairway seems to elongate and drop beneath him, enhancing the sense of height. The push-in portion of the camera movement keeps the figures in the foreground in place within the composition, while the zoom-out separates the distance between the compositional elements. The viewer experiences Scotty's fear of heights through this eye/camera shot. Hitchcock also creates visual interpretations of perspective in drunken driving sequences in both *Notorious* (1946) and *North by Northwest* (1959). In both of these films, we experience driving after drinking heavily through eye/camera shots, filmed from the driver's seat of a car. The movement of the composition reflects the movement within a car. Hitchcock's camera uses a slower shutter speed to create a more disjointed and shaky image. The shots are not clearly focused.

These examples indicate an early playfulness with film style, up through classical Hollywood. They also show a clear preoccupation with creating a visual experience resembling that of a figure in the movie. This isn't necessarily new; writers have long written in the first-person, going at least as far back as the Bible, and likely before that, whether as biography or not. However, these cinematic tropes show clear development and consideration, which has filtered into the way first-person experiences are depicted in slasher movies.

Seeing in a slasher

Hitchcock's film *Psycho* has clearly influenced slasher films, and innumerable scholars have written about it at great length. In this film, Hitchcock recreates some of the point-of-view techniques going even as far back as early primitive shorts. After eating with Norman Bates in the Bates Motel parlor, Marion Crane retires to her room. Norman removes a picture from the wall to reveal a hole that provides visual access to Marion's room. We see an extreme close-up of his eye as it looks through the hole in the wall, which cuts to an eye/camera shot (figure 1.9). This shot captures the action from the same perspective of the character we know we inhabit, including height and direction. Additionally, Hitchcock borders the image with black to reflect the hole in the wall that we have already witnessed. Although Hitchcock does not use the shaky handheld camera, the framing of the hole along with the awareness of the character perspective identifies this clearly as an eye/camera shot, similar to those in *As Seen Through a Telescope* (figure 1.10) or of the keyhole spying sequence in *And Then There Were None* (1945) (figure 1.11).

Although this film provides a strong template for the modern slasher film, a different genre is responsible for many of the stylistic qualities of the slasher, particularly those of the late 1970s and early 1980s. The Italian giallo film exhibits stylistic elements that crop up in slasher movies, particularly those of Mario Bava and Dario Argento as well as some of their gothic horror films. Italian giallo movies are often murder mysteries that feature a series of graphic, brutally violent death sequences. "Giallo," the Italian word for "yellow," refers to the color of the pulp novels published by Mondadori that frequently

Figure 1.9. *Psycho* (1960)—Norman Bates watches Marion Crane through a hole in the wall. (Shamley Productions, 1960)

featured this type of story.[8] Critics often consider Bava and Argento two of the great masters of the Italian giallo film, and both directors tell mystery stories, which include inventive set pieces that involve gruesome and creative death sequences. The early films of each director, Bava's *The Girl Who Knew Too Much* (1963) and Argento's *The Bird with the Crystal Plumage* (1970), provide examples of the standard giallo narrative conventions of murder mysteries with sometimes elaborate and often graphically violent death sequences. They also retain a more stylistically straightforward approach to presenting the narrative. The stalking camera is featured in these films but without seeming to challenge the boundaries of visual understanding. However, if horror filmmakers use stalking so frequently, is the act of stalking by itself meant to scare us?

In much of the writing on first-person point-of-view, critics appear to consistently ignore or overlook one important thing essential to the emotional impact of the horror film. The eye/camera creates a sense of proximity, or distance, between the character looking and the subject of the camera's gaze. Whether we see the stalker's eye/camera with the victim as the subject or the victim's eye/camera with the stalker or killer as the subject, the audience gets a clear sense of the distance from one to the other. When we see Michael Myers's eye/camera in the opening shot of *Halloween* (1978), the film gives us no information regarding who the stalker is until just before the murder. But this disorientation does not change the fact that we know the young couple is being watched, and only a window and a few feet of space separate them from

---

8. See Mikel Koven (2006, 2) for a more detailed explanation of the term "giallo."

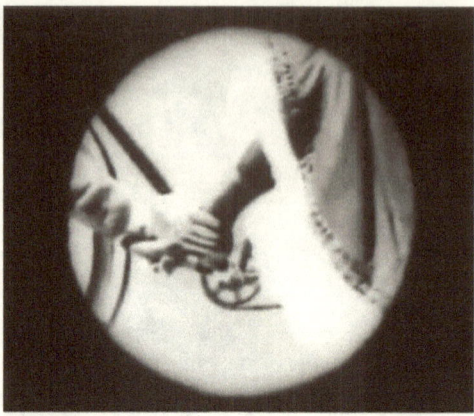

Figure 1.10. *As Seen Through a Telescope* (1900)—Watching another man fondling a woman's foot. (G. A. S. Films, 1900)

Figure 1.11. *And Then There Were None* (1945)—Watching someone watch someone. (Popular Pictures, 1945)

an ominous presence, as indicated by the music. In the opening sequence of *My Bloody Valentine* (1981), the first victim's eye/camera reveals the killer filling the frame and lunging even closer to the victim in a threatening way. In those few moments, the threat is too close to run away from or defend against, and this frightens us. This "proximity fear" is much more tangible. While the eye/camera itself gives us little information about the characters involved, this device shows us how close the character we see through might be in relation to the person or object they are watching.

With this proximity fear in mind, each director exploits this device to subvert our expectations. Mario Bava's *Twitch of the Death Nerve* (1971) provides an excellent example of this. The movie takes place in an elaborate estate on a desolate lake, and the opening sequence shows the murder of an old lady in a wheelchair. The camera not only stalks her, but moves towards and away from her at unusual speed and from strange angles. We see the killer's hands in black gloves so we are aware that they are human, and the familiar shaky handheld camera is used. Despite the unusual angles and speed, the audience distinctly interprets the images as eye/camera shots.

The immediate predecessors to the modern slasher film become elemental prototypes of what is to come. *The Texas Chain Saw Massacre* (1974) is a film that contains the narrative elements of the slasher film, using a unique stylistic approach. Director Tobe Hooper shot the movie with a detached stalking camera, largely without using eye/camera coding. By this point in film history, the eye/camera was a mainstay technique in horror, and its absence leaves the audience with a heightened fear of proximity, because it fails to give precise spatial relationships. In contrast, another significant modern slasher predecessor is *Black Christmas* (1974), which places heavy stylistic and thematic emphasis on seeing and vision. Here, the eye/camera plays a prominent role, and is the only way to identify the stalker; we never see the stalker, only his point-of-view. A wide-angle lens distorts the image, which is shot with a handheld camera. The sounds of loud breathing, swallowing, and muttering accompany eye/camera shots, furthering the illusion of being inside the eye of the character. The one time we see the stalker, he is standing in complete darkness, with light shining only on a single eye. *Black Christmas* gives us no bearings as to the identity or motive of the killer, and essentially is only a pair of eyes, by which we know the location and proximity of the threat to the victims at all times.

Eyes of Laura Mars (1978) was released at the height of this premodern slasher cycle and is emblematic of the movement toward a newer, but more formulaic approach to the horror film. *Eyes of Laura Mars* stands as an example of a mature aesthetic approach to the eye/camera. The John Carpenter-scripted movie tells the story of a photographer named Laura Mars who sees visions of the first-person perspective of a stalker and killer. This film does not simply contain the eye/camera, but the plot entirely revolves around it. The eye/camera limits itself even more by blurring the edges of the composition to create an almost indecipherable frame. The clear image is almost contained within an iris that all but removes everything around the edges. While this composition asserts a distinct perspective, it proves the eye/camera is extremely limiting and frustrating. Not knowing whose eyes she sees through while this more restrictive and mysterious viewpoint usurps her own vision reflects the experience of Laura Mars.

The eye/camera brings with it the same sense of proximity fear as we watch victims we are increasingly more familiar with become the object of stalking and killing. But this proximity fear takes a unique turn when Laura Mars, overcome with the sight of the attacker, sees that the stalker is coming up the stairs to her studio where she is at that very moment. Laura is aware of the proximity of the threat to her and is able to escape the threat with this knowledge. This sequence uses the viewer's experience of the eye/camera to benefit the protagonist and create a new dimension to the suspense created with the device.

John Carpenter had a very successful year in 1978. Apart from the release and relative success of *Eyes of Laura Mars*, Carpenter's directorial effort that year, *Halloween*, met with surprising success for an exploitation movie. *Halloween*'s financial success provided a generic template—a prototype or outline that future films copied—for the cycle of slasher films to come. Considering its significance in the rise of the slasher film, I must explain what it brings to our understanding and analysis of the eye/camera, or, rather, why Carpenter's movie is so important to this device. The opening shot is an extended eye/camera shot beginning with an establishing view of the Myers house. A handheld camera captures this scene, which is similar to the appearances of the stalker in *Black Christmas*. Unlike *Black Christmas*, however, the edges are not blurred, and a wide-angle lens isn't used. In fact, the anamorphic lens used creates a widened panoramic field of vision, separating its eye/camera shots from the extremely limited perspective of *Black Christmas*. The technical aspects of the frame combined with the immediate presentation of the eye/camera overwhelm the viewer from the outset of the film, entirely drawing the audience into Michael's perspective.

Significantly, however, the opening eye/camera shot establishes a subjectivity, a style linked to a particular point-of-view, which permeates the entire film. Whether the shot inhabits Michael or sits near Michael, the viewer understands the overall perspective established in the film relates to that character. *Halloween* reveals how the eye/camera can establish the perspective of a film, without being used all the time.

Giallo films also influenced the use of the eye/camera in mainstream American horror from the late 1970s. Whether films drew directly from the giallo movement or imitated films that had the co-opted giallo form, the influence is palpable. *Hell Night* (1981), *Happy Birthday to Me* (1981), *Maniac* (1980), and *My Bloody Valentine* stand as a small sample of a body of genre films that, like giallo, use the eye/camera to create suspense and proximity fear in addition to providing a way to disorient the viewer through distorting time and space.

Losing an eye

The Blair Witch Project (1999) spearheaded the wave of victim-camera films, sometimes called "found footage films," that went out of fashion within the last decade. Here, I'd like to make clear my distinction between the two terms. "Found footage," for me, describes how the shots work within the story, with a focus on the relationship of the footage to the fictional world. "Victim-camera," on the other hand, describes the type of shot: a camera captures images in a particular way, as only a fictional camera could. It may be a subtle distinction, but it's a useful one. "Found footage" references the story that frames it, whereas "victim-camera" references the style of the shot.

The popularity of this type of movie provides a significant link in the developing visual style of horror, particularly in the way it links visually to the eye/camera. A primary forerunner to this phenomenon is *Cannibal Holocaust* (1980). This movie acts as a primary precursor to *The Blair Witch Project*, which was by no means the first film to use such a visual perspective. The story of *Cannibal Holocaust* revolves around the members of a film crew that travel to the territory of a South American cannibal tribe and become their victims. The film focuses on the search for these missing filmmakers, and the audience discovers their fate through the footage discovered in the jungle. Only a few shots in *Cannibal Holocaust* involve people watching the found footage. The viewing of the found footage acts as the film's climax. The story of a man going to the last known location of the missing crew to find them frames the found footage. While the found footage works as a "film within a film," this becomes *Cannibal Holocaust*'s central focus, the acknowledgment of the camera within the film text creates a heightened sense of "reality"—a specious concept if ever there was one.[9] Acknowledging the presence of film equipment is a recognizable element of documentary, amateur film, and home movies, all of which include the camera within the universe it represents. Although the violence witnessed is fictitious, the convincing portrayal of violence in movies that share a documentary or amateurish awareness of the camera strikes us as, at minimum, slightly more real than in mainstream narrative filmmaking.

Most importantly, though, victim-camera's stylistic acknowledgment of the existence of filmmaking equipment and crew fractures the eye-camera-eye model. When the camera acts as eye, this creates, unknowingly, a comfortable transition for the viewer to accept this eye/camera compression. We know what looking through eyes is supposed to look like. It's not a huge leap for us with victim-camera films. From the outset, we know, or the film makes us know, that a camera is capturing these images. This removes one of the eyes from the eye-camera-eye model, leaving not an eye/camera, but two separate visual filters: an eye and a camera. The character, by way of an eyepiece or a digital viewscreen, becomes a viewer like the audience. In fact, there are sequences in *The Blair*

---

9. See any film studies textbook—literally.

Witch Project and *Cloverfield* (2008) in which the fictional characters are running with camera in hand, and the shots we see quickly swing pendulum-style (a sort of snap-tilt at roughly a 180-degree angle), mostly capturing images of the ground. And during this time, the characters are almost certainly not watching what they are recording.

This style acts as a directly exaggerated extension of the eye/camera in terms of effect. We view events from an extremely limited perspective since the camera does not move on its own and lacks the swiftness of the human eye. The events captured are a few fractions of a second behind what the firsthand viewer sees. This enhances the proximity fear, as a swift move of the camera could easily mean a slow response to a violent attack, resulting in fatal injury for the person holding the camera by the time the audience sees the threat (as the final moments of *The Blair Witch Project* demonstrate).

The way the eye/camera developed over the history of cinema is a useful way of showing the history of film style and provides a useful timeline for the way horror has developed. Furthermore, we can see how eye/camera shots are quite multifaceted in how they create perspective and emotional impact. But while I have discussed the many ways that first-person framing of an image impacts the viewer as well as the way movies tell stories, critical discussions of this perspective around horror tend to focus on very different concerns.

In a discussion of *Halloween*, Reynold Humphries asserts that "the spectators can both enjoy the earlier sight of the girl undressing and later feel safe from any danger insofar as we can identify with her, while knowing we are safe. [. . .] Spying on girls undressing is fine, provided the looker is not a psychotic" (143). Then, Humphries makes a firm but common claim: first-person camerawork gives the viewer an excuse to comfortably engage in sadistic viewing. Humphries's reasoning is that a viewer can enjoy watching a vulnerable subject through a sadistic character, while being able to condemn the actions of the character that is looking (143–44). And much like Humphries's example, critics often centralize *Halloween* in discussions of the eye/camera and vice versa. This is largely due to the distinctive and iconic opening sequence, which makes it a significant film particularly where the eye/camera is concerned.

Robin Wood also writes about the eye/camera, reaffirming this negative reading, but recognizing a greater complexity:

> A simple alternative explanation for the device, which in fact works with rather than against (the critical accusation that the eye/camera is an invitation to sadism), is the need to preserve the secret of the killer's identity for a final "surprise." The latter motivation might be seen merely as supplying a plausible alibi for the former: the sense of indeterminate, unidentified, possibly supernatural or superhuman menace feeds the spectator's fantasy of power, facilitating a direct

spectator/camera identification by keeping the intermediary character, while signified as present, as vaguely defined as possible. (2003, 177) [parenthesis mine]

Here, Wood takes the time to examine this device in terms of narrative function before moving on to discuss the psychological issue of viewer sadism. While there may be an element of truth to this argument, Wood fails to acknowledge the fact that the eye/camera actually communicates a great deal of very complex information. In particular, Wood neglects to address the complex emotions that come with combining sadistic pleasure with the suspense that comes with disorientation. This is especially evident in his statement regarding a "plausible alibi." The eye/camera fuses complicated story information and emotional sensation. Reducing this device to a few abstract concepts fails to address why the eye/camera is both popular and prevalent in cinema.

Wood also does not mention the tension and suspense created through use of the eye/camera. In fact, Wood seemingly contradicts much of his own argument in his discussion of point-of-view in relation to the work of Alfred Hitchcock. Wood states:

> The power of the POV shot in constructing identification has been greatly exaggerated (by myself, among others): it is simply not true that to stick in a shot from a given character's point of view automatically identifies the spectator with that character, beyond the obvious enforced identification with a physical position (we see what the character sees). (1989, 308) [parenthesis in original]

The disparity in his two explanations raises questions regarding Wood's consideration of "worthiness": he seems to consider Hitchcock's films more worthy, artistic, and complex than the 1980s slasher films addressed in *Hollywood from Vietnam to Reagan*, which he considers to be merely sadistic. And while Wood seems to admit his role in exaggerating what those films do—"by myself among others," he writes—Wood revised *Hollywood from Vietnam to Reagan* years after *Hitchcock's Films Revisited*. In that revised book, he could have easily used his awareness for exaggeration that he addressed in his work on Hitchcock to reconsider his argument of '80s-era horror films (although, to be fair, that would be very inconvenient to his greater argument in that essay).

Clover notes the separation between critical analysis and viewer reception. Clover responds to certain critics, arguing that a limitation of the first-person camera is:

> it does not see well—at least not since 1978, when John Carpenter popularized the use of the unmounted first-person camera to represent the killer's point of view. Although critics tend to assign a kind of binding power to marked first-

person cinematography, the fact is that the "view" of the first-person killer is typically cloudy, unsteady, and punctuated by dizzying swish-pans. Insofar as an unstable gaze suggests an unstable gazer, the credibility of the first-person killer-camera's omnipotence is undermined from the outset. One could go further and say that the assignment of "real" vision to "normal" characters draws attention, in the hand-held or Steadicam sequences, to the very item the filmmaker ostensibly seeks to efface: the camera. (186–87) [parenthesis in original]

Vera Dika discusses the eye/camera very early in her book *Games of Terror: Halloween, Friday the 13th and the Films of the Stalker Cycle*, but makes no statement nor allusion as to the link between first-person camerawork and morality. Instead, Dika reads the eye/camera as a distinct generic signifier; if you see an eye/camera shot, you can be pretty sure you're in a horror film (1990, 14). Here, Dika shows that the eye/camera is not only important to understanding the genre, but drives narrative, without which the films could not operate.

Writers like Wood—as well as Lucy Fischer and Marcia Landy, who wrote an article about point-of-view shots in *Eyes of Laura Mars*—do discuss the basics of the eye/camera's relationship to narrative. However, they eschew detailed formalist analysis for an observation of the problematic psychological and social implications of the eye/camera's positioning within a film. Clover responds to this negative critical stance, providing an alternate reading, while Dika ignores such criticism and seeks to understand why the eye/camera predominates within the genre. Following on from Dika's work, the essential question I seek to address is: why is the eye/camera used so often within the slasher film? The simplest answer is that it is frightening by showing precise proximity between victim and threat. And, of course, we want our horror films to be frightening. Even our *Friday the 13th* movies.

Jason Voorhees: A Biography

Friday the 13th and its related franchise films center on the killings that occur around a summer camp, Camp Crystal Lake, primarily executed by a seemingly invincible man in a hockey mask, Jason Voorhees. I will here pretend that I chose the *Friday the 13th* series for discussion because the series provides a unique opportunity to observe the development of slasher film aesthetics. This is true, but honestly, I just love the movies to bits. But that aside, the series does have many qualities that make it a useful case study.

Firstly, the release dates for the *Friday the 13th* films range from 1980 to 2009. Paramount Pictures released eight of the films between 1980 and 1989.

Paramount then sold the franchise to New Line Cinema, resulting in the release of *Jason Goes to Hell: The Final Friday* (1993) and *Jason X* (2002). New Line released a franchise crossover of the Jason films and another New Line property, *A Nightmare on Elm Street*, which resulted in the film *Freddy vs. Jason* (2003). Finally, in 2009, New Line and Paramount co-produced a remake: *Friday the 13th* (2009). In other words, there have been eleven films in the *Friday the 13th* series alone, with an additional franchise crossover film, all within the span of just under thirty years, with another movie hoped for but consistently meeting with obstacles standing in the way of its production.[10]

The *Friday the 13th* films prove excellent examples of contemporary aesthetic trends within the slasher while also being consistently innovative. However, this series uses these trends in such a significant and concise way that almost any given film in the *Friday the 13th* series acts as a prime example of how these contemporary trends can be made most effective. However, in a discussion of the entire series, you could easily get lost if you have only seen them casually and out of order, so here I will briefly go through the narratives of the films in an attempt to demonstrate how they all work in the (admittedly sloppy) context of the larger story of the series.[11]

Friday the 13th, the first film, centers on a group of teenage counselors at a summer camp, called Camp Crystal Lake, and the systematic stalking and slaying of each by Mrs. Voorhees as revenge for her son drowning under the supervision of irresponsible, horny counselors thirty years earlier. *Friday the 13th Part 2* (1981) follows the stalking and killing of another group of camp counselors at a Camp Crystal Lake adjacent summer camp, this time by Jason Voorhees, the son of the killer in the previous film. *Friday the 13th Part III 3-D* (1982)[12] sees the return of Jason as the killer of a group of friends visiting a holiday cabin by Crystal Lake, ending with Jason's supposed demise. *Friday the 13th: The Final Chapter* (1984) introduces a young boy, Tommy Jarvis, and his family along with a group of visiting teenagers at a nearby house. A still-living Jason terrorizes all of these characters, and Tommy verifiably kills Jason at the end of the film.

---

10. See Sprague (2018).

11. See appendix 1 for a more detailed description of the film narratives.

12. The film has this title because, of course, it was shot and released to be a 3-D feature. Most VHS, DVD, and Blu-ray versions of the film, without the 3-D option,[a] tend to go by *Friday the 13th Part III*, reasonably enough.

[a.] The 2009 US Special Edition DVD reissue of the film has both 3-D and 2-D options, with the old red-and-blue lens 3-D glasses as per its original exhibition. It was also shown on UK television in November 2009 in 3-D during a 3-D season—anything to promote the remake.

In *Friday the 13th Part V: A New Beginning* (1985), Tommy, now a teenager and still disturbed by the events of *The Final Chapter*, is transferred from an institution to a halfway house for troubled teens where Jason-style murders occur after his arrival. *Jason Lives! Friday the 13th Part VI* (1986) again follows Tommy, still a teenager but no longer disturbed to the extent of institutionalization. He inadvertently brings Jason back to life, and then attempts to find and destroy Jason, who is now attacking a new set of camp counselors. *Friday the 13th Part VII: The New Blood* (1988) follows Jason's efforts to terrorize a telekinetic teenager along with her mother and a group of teenagers in a nearby cabin. *Friday the 13th Part VIII: Jason Takes Manhattan* (1989) centers on Jason's attacks on a group of high school students who are traveling, by boat, to New York City.

In *Jason Goes to Hell: The Final Friday*, the FBI destroys Jason, but his spirit passes between people who then attempt to kill others upon being possessed. At the end, Jason is killed and his spirit taken to Hell. *Jason X* ignores the events of *Jason Goes to Hell*, following Jason as he is cryogenically frozen and reawakened in the year 2455, where he begins killing students on a scientific exploration in a spaceship. *Freddy vs. Jason*, ignoring the events of *Jason X*, sees serial child-murderer Freddy Krueger, antagonist of the *A Nightmare on Elm Street* films, bringing Jason back from Hell to kill for him, so that the residents of Elm Street will remember Freddy, thereby bringing him back to kill again. However, Jason becomes uncontrollable, resulting in a showdown between the two characters. Finally, *Friday the 13th* (2009) follows two groups of teenagers camping near Crystal Lake as Jason kills them one by one. This last film acts as a remake of the first three films and an attempted reboot of the franchise.

While the overarching strand of Jason killing people in response to his mother's death carries a large number of the films through the series, a select few, notably *A New Beginning* and *Jason Lives!*, incorporate other narrative strands, such as the story of Tommy Jarvis. However, the minimalist thread of narrative continuity allows each film to create its own themes and design.

Jason plays well with others

Friday the 13th and *Friday the 13th Part 2*, more than most slasher films, have close ties to the Italian giallo genre, both owing a particular debt to *Twitch of the Death Nerve*. This makes both movies unique amongst their contemporaries, which draw from this tradition somewhat but not as extensively as the first two *Friday the 13th* movies. While director/producer Sean S. Cunningham and screenwriter Victor Miller based the immediate business model for

Friday the 13th on the production, narrative, and marketing of *Halloween*,[13] the film actually adopted the style and stylistic framework of the giallo. Its contemporaries opted for aesthetic replication of *Halloween*, which was an unexpectedly successful independent film. We could make an exception from this period for Brian De Palma's *Dressed to Kill* (1980), which doesn't appear to emulate *Halloween*'s style. However, as his earlier quotes indicate, De Palma clearly owes a debt to Alfred Hitchcock's films. *Dressed to Kill* closely mirrors *Psycho* (1960) in both style and story.

Moreover, some giallo filmmakers, particularly Argento, owe much of their stylistic tendencies to Hitchcock, too. One of Mario Bava's earliest films is entitled *La ragazza che sapeva troppo* which can be directly translated to *The Girl Who Knew Too Much* (1963), a title that alludes to Hitchcock's *The Man Who Knew Too Much* (first made in 1934 in the UK and remade by Hitchcock himself in 1956 in the US). Argento more recently made a film for Italian television entitled *Ti piace Hitchcock?* (*Do You Like Hitchcock?*) (2005), revolving around a film student who becomes entangled in the activities of a serial killer, and during the course of the film, a large number of set pieces are transposed onto the narrative from a multiplicity of Hitchcock films. Even John Carpenter acknowledges a debt to Hitchcock's filmmaking, in addition to highlighting his intention to favor cinematic suggestion of violence rather than overt portrayal.

Immediate predecessors to *Halloween*, like *Black Christmas*, *Eyes of Laura Mars*, and *The Texas Chain Saw Massacre*, also rely on aesthetic suggestion as a preference to graphic depiction of violence. Films such as *The Toolbox Murders* (1978) and even *Dawn of the Dead* (1978) owe more to American exploitation aesthetics, despite the extent of their artistic innovations. This shows that some films we consider a part of the slasher's development in fact come from an entirely different tradition.

Halloween effectively works as the prototype for this new wave of slasher film that includes such *Friday the 13th* contemporaries as *Prom Night* (1980), *Terror Train, Hell Night, Happy Birthday to Me,* and *The Burning* (1981), to name just a handful. I can't overstate just how incredibly popular these movies were and how many were produced in a few short years. *Friday the 13th*, however, openly acknowledges its roots in this Italian movement, its graphic depictions of violence stemming directly from this genre. *The Burning* also demonstrates this tendency to portray graphic violence. This connection is largely due to practical makeup and special effects artist Tom Savini, who gained attention because of his detailed recreations of bodily mutilation in *Dawn of the Dead*. We

---

13. See Bracke (2005) and Nowell (2011).

can see the influence of *Friday the 13th*, along with immediate contemporaries like *Prom Night*, in several of the films released in 1981, such as *Hell Night* and *Happy Birthday to Me*, and even *Halloween II* (1981), which contains set pieces more closely reminiscent of these 1980 slasher films than its actual predecessor, the original Carpenter-directed *Halloween*.

The success of the first two *Friday the 13th* films, and the return of director Steve Miner, resulted in little stylistic difference in *Part III 3-D*. The use of 3-D appears to be the biggest development between the first two sequels. This led to adjustments in framing and, as I will show, a shift to a victim's perspective to accommodate the tendency towards spectacle allowed by 3-D. The process of shooting in 3-D resulted in increased expenses, and the film's poppy music demonstrates an attempt at wider appeal to young audiences.[14] These elements show the filmmakers were investing more financially and creatively at this point, in hopes of a larger audience.

Consider the similar tendency within other mainstream productions of the same year, such as John Carpenter's *The Thing* (1982), which stars Kurt Russell, a growing celebrity at the time, and Tobe Hooper's *Poltergeist* (1982), a horror film rated PG in the US and produced by Steven Spielberg. Box-office reception aside, the fact that major studios, Universal and MGM, respectively, decided it potentially lucrative to produce and release these films shows how horror had become a large part of the filmgoing consciousness. Indeed, it is Jason's acquisition of his hockey mask in *Part III 3-D* that helped the film series reach iconographic status in popular culture. There were other films released at the time that assumed elements of the style established by films from 1980 to 1981, such as *The Slumber Party Massacre* and *Pieces* (1982), with success linked to home video releases. However, the notable trend of this year is the movement of horror further into the mainstream. The increased investments in horror films made by major studios points to this, and the *Friday the 13th* series is a clear part of these investments.

The Final Chapter and its success was unusual for box-office trends at the time. The makers of the film claim that the slasher was in decline at this point. Although *A Nightmare on Elm Street*, released later that same year, revived the slasher subgenre for mainstream audiences, it also reinvented the form. *Nightmare* brought elements of the supernatural even more into slasher storylines. In films like *Friday the 13th* and *Halloween*, supernatural elements were left either implied or ambiguous, while *Nightmare* intertwined generic

---

14. Harry Manfredini's music over the opening and closing titles bears strong similarities to Michael Jackson's horror-themed smash hit single "Thriller," which was released the previous year—yet another indication of the extraordinary popularity of horror at this point in history.

conventions of the slasher with overt elements of the supernatural, having a strong effect on horror film production for the next decade.

A New Beginning came out the following year, and the story itself played upon this increased tendency toward supernatural storylines, teasing viewers with questions of the killer's identity—a game which was lost heading into the first sequel's second act. In this case, it could be Tommy, or Jason could have come back from the dead, or it could be another, less obvious character. Although the climax reveals that it is the latter of the three, the supernatural explanation exists as a possibility until the film reveals the identity of the killer. Even throughout the climax, when we see Tommy struggling with Jason, the supernatural answer seems to be the most likely. This exploitation of the trends and overarching storyline of the *Friday the 13th* series, along with the contemporary tendency toward supernatural horror, again contributes to the viewing of *A New Beginning* as a unique and complex example of the genre.[15] The relative financial failure of the film,[16] however, demanded adjustments to the series to justify making more entries, and the strong supernatural narrative of *Nightmare* did for the second slasher cycle what *Halloween* did for the first.

As *Jason Lives!* adapted *Frankenstein*'s (1931) use of lightning to bring the dead to life, other horror films of the period relied heavily upon the use of the supernatural and science fiction in their plots. While *Aliens* (1986), *Critters* (1986), and *The Fly* (1986) used science fiction, the supernatural was prevalent in films like *Troll* (1986), *Poltergeist II: The Other Side* (1986), and even Steve Miner's film *House* (1986). While there were slasher films closer to the *Friday the 13th* model, some of these used supernatural plot points, such as *Sorority House Massacre* (1986) which contains a protagonist who has telepathic visions. *The Texas Chainsaw Massacre 2* (1986) incorporated no supernatural elements, but undercut the horror with both overt sociopolitical statements and broad comedy. *Jason Lives!* advanced the slasher by applying supernatural elements in order to revitalize a financially diminishing franchise, but this innovation only occurred in response to other more innovative films and franchises, particularly the *A Nightmare on Elm Street* films.

The New Blood incorporated more supernatural plotting into the narrative by making the protagonist, Tina, telekinetic.[17] This follows on from the story line

---

15. To date, I'm the only person that has academically defended and praised *A New Beginning* based on artistic merit (see Clayton 2015b). Make of that what you will.

16. $21.9 million, according to Bracke (143).

17. Caryn James's contemporary review of the film for the *New York Times* describes Tina, the protagonist, as "a Carrie clone" (1988), in reference to the telekinetic protagonist from the Stephen King novel (1974) and Brian De Palma's 1976 film adaptation.

of *A Nightmare on Elm Street Part 2: Freddy's Revenge* (1985), in which Freddy kills his victims by possessing a teenage boy. While this plot point in *Freddy's Revenge* directly translates into the later *Jason Goes to Hell*, it still indicates the divergence of the *Friday the 13th* series from the types of slasher stories that appear in the earlier films. There is also a close link to *A Nightmare on Elm Street 4: The Dream Master* (1988), in which the female protagonist, Kristen, has the ability to draw others into her dreams, allowing her to assemble a group of people to defeat Freddy. This shows a clear interest in the use of psychic powers as a supernatural antidote to supernatural evil during this period, which we can see in *Sorority House Massacre,* and even as far back as *Eyes of Laura Mars*. Yes, John Carpenter is quite an important figure for the slasher.

The New Blood was also released the year following *Evil Dead 2* (1987), which simultaneously demonstrates the influence of *Friday the 13th* and the increasing unfashionability of slasher subgenre. *The Evil Dead* (1981), which came out a year after *Friday the 13th,* similarly follows a small group of teenagers who go camping at an isolated spot in the middle of the woods. While the overtly supernatural narrative of *The Evil Dead* stands in contrast to the mainstream films released at the time, the early portions of the film share similarities in *mise-en-scéne* (all the stuff in front of the camera) and sound design with such films as *Friday the 13th*. *Evil Dead 2*, however, appears to go along with contemporary horror film trends, and even incorporates strong elements of comedy, similar to *Texas Chainsaw Massacre 2*. However, a film like *The Stepfather* (1987) includes no supernatural elements; instead, as with *Henry: Portrait of a Serial Killer* (1986), it more closely focuses on the psychology of the killer. We can see these mind-of-a-killer stories in movies linked to the slasher going back almost a decade in *When A Stranger Calls* (1979), famous for the "have you checked the children?" phone calls and "the caller is coming from inside the house!"[18]

These films closely establish the perspective of the killer, both as aggressor and victim, and at the same time attach themselves to the perspective of the victim of the killer's violence and terrorism. At this point, however, the *Friday the 13th* series is primarily focused on creating generic orientation, clearly establishing the tropes of the genre so we don't get too lost in the unusual experiments. This phase of *Friday the 13th* places narrative identification with the protagonist, which puts Jason, like Freddy in *A Nightmare on Elm Street*, firmly in the position of the villain, the dangerous and unknowable entity, by removing the aspects of his character that arouse pity in the earlier films.

---

18. Similarly used in *Black Christmas,* and generally drawn from campfire ghost stories and contemporary Western folklore.

During what Ian Conrich describes as the "shocking reveal" (2010, 180) of *The New Blood*, Jason's ugliness does not incite pity,[19] but creates an advantage for him by disarming the protagonist with shock and fear, and making him appear even more monstrous.

Jason Takes Manhattan renews the eliciting of pity through Jason's condition, as several sequences show Rennie observing Jason as a crying, deformed boy. These moments work as an extension of Rennie's clairvoyance, which clearly demonstrates the continuing use of the supernatural in the series. Additionally, the movie features the added novelty of moving Jason away from Camp Crystal Lake, a generic rural setting, to a specifically recognizable urban setting: Vancouver. Well, er, Manhattan. Which is actually Vancouver. And Times Square.

While moving a franchise out of its recognizable location is not repeated across other horror films released at the time, others also told stories where psychic phenomena become intertwined with horror narratives. *Halloween 4: The Return of Michael Myers* (1988) attempts a closer return to the early 1980s slasher formula, introducing the character of Jaime, the daughter of Laurie from *Halloween* and *Halloween II*, who has died before the events of *Halloween 4*. Jaime, however, through nightmares, has the ability to foretell the danger presented by Michael. Following this, *Halloween 5: The Revenge of Michael Myers* sees Jaime rendered mute by the traumatic experience of the previous film. However, she shares a psychic connection with Michael, much like Rennie's psychic connection to Jason in *Jason Takes Manhattan*, released the same year. This illustrates little change in the slasher's infusion of the supernatural into its plotlines and an increased sympathy for the killer, while favoring the perspective of the protagonists.

Two years following the release of *Jason Takes Manhattan*, New Line released *Freddy's Dead: The Final Nightmare* (1991), which can be taken as evidence of the unprofitability of the running horror franchises. While *Freddy's Dead* director Rachel Talalay clearly aims at radically subversive fun, it also contains multiple elements designed to increase the novelty factor of the film. This suggests an effort to reach for mainstream appeal and high box-office receipts.[20]

---

19. I certainly cannot make a claim that the franchise's disability politics are in any way progressive. Whether Jason's deformity causes fear or pity, it is still a tough nut to slice, if you'll forgive my mixed and pointless metaphor.

20. In her keynote at the DePaul University Pop Culture Conference titled "A Celebration of Slashers" on April 28, 2018, Talalay firmly confronted critics of the film, and argued that its structure, flaws, and successes all relate to the business practices and historical context of the period. It's also worth noting that Talalay, a truly wonderful and generous person, has a history of working with John Waters prior to this—a filmmaker who has relished the subversive possibilities of novelty.

First, as indicated by the title, the film promises the end of the culturally significant *A Nightmare on Elm Street* franchise, telling viewers that they should expect to be witness to the end of this cultural institution. Secondly, the film includes cameos from US television celebrity couple Roseanne Barr[21] and Tom Arnold.[22] Roseanne at this point had one of the highest-rated sitcoms on American television, and *Freddy's Dead* appeared one year after her much-publicized, high-profile marriage to comedian Arnold. We can interpret the inclusion of the couple in the film following the amount of media coverage of their relationship as an effort to increase ticket sales. In addition, *Freddy's Dead* featured a climax shown in 3-D in theaters, promising a unique viewing experience. 3-D was (still) not frequently used at this point, and the VHS home video format rarely, if ever, released films in 3-D, opting instead for 2-D transfers, as happened with *Friday the 13th Part III*. While *The Final Chapter*, like *Freddy's Dead*, also promised to be the last of the *Friday the 13th* franchise, it did not use similar attempts at novelty, aside from featuring this finality in its title. The fact that *Freddy's Dead* tried so many different things to sell itself points to the large amount of effort the producers deemed necessary to attract an audience.

The attempt was successful, and *Freddy's Dead* turned a greater profit than its predecessor, *A Nightmare on Elm Street: The Dream Child* (1989). According to J. A. Kerswell, "Freddy also lost his sparkle in *A Nightmare on Elm Street: The Dream Child*; it proved to be a sequel too far, taking $22,168,359, less than half what its predecessor had barely a year ago" (161). *Jason Takes Manhattan* also turned a low profit,[23] and Paramount Pictures sold the franchise to New Line Cinema, which also owned the rights to *A Nightmare on Elm Street*. The success of *Freddy's Dead*[24] prompted New Line to develop another closing film for the *Friday the 13th* franchise, resulting in *Jason Goes to Hell*.

Instead of relying on cameo appearances or 3-D sequences, *Jason Goes to Hell* again announced the finality of the series through the title; the film also tried to explain the logical gaps in the overarching story. *Jason Goes to Hell* applies an explanation that Jason's essence is a demonic worm that uses human bodies as hosts, and only a special dagger wielded by a relative can kill him,

---

21. As of the week that I am rewriting this sentence, a tremendously problematic and infamous personality.—WC 05/31/18

22. Infamous since 1994.

23. *Jason Takes Manhattan* took in $14.3 million in US box-office receipts on a $5 million production budget. This is less than its predecessor, *The New Blood* ($19.2 million on a $2.8 million budget) and the film that followed *Jason Takes Manhattan*, *Jason Goes to Hell*.

24. $34,872,033, according to Kerswell (2010, 161).

explaining why he keeps returning from the dead. This overtly supernatural development shares similarities with the *Halloween* sequels. Similar plot points are seen in the last two (at the time of *Jason Goes to Hell*'s release) *A Nightmare on Elm Street* films, where the bloodline of the killer is his fatal weakness. The *Friday the 13th* films alternate perspective frequently during this period, all with the apparent goal, again, of providing generic orientation, which seems necessary considering the radical narrative experimentation.

Nineteen ninety-three, the year that *Jason Goes to Hell* came out, proved a low point for slasher films, with the only significant addition being *Leprechaun*, a film in which a leprechaun kills people in order to defend and retrieve his gold. This film included a centrally supernatural storyline, as well as strong ties to comedy, though structurally it retained slasher elements. *Leprechaun* became one of the more significant horror films from the early 1990s, launching a series of sequels throughout that decade and into the early 2000s.

A more "serious" (that is, less comedic) franchise which began in the early 1990s was *Candyman* (1992), which also retained structural similarities to the slasher but remained firmly within the supernatural, with many similarities to the *A Nightmare on Elm Street* films but fewer ties to *Friday the 13th*. A made-for-television sequel to *When A Stranger Calls*, entitled *When a Stranger Calls Back* (1993), as well as *Maniac Cop 3: Badge of Silence* (1993), also came out that year, which were sequels to previous films using the slasher formula. The minimal success of these films demonstrates the diminishing cultural relevance of the genre during this period. I should note, however, that during 1993, Dario Argento released *Trauma*, which signaled a return to the murder-mystery-style giallo film, in a similar vein to his films *Bird with the Crystal Plumage* and *Deep Red* (1975), for the first time since 1982's *Tenebrae*.

Between *Tenebrae* and *Trauma*, Argento returned to supernatural-based narratives, the only possible exception being 1987's *Opera*, which still retained an exaggerated Gothic melodramatic sensibility. This makes a fair bit of sense as Argento based the film on Gaston Leroux's novel, and early cinematic adaptations of, *The Phantom of the Opera*. Argento's decision to return to the format that inspired and informed the *Friday the 13th* films proves an interesting choice at this point in time, when the slasher was in the midst of a significant decline.

Halloween: The Curse of Michael Myers (1995) maintained the franchise's tendency toward the supernatural. However, like *Jason Goes to Hell*, it tried to fill gaps in the overarching plotline. In the case of *The Curse of Michael Myers*, which Adam Rockoff describes as "a film so bad and disrespectful to the franchise that it's a mystery how anyone could have even allowed it to be made" (173), the film employed an occult fantasy narrative. In this movie, a group of people who consider Halloween a dark, holy day lionize Michael as its physical embodiment. Jamie, now a young woman, is impregnated by the cult which wishes to infuse the child with Michael's powers. This narrative contains multiple points of contact with *Jason Goes to Hell*, and its subsequent financial failure[25] echoes that of its *Friday the 13th* counterpart. I don't recommend blaming Paul Rudd for the film's failure, though.

During this period of decline, the slasher film began toying with self-referentiality, looking at the tropes we are all familiar with and pointing them out. Wes Craven pioneered the mainstream wing of this trend with *Wes Craven's New Nightmare* (1994), his attempt to revive the *A Nightmare on Elm Street* series. In this film, Heather Langenkamp, the actor who performed the role of final girl Nancy in *A Nightmare on Elm Street*, plays a fictionalized version of herself who begins to have nightmares about a Freddy Krueger-type character. In order to save herself and her son from danger, Heather talks to other cast and crew members from the original film about their experiences with this mysterious figure. Heather encounters people such as Robert Englund and Johnny Depp, eventually asking for help from Wes Craven, who reveals that he drew the idea for the screenplay from his own dreams, verifying the existence of this threatening figure. Craven here develops a narrative that acknowledges the fictitiousness of the original series, and attempts to bring Freddy Krueger into real life. This heightens the potential horror of the situation by breaking away one element of artifice, and at the same time draws attention to the behind-the-scenes element of filmmaking, exposing the inner workings of this process.

Although *New Nightmare* did not prove successful enough to warrant a sequel,[26] Craven further developed this metanarrative design in *Scream* (1996), which centers on a killer who is apparently obsessed with horror films. Instead of taking us behind the scenes of slasher films, *Scream* draws attention to the subgenre's formula. Characters in *Scream* manage to survive attacks through a familiarity with specific films and generic conventions. The success of *Scream* resulted in a sequel released the following year. *Scream 2* (1997) furthered the use of metanarrative, or self-referential, storytelling. The movie accomplished this first, by focusing on slasher sequels and how they work. Secondly, *Scream 2* used the narrative to reference itself—not just the genre—specifically. In the film, Gayle, the journalist from *Scream* played by Courtney Cox, has written a book about the events of the previous film, resulting in a film adaptation which is not only central to the story but also a strong point of self-referencing.

In the wake of *Scream*, two other slasher series began, both significant for different reasons, in that they both represent key trends within this period. One continues in the metanarrative slasher vein of *Scream*, and the other

---

25. According to Muir (33), *The Curse of Michael Myers* only brought in $14.7 million.
26. See Fuchs (2010, 82).

demonstrates a return to traditional slasher formulas. A direct relative to *Scream* was 1998's *Urban Legend*, which tells the story of a stalker who kills people according to popular urban legends. While *Urban Legend* does not approach the level of self-referentiality of *Scream* and *Scream 2*, it features a cameo by Freddy Krueger himself, Robert Englund, and the narrative centers on the concept of stories, elements of which we assume are general knowledge as the *modus operandi* of a killer. And as in *Scream*, familiarity with these stories increases a person's chance of survival.

The year before that, *I Know What You Did Last Summer* (1997) came out, which signaled a return to the slasher formula of the early 1980s. The story has similarities to *Terror Train* and *The Burning*, in which the protagonists directly harm the killer in the first act, and his killing spree is vengeance for this harm. The sequel, released in 1998, *I Still Know What You Did Last Summer* retains the generic formula, displacing the surviving characters from the first film to an exotic island.

We can see this return to formula in *Halloween H20* (1998) which also saw the return of star Jamie Lee Curtis to the franchise for the first time since *Halloween II* in 1981. The movie, however, toys with self-referentiality, as *Halloween H20* also features a cameo by Janet Leigh, who is Curtis's real-life mother and star of *Psycho*. In *Halloween H20*, Laurie Strode is now a grown headmaster of a private school after going into the witness protection program following the events of *Halloween II*. Her son attends the school, and is now in danger from the homicidal nepotism of Michael.

While this return to formula in slasher movies did not see as much use as the metanarrative trend initiated by *Scream*, it was not limited to just a few flicks. Movies like *Joy Ride* (2001) and *Valentine* (2001) both used a similar narrative structure and style to the early slashers. *Urban Legend* resulted in a sequel that explored self-referentiality more intricately. *Urban Legends: Final Cut* (2000) focuses on a series of killings on a Hollywood film set, each one based on an urban legend. The lead character is a postgraduate student completing her thesis on urban legends, closely resembling *Scream 2*, in which the killer is a film student. This not only establishes a character with a greater familiarity of the killing methods, but also addresses the process of filmmaking at the same time.

Urban Legends: Final Cut, released the same year as *Scream 3* (2000), used a similar story of killings occurring on a film set. *Scream 3*, however, directly incorporates more self-referentiality, as the film being made is a sequel to the film that appears in *Scream 2*, which is an adaptation of the events in *Scream*. In *Scream 3*, all of the surviving characters come to the film set to investigate the murders that are happening around fabricated locations of events in which they participated. The film also uses the opportunity to discuss narrative tendencies of final installments of trilogies.

Also in 2000, *Jason X* was completed and intended for release, but did not see distribution until 2002 due to restructuring in the upper management of New Line Cinema (Bracke 263–64). Multiple self-referential elements appear in *Jason X*, and were it released in 2000 as planned, it would have thematically fit alongside *Scream 3* and *Urban Legends: Final Cut*. *Friday the 13th* historian Peter Bracke writes, "By the time New Line released the film on April 26, 2002, much had changed both in the world of digital filmmaking and in the sensibilities and expectations of the moviegoing public" (263). Bracke also addresses the advances made in special effects, in addition to questioning the potential of the *Friday the 13th* franchise to still draw in audiences. Releasing the film in 2000 would only leave a seven-year gap in installments for the series. Ultimately, *Jason X* was released after nearly a decade since the previous film, in a franchise that had seen no more than a four-year gap between movies. The difficulty of being heavily reliant on special effects that had become dated further complicated matters.

One year after New Line released *Jason X*, *Freddy vs. Jason* managed a large box-office take[27] by adapting the tendencies of the "postmodern", or rather, self-referential slasher to a deceptively straightforward story. The crossover appeal didn't hurt either. The meeting of both the *Friday the 13th* and *A Nightmare on Elm Street* franchises allowed the film to directly address different killing styles of the antagonists. The movie further defined the killers' motivations and allowed each franchise to comment on the other, without drawing as much attention to the artifice as *Scream 3* or even *Scream*. *Freddy vs. Jason* used this metanarrative approach as a subtext to heighten the antagonism between the two killers. We can see another effort at franchise crossovers a year later with *AVP: Alien vs. Predator* (2004).

During this time, we can also see the advent of two popular movements in horror that would dominate a large proportion of the genre's releases. As mentioned, *The Blair Witch Project* not only brought the victim-camera movement into the mainstream, but also demonstrated the potential for a return to low-budget filmmaking in horror. One significant follower of this movement is *Halloween: Resurrection* (2002),[28] in which a group of students volunteers to participate in an internet broadcast where they stay in the Myers house with head-mounted and house-mounted cameras recording the events. We see a lot of the head-mounted camera footage in this movie incorporating the style of victim-camera as seen in *The Blair Witch Project*.

---

27. $82,622,655, according to Kerswell (178).

28. *Halloween: Resurrection* is a brilliant and deeply underappreciated film—and shame on you for not believing me.

However, *Halloween: Resurrection* also incorporates a sense of metanarrativity within the framework. In the movie, Michael and his killings are not only matters of general knowledge, but have attained a position of legend, much like the myth of Jason and the increased awareness of this myth by the characters within the *Friday the 13th* series. In order to increase hits on the webpage broadcasting this, the producer/director, Freddie, sets up fabricated booby traps in the house to frighten the participants. In one unsettling moment of self-referentiality, we see Michael from behind with a knife stalking around the lower level of the house with everyone else upstairs, when another Michael appears in the frame stalking behind the first Michael. Seeing one Michael following another is disorienting until it is revealed that the first Michael is Freddie dressed as Michael to frighten the participants, berating someone whom he believes to be a technician also dressed as Michael, when it is, in fact, Michael himself. *Halloween: Resurrection* historically marks the dying out of the popular metanarrative slasher and the rise of the use of victim-camera.

The other film from this period that initiated a popular trend in horror is Gus Van Sant's remake of *Psycho* (1998), bringing self-referentiality to its logical conclusion by overtly replicating known properties in their tiniest details.[29] This version of *Psycho*, while eluding financial success,[30] gained much publicity for its close shot-for-shot approach to remaking. Although there was not an immediate wave of slasher remakes, the Van Sant-directed *Psycho* generated a significant amount of public conversation about the possibilities of remaking. The movie also marks a key transition point between the tendency towards self-referencing in contemporary horror and the potential to extend this into film remakes.

The Texas Chainsaw Massacre (2003) became the direct model for the trend of slasher remakes. While not precisely faithful to its source material, *The Texas Chainsaw Massacre* streamlined a style for remaking that worked outside of the trends of its contemporaries, becoming, in the process, a trendsetter in its own right. Instead of Leatherface relegated to an easily recognizable, awkward, menacing character in a family of equally threatening characters, as in the original films, he became the central threat, with other characters facilitating his bloodlust and occasionally fulfilling their own.

Following this, filmmakers revived and adapted multiple slashers for contemporary audiences, resulting in *The Hills Have Eyes* (2006), *Black Christmas* (2006), *The Hitcher* (2007), *Halloween* (2007), *Prom Night* (2008),

---

29. The official production website, http://www.psychomovie.com/production/production-why.html, is sadly now defunct, but had some wonderful material about the remaking process.

30. According to *Box Office Mojo*, the 1998 version of *Psycho* earned a lifetime worldwide gross of $37.1 million on a production budget of $60 million.

My Bloody Valentine 3-D (2009), *Friday the 13th* (2009), and *A Nightmare on Elm Street* (2010), among others. These remakes are notable for making the stories and set pieces even more unpleasant than before, as identified by Sarah Wharton. Some of the deaths that occur in these films linger on the extreme brutality and violence, occasionally highlighting the fragility of the body of the victim. This dark violence tends to follow sequences that provide richer character development than what we see in earlier slasher films. Examples of this include many of the deaths in Rob Zombie's remake of *Halloween* and its sequel, *Halloween II* (2009), particularly with Annie and Lynda, whose attacks are shown with extensive graphic and visceral detail, with their pain and fear registered during extended amounts of screen time. The deaths of Andy and Morgan in *The Texas Chainsaw Massacre* create a similar effect, as do the deaths of Chewie and Amanda in *Friday the 13th* (2009).

Amanda's death is a particularly illustrative example as it reimagines and adapts a famous death sequence in the series. In *The New Blood*, Jason picks up Judy while she is still in her sleeping bag and hits her against a tree to kill her. The sequence contains a few short shots cut together of Jason swinging the sleeping bag, the sleeping bag hitting the tree, and then Jason dropping the bag. We see a comedic version of this in *Jason X*, in a long shot captured in a continuous take. In *Friday the 13th* (2009), however, Jason traps Amanda in her sleeping bag, suspending it from a tree branch directly over a campfire. The camera cuts between shots of the sleeping bag as Amanda screams and thrashes trying to get out, and shots within the sleeping bag, showing the obvious panic and desperation on her face as she struggles. We hear the crackling of the fire and the sizzling of her flesh, and at the end of the sequence, she falls out of the bag, her body burnt beyond recognition. The sequence is also longer than the sleeping bag set pieces in *The New Blood* and *Jason X*, prolonging the focus on her pain and suffering.

Referencing and adjusting elements of earlier films, then, proves a key part of remaking the slasher. *The Hills Have Eyes* updated the story of the original (1977), addressing the potential ramifications of the contemporary political climate. *Black Christmas* takes the intrinsic aesthetic theme of vision and seeing and overtly makes it part of the story as the killer's MO involves removing their victims' eyes. Furthermore, *Black Christmas*, *Halloween*, *My Bloody Valentine 3-D*, and *A Nightmare on Elm Street* dedicated more screen time to character backstories than their source texts. Many of these remakes have resulted in another series. We end up with film sequels such as *The Hills Have Eyes II* (2007) and *Halloween II*, and the prequel *The Texas Chainsaw Massacre: The Beginning* (2006).[31]

---

31. George Lucas's poor reviews be damned.

A final significant trend in slashers is the advent and subsequent decline of "torture porn,"[32] otherwise known by my preferred term, "torture horror,"[33] particularly as it runs concurrently with the recent cycle of slasher remakes. The "darker" stories and greater focus on suffering work as a point of overlap between these two movements. The primary elements of torture horror have closely informed slasher remakes, as can clearly be seen in *Friday the 13th* (2009).

The *Friday the 13th* franchise has held an incredibly important role in the evolution of the slasher film. The series has both responded to and influenced contemporary trends in film style. It naturally follows that the apparent influence of *Friday the 13th* in terms of story or plot would also extend to subtler elements of how the stories are told. In addition, while there is some crossover concerning the perspectives used in the movies, the slasher's evolving style is, of course, going to include examples that are nowhere near mainstream trends. If nobody took stylistic risks, we'd still be watching people wandering out of factories. However, what this does show is that it is not the specific perspective that is significant, but how this perspective is rendered through the film's form. The aesthetic similarities between the films of this genre create a picture of dominant stylistic trends, and the development of less solid, tenuous aesthetic elements into a fluid progression of simultaneous stylistic advance. Somebody will take risks, and some of these risks filter into the wash cycle, until all of our work shirts end up pink.

Since the beginning of the *Friday the 13th* film series, movies outside of the franchise reached the status of "classics" within the subgenre and even received acknowledgment for their originality or significance. Critics, both academic and mainstream, frequently derided and overlooked the *Friday the 13th* series. Even Roger Ebert's review of the 2009 reboot reflects the amount of contempt he holds for it: "I know what you're thinking. No, I haven't seen them all. Wikipedia saw them so I didn't have to." Ebert clearly thought it was unnecessary to even see the movies to be qualified to sit in judgement of them. But in spite of this poor reception, the series still stands as an effective barometer for developments within the genre over this thirty-plus-year period. And those other critics aren't me, poor bastards.

---

32. Coined by David Edelstein (2006), this term suggests sexual gratification and has been examined in great depth by Steve Jones (2013).

33. Coined by Jeremy Morris (2010, 54) as a more accurate term than "torture porn."

Chapter 2

Jason's Mechanical Eye

The original screenwriter of *Friday the 13th*, Victor Miller, once recalled that producer/director Sean S. Cunningham "called me up and said, '*Halloween* is making a lot of money at the box office. Why don't we rip it off?'" (quoted in Bracke 2005, 17). Few researchers hit such a jackpot in tracing a movie's stylistic antecedents. However, in all the firsthand accounts of the first film's production, there is, what TV cops like to call an "orgy of evidence."

Associate producer Steve Miner similarly explained:

> I loved the original *Halloween*. It was a breakthrough for American cinema really. It pioneered several concepts, of the independent film having mainstream success, and of a certain type of horror film as a genre. And it was really well done, a really terrific film. It relied on classic suspense and situations, and not gore. With *Friday the 13th*, we tried to copy the success of *Halloween*, clearly. (ibid.)

Cunningham further describes the inspiration for *Friday the 13th*, saying, "Obviously, from a financial standpoint, which was the most important factor at the time of making *Friday*, the success of *Halloween* was the main inspiration. I think Bava certainly inspired me. His films were shocking and really visually-stunning and they made you jump out of your seat, which was what I wanted *Friday* to be all about" (quoted in Grove 2005, 11–12).

Theorists and critics also note the background of *Friday the 13th*'s business and aesthetics. Kevin Heffernan discusses this business model as well, saying, "Paramount's *Friday the 13th* series follows the time-honored fifties and sixties tradition of a major studio knocking off the genre success of an independent production (in this case, John Carpenter's independently produced *Halloween*)" (223).

Clearly, *Halloween* was incredibly important to the development of *Friday the 13th*. As Cunningham revealed, however, the acknowledged inspiration of Mario Bava's films shows that *Halloween* alone is not solely responsible. As Dika writes:

> *Friday the 13th* was the first film to reproduce the success of *Halloween* by copying its intrinsic elements. Although *Friday the 13th* is a minimalization or reduction of *Halloween*'s essential structure, it incorporates elements from other successful films (e.g., *Dawn of the Dead*, *Last House on the Left*) and so is an amalgam of visual and narrative motifs that significantly add to the formula. (1990, 64) [parenthesis in original]

All of these influences partly dictate the way *Friday the 13th* and its sequels use first-person camerawork. *Friday the 13th*, like *Halloween*, even like *Twitch of the Death Nerve*, features the eye/camera from the start of the film, and the device remains prominent throughout. The basic function of the eye/camera aligns with Wood's "alternative explanation," the need to disguise the identity of the killer. Clover also elaborates on the use of the eye/camera as a device used to disguise the killer:

> Again, *Friday the Thirteenth I*, in which "we" stalk and kill a number of teenagers over the course of an hour of movie time without even knowing who "we" are; we are invited, by conventional expectation and by glimpses of "our" own bodily parts—a heavily booted foot, a roughly gloved hand—to suppose that "we" are male, but "we" are revealed, at the film's end, as a woman. (56)

Clover's assessment identifies *Friday the 13th*'s debt to *Psycho*, *Black Christmas*, and *Twitch of the Death Nerve*. These, in addition to the opening sequence of *Halloween*, are other movies which hide the killer's identity, often using the eye/camera, to create a final surprise.[1]

---

1. *Black Christmas* proves a significant variant to the murder mystery formula of these earlier films, in that there are, in fact, two final surprises. In the climax, the "final girl," Jess, concludes that her temperamental artist boyfriend, Peter, is the killer, as he appears at the house before the police have been able to arrive. The film frames Peter in a very sinister and imposing manner, and Jess suddenly kills him to defend herself. The end of the film, however, reveals that he was not the killer.

The identity of the killer (Mrs. Voorhees) in the first *Friday the 13th* movie is hidden until the end. Therefore, like many early slashers, the movie structurally resembles a mystery story, similar to *And Then There Were None*. *Twitch of the Death Nerve* has a similar structure, but surprises the viewer in revealing that not *one* of the central characters, but *two*, are the killers. In this movie, the eye/camera also acts, as discussed by Wood, as a method of disguising the identity of the killer.

However, Mrs. Voorhees is not a central character in *Friday the 13th*. In fact, she does not appear in the film until Alice is the only living character remaining, or if you prefer, the final girl. In this way, *Friday the 13th* follows the structure of *Black Christmas*, in which the killer, dubiously attached to the name "Billy," is never fully identified. We only know who "Billy" is through his repetition of this name in the muddled personalities of his garbled phone calls that always follow a murder he has committed. The only part of him we ever see is his eye. *Black Christmas* acknowledges the mystery structure by revealing Peter, an emotionally volatile character, as the only other person near the house. Jess kills him, suspecting he is "Billy," but the film ends with Jess sleeping under sedation alone in the house, and as the camera shows the outside of the house, the repeated, unanswered ringing of the phone indicates the high probability that "Billy" is still alive—and has just killed Jess.

Black Christmas attaches the eye/camera to a character who is never properly identified throughout the course of the film. *Friday the 13th* develops Mrs. Voorhees much as *Black Christmas* develops "Billy." And, although she is eventually identified as the killer and her motivation is explained, no previous sequence really gives the viewer a chance to guess "whodunit," resulting in the killer's identity being fundamentally enigmatic.

Clover also identifies the misleading gender game played by *Friday the 13th*, which can be traced to both *Psycho* and *Twitch of the Death Nerve*. *Psycho*'s Norman Bates identifies as a man, but when he kills, he embodies the personality of his mother, a woman. This approach to gender identity is a way to mislead the viewer from guessing the identity of the killer. *Friday the 13th* shows glimpses of the killer, and these glimpses (and genre tropes) suggest the killer is male: masculine hands, heavy boots on the feet, androgynous camper clothes. The revelation that the killer is a woman replaces the surprise that traditionally comes with the revelation that a trusted character is the killer in mystery stories. *Twitch of the Death Nerve* tends to remove itself from creating gender assumptions within the viewer, but the revelation that there are two killers, one male and one female, justifies this ambiguity.

The vague identity of the killer in *Friday the 13th* creates a challenge to the issue of character perspective and its relationship to the audience. The eye/

camera shots intentionally distance viewer perspective, without excluding the viewer from complete understanding. These shots prevent a full sense of identification as the viewer does not know who they are seeing through. However, the banality of the events viewed, combined with the menacing score, provide an understanding of the seer's motivation. These qualities of the image encompass the narrative drive of the film, through this particular perspective positioning.

The opening sequence, depicting what Dika categorizes as the "past event" (1990, 59), is reminiscent of the single-shot eye/camera opening of *Halloween*, as noted by Cunningham: "Working on a limited budget, there wasn't much choice other than doing it that way. I'm hoping that people can take it as sort of a tip of the hat to Mr. Carpenter" (quoted in Martin 1980, 64). Unlike *Halloween*, the opening of *Friday the 13th* breaks up the eye/camera shots with third-person shots that establish the location and potential victims in more detail.

The film begins, establishing Camp Crystal Lake in 1950 as populated by a number of campers. It's nighttime and a group of counselors sing "Michael Row the Boat Ashore" and "Tom Dooley" by a(n indoor) fire. Two of these counselors, clearly attracted to one another based on the googly eyes they make at each other during the song dictating Michael's nautical efforts, sneak off to be alone. Within this establishing sequence we see an eye/camera shot, taking the first-person perspective of someone stalking through the cabin of the young campers, who are asleep in their beds. The proximity fear is immediate, as we know that all of these young children are vulnerable to attack specifically due to the eerie and threatening music accompanying the shot, along with the fact that it is night and they are asleep. Although nothing happens, this device creates tension through all of the sinister stylistic elements.

The two amorous counselors sneak off to a nearby barn and go to the upstairs room, where they begin to have sex. The eye/camera stalks them, following the sounds of their voices up the stairs until they come into view. The two counselors notice the stalker and quickly stand up to straighten their clothes, embarrassed. The eye/camera pushes toward the boy, who is stuttering trying to explain what they were doing. The camera lunges toward the boy as he doubles over, apparently struck in the stomach.

After this long, continuous eye/camera take, the film suddenly cuts to a long shot of the boy, who stumbles backwards, holding his bleeding stomach as he falls over. The audience is presented with the attack and death of the boy from two perspectives: first-person and third-person. Through this moment, *Friday the 13th* challenges the viewer to decide which perspective is more frightening. The movie answers its own question in two ways: first through creating a detached and ambivalent third-person camera shot that is shocking in its lack of intensity of movement in comparison with the previous shot; and second through an immediate return to the eye/camera. This transition between perspectives feels disjointed and creates a sense of disruption. The sequence ends with this eye/camera shot, slowly chasing the terrified surviving girl around the room into a corner, ending in a gradually enlarging and fading freeze-frame of the girl's final scream. The entire sequence gives you the very important first fright of the film, setting the mood almost entirely through the first-person perspective.

The dissolve on the freeze-frame leads directly into the opening credit sequence, which begins with the title "*Friday the 13th*" in large three-dimensional font moving quickly from a point in the distance toward the audience. As unsettling as the swift movement of the title may be, the movie assumes the viewer feels protected by the cinema screen. At the very least, it presupposes you do not anticipate a scare from the credits. Cunningham, however, uses the eye/camera from the previous sequence to his advantage, as the eye/camera shot works to make the viewer feel directly involved with the action within the film.

When the title has filled the screen, it stops suddenly. A pane of glass seeming to separate the audience from the title unexpectedly shatters with a loud crash on the soundtrack. The film confronts us with the last thing we actually expect to be confronted with: the opening title. And, here, the eye/camera compression model ingeniously breaks apart. The movie interacts with us directly, without using the point-of-view of a character within the film. This specific moment does not try to make us feel involved through a mediating character, but directly involves us in the action on-screen. The movie does not provide a direct address, a point at which a character speaks to the cinema audience. However, creating such an effect so close to the start of the film pointedly draws us closer to the action by breaking through the limitations of the eye/camera and engaging us directly.[2]

While these elements demonstrate the unique and aggressive approach that *Friday the 13th* takes with the eye/camera, critics such as Wood and others insist upon describing the eye/camera of the film in the same negative way

---

2. Other films have recreated and adapted this use of the opening credits to create a visceral response. An example is *Final Destination 5 3-D* (2011), in which the titles appear to be printed on transparent glass. Objects that appear in the background move toward the viewer, such as lead piping, nails, dismembered body parts, and charred corpses. As these items reach the titles, the glass panes shatter, and the objects, as well as small shards of glass, appear to move toward the spectator.

as other slasher movies of the period. Before providing an analysis of eye/camera sequences in *Friday the 13th*, Reynold Humphries deconstructs the eye/camera's function by discussing the effect of shifting perspectives on the viewer. In essence, Humphries sees the eye/camera as giving the viewer the illusion of power while simultaneously creating empathy for the victims of this power. Humphries argues that these juxtaposed sensations blunt the negative aspects of both. The movie simultaneously excuses us for relishing in the sadism of the aggressor while protecting us from the experience of victimization. He then summarizes by saying that this ultimately places the viewer in a position to experience an event where, in reality, they are more likely to be the victim (143–44).

Despite his critical view of the eye/camera, Humphries defends *Friday the 13th*'s innovative use of the eye/camera through the examples of two sequences:

> It is here that *Friday the 13th* fails to play the game. At one point a girl at the camp goes to the toilet after having sex. The camera tracks in slowly towards her from our point of view, as if someone is/we are approaching her. She looks up, not into the camera but off-screen left in the direction of a sound. This is repeated in an almost identical fashion shortly after where another girl goes to the toilet: the character does not look into the camera and there is no shot-reverse shot indicating some menacing figure about to stab her. Thus the film places the spectator in a position of potential aggressor, only to reveal that the danger lies off-screen. By so doing it suggests that the danger exists for us too—the off-screen being the favourite place for lurking monsters—and that our supposedly homogenous subject position is in fact a split one, a split which corresponds to our split position as spectators outside the text and as spectators inscribed within the text by various modes of identification. (144)

Humphries acknowledges the challenging use of the eye/camera within the film. His observation creates a stronger sense of how *Friday the 13th* uses the eye/camera in a stylistically unique and innovative way, suggesting its significance to the development of slasher aesthetics. The sophistication of eye/camera usage in *Friday the 13th* provided a strong stylistic foundation for the following films in the franchise, which is why I'm discussing it here. This movie is a clear starting point to show how use of the eye/camera can be advanced and varied, and while it is more consistent in some films, others prove more playful.

Although Cunningham revealed himself as inventive with the eye/camera structure, the earliest eye/camera shots in the film, including the pre-credit sequence, are representative of what I will call "direct" eye/camera shots. These are shots that clearly correspond with the viewer eye/camera lens/character eye model shown in my cute little drawing. In direct eye/camera shots, the image is designed to precisely correspond, occasionally with some small variation, with the precise eye position of a character. These direct eye/camera shots continue to appear throughout the *Friday the 13th* films, and while the stylistic variants are usually minor, specific variations tend to go through phases, which I will explore. However, the important questions moving forward are: who are we looking through, and what does it do for our viewing experience?

Kill or be killed

With so many critics suggesting first-person camerawork is an excuse to indulge in our nasty little sadistic fantasies, it is useful to discuss the films which use eye/camera shots from an aggressor's perspective. I am using the term "aggressor" loosely. Here, I mean someone who has some form of power or control, whether it is one of actively or inconspicuously watching, attacking, or simply *moving forward* towards its subject. It should be noted that inconspicuous watching can take the form of aggressor or victim, depending on how the rest of the eye/camera shots in the film are framed. Here, when padded with eye/camera shots that attack or move forward, the act of watching becomes aggressive and sinister. Like a shark in an ever-moving, predatory position, the aggressor eye/camera is likely the type of shot writers think of when considering this device as a vehicle for sadistic voyeurism.

Friday the 13th Part 2, for example, predominately places the eye/camera in positions of power, over both the characters and events in the film as well as the audience. The eye/camera's power over the characters and events is overtly recognizable, positioning the viewer in the place of an acknowledged or known character, whether the killer or one of the many victims, in a situation where they actively control the action. In one of the more banal eye/camera sequences, the viewer sees through Jeff's[3] point-of-view as he drives the truck into the woods and approaches a rotting log in the middle of the road. As we see through him, Jeff is driving the truck towards the log. Jeff stops, and, along with Sandra and Ted, he gets out of the truck, pondering the object. Ted asks, "What's that?" Jeff responds, "Where'd that sucker come from?" Ted replies, "I don't know. Let's move it." As this brilliantly superfluous exchange occurs, the viewer is placed in a stalker's, most likely Jason's, eye/camera, watching

---

3. See appendix 2 for a full list of characters from each film, so you hopefully are not too disoriented by interchangeable names.

the unsuspecting characters as they move about. This places the watcher in the film in a more powerful position than the characters they are watching.

Later in the film, Deputy Winslow, in the midst of chasing Jason through the forest, comes upon Jason's makeshift shack. We see through Deputy Winslow's eye/camera as he explores the cabin, actively looking around this location. Although he is investigating the premises, the fact that he is killed in the process implies that there is somebody around who is much more active than Deputy Winslow. His death also indicates he did not see something important. His actions may be proactive, but his perspective is fallible. Therefore, the question of the power that the eye/camera holds is ambiguous. The character we see through may be powerful and active, but is also at a disadvantage—as are we. Our periphery is very limited.

The Final Chapter contains several eye/camera shots, mostly framed in three different ways. Firstly, there are shots in which a character from a singular position either watches other characters or examines their surroundings, such as Tommy looking around the basement with a flashlight or Trish examining the bathroom after Doug's murder. The second framing is one in which a character actively moves forward, such as Pam and Paul individually swimming toward the raft in the lake, or Tommy walking downstairs in the dark. The third framing is one in which Jason specifically looks at a character as he kills them, such as his first strike with the saw as he kills Axel, the orderly.

And it is only these films—*Friday the 13th*, *Friday the 13th Part 2*, and *Friday the 13th: The Final Chapter*—that prefer the aggressor perspective surrounding eye/camera shots as popularized by *Halloween*. While other features of film form and style, such as editing and sound, complicate this, as we will see in later chapters, we can at least say that it is not inaccurate for critics to pinpoint the use of aggressor eye/camera as common to the slashers. Indeed, it can be thought of as morally, politically, or socially problematic. However, when a consideration of proximity fear is brought into play, this reading becomes far more complicated. Furthermore, the idea that, while we see through the aggressor, we still empathize with and fear for the victim calls the whole idea of "identification" into question and blurs these lines.

If the intention of horror is to instill fear, then in simplest terms—the terms Hollywood prefers to play with—shots such as these are meant to make us afraid. And what is scary about having control over a violent situation without digging into some heavy-duty psychoanalysis? With this in mind, the other films in the series complicate the assumption that this aggressive framing is common, and such criticism would only be accurate if you'd stopped watching these movies as the first wave of slashers drew to a close.

I could argue that using an aggressor perspective is a far more complex way of creating empathy for a victim than by placing the viewer in the shoes of a victim. But a victim's shoes are still a useful place to put our eyes, especially if they wear shoes on their face.

With *Friday the 13th Part III 3-D*, Steve Miner firmly places the viewer in positions of vulnerability, which is further enhanced by the 3-D effects used in the film. This, in turn, places the film in a position of power over the audience, challenging us to withstand frequent childish taunts of "I'm not touching you." Regarding the decision to shoot *Friday the 13th Part III* using 3-D devices and aesthetics, Miner said, "With the *Friday the 13th* films, we had always made a conscious decision to make the same movie over again, only each one would be slightly different. [. . .] So it occurred to me that a *Friday the 13th Part 3* and 3-D would be a perfect combination" (quoted in Bracke, 74). Using 3-D provides an excuse for aligning perspective with the victim, unlike the tendency to place the eye/camera in positions of power in the first two films while still using similar story structures. Thomas M. Sipos directly compares 3-D to victim point-of-view shots: "Like 3-D photography, a victim's POV helps audiences experience scary events firsthand" (83). And Frank Mancuso Sr., the vice president of distribution at Paramount Pictures at the time of production, said, "The idea for the 3-D was born out of the fact that the process is so visceral, and horror movies are so visceral" (quoted in Bracke, 74).

The connection between the horror film and 3-D also extends to the tendencies in the genre's narratives. According to Kevin Heffernan: "The generic norms of the horror film were uniquely suited to achieving a balance between integrated narrative and scenes of shock or spectacle, an obsession of industry discourses on 3-D during the period of *House of Wax*'s (1953) production and reception" (27). Miner utilizes such "scenes of shock or spectacle," or novelty shots that involve objects leaping out at the viewer,[4] in *Friday the 13th Part III 3-D*. This reinforces expectations created by previous 3-D films, thereby creating a sense of comfort in familiarity.[5]

After the opening flashback sequence which consists of a condensed version of the last fifteen minutes of *Friday the 13th Part 2*, the opening credits appear from a distance, moving toward the viewer. However, Miner plays with this

---

4. An example of such a novelty shot from *House of Wax* features a man, using his best carnival-barker tone of voice, demonstrating a paddle-ball game to people standing in a queue to enter the titular House of Wax. In a sequence of little narrative import, though it is highly informative, he spends a large amount of time demonstrating the paddle-ball game, bouncing the ball directly at the camera.

5. To simplify the description of 3-D imagery, I will discuss the viewing experience of 3-D in terms of proximity to the viewer, although this proximity is entirely illusory. If it wasn't, I would probably avoid 3-D horror films.

in order to shock the audience. The final shot of the flashback sequence, as in *Friday the 13th Part 2*, is a close-up of Mrs. Voorhees's severed, rotting head on the homemade shrine surrounded by candles. The first part of the title, "*Friday the 13th*," comes out of the eye to the left of the viewer and stops at a moderate distance. Then from the eye to the right of the viewer, "*Part III*" comes toward us. As "*Part III*" reaches the same distance as the "*Friday the 13th*" title, they both continue moving closer to us, stopping at what appears to be a close distance (figures 2.1–2.3). Miner has created the expectation for "*Part III*" to stop at the same distance as "*Friday the 13th*," and the continued movement of both titles comes as a surprise to us. After this, the rest of the titles come at the viewer and then recede to make way for the next set of titles. This creates a consistent rhythm of expectation that continues through the opening credit sequence.

The first scene focuses on a couple, Harold and Edna, who run a convenience store, which doubles as their house. Miner establishes this first through a crane shot that descends on the convenience store and then moves to the side of the building. Here there is laundry drying on clotheslines, flapping in the wind, the corners of bed sheets coming within close proximity to the viewer.

Harold walks through the laundry and knocks over a supporting pole, and Edna immediately yells at him for being clumsy. He picks up the pole, and while in the process of repositioning, conspicuously points the end of the pole toward the viewer, which comes out at us. As this is not an eye/camera shot, it creates an awareness of how parts of the *mise-en-scéne* will interact with the camera and hence us as viewers. There is no narrative significance to this shot, which creates an emotional distance from the characters in the text, through both its superfluous nature coupled with the obvious usage of the 3-D technology for our benefit. Our awareness of the artifice, as hackneyed and obvious as it is, only momentarily threatens to intrude on our universe. This shot creates a visceral effect to make us flinch at the illusion of how close the pole is to your eyes.

In a similar shot, Edna, while watching news reports recounting the deaths that occurred in the previous movie, turns the rabbit ear antenna on top of the television for a better reception, stopping it in a position close to the audience. Other shots in this opening scene are similar in effect, despite the fact that they are specifically eye/camera shots, such as a snake striking at Harold/us and a mouse walking on a plank in close proximity to Edna/us. Even with the eye/camera positioning included, the narrative irrelevance of these shots creates a sense of separation between the characters and the viewer, but provides a visceral spectacle. Things casually poke at your eyes, without actually touching you.

If you expect this pattern of distancing spectacle throughout the film, then you're in for a bit of a surprise. Miner subverts this expectation as the film

Figures 2.1, 2.2, and 2.3. *Friday the 13th Part III 3-D* (clearly)—Miner plays with your expectations around how far the titles come toward you. (Paramount Pictures / Georgetown Productions Inc. / Jason Productions, 1982)

continues. The eye/camera in the rest of the film alternates between characters, both Jason and the victims, watching events from a distance, and the position of a victim of an act, usually violent. As stated earlier, it is necessary to place the act of viewing into the context of the surrounding eye/camera shots. Here, with it standing alongside shots from the perspective of the victim, the act of watching makes us vulnerable, passive.

This overtly links the camera to the viewer. Miner occasionally uses this position of victimization, or more appropriately the object of an action, to highlight the difference between character and audience perspective. One of these sequences involves Debbie lying on the ground sunbathing as Andy sits above her, playing with a yo-yo close to her face. The audience sees the yo-yo coming toward them through Debbie's eye/camera from an extreme low-angle, looking directly upwards at Andy. This combines the novelty 3-D effect of an object coming within close proximity and simultaneously inhabiting the perspective of someone lying horizontal. The horizontal position works in direct opposition to the vertical seating position of the film viewer,[6] creating a disorienting effect.

The same disorientation occurs in a shot where Chuck, making popcorn, removes the lid of the kettle and tries to catch the popcorn in his mouth as it flies upward. The viewer sees through Chuck's eye/camera looking directly downward into the kettle as the popcorn jumps towards the audience. This effect occurs again after Debbie notices blood dripping on the magazine she is reading; the viewer experiences her eye/camera as she looks directly up and sees Andy's bisected body dripping with blood.

These are extreme examples of positional disorientation, but the victim's eye/camera provides the expected visceral shocks that are narratively significant and highlights viewer vulnerability. Examples of these shots include Harold's eye/camera as a butcher knife comes toward him, Shelly's eye/camera as Ali punches through the car window toward him, the harpoon coming toward Vera, stabbing her through the eye, and Jason while books from a tipped bookcase fall on him.

Jason Takes Manhattan contains a little more variety, and on the heels of several years of tired tropes and development, plays with eye/camera shots in rather fun ways. However, the primary function of the eye/camera in this movie is to align us with the victim, or characters who pose less of a threat than Jason. There are only three eye/camera shots from Jason's vantage point, but these place him as a victim of aggressive action. In addition, this movie contains a few *misleading* shots of a character approaching other characters, framed in an aggressive or stalking manner. However, these shots provide a counterpoint to the victim eye/camera shots. As the character housing the

---

6. Unless you are a member of the target demographic "watching" the movie on home video (or movie theater, if you are adventurous) with another person who instinctively sets off the klaxons of your explosive, burgeoning biological impulses.

eye/camera in such misleading shots is initially unidentified, we think we are seeing from the perspective of Jason, which is usually not the case.

Examples of this include two sequences shot from Charles's eye/camera. The first occurs as he approaches Tamara and Eva, who have drugs in a cargo room, and second as he slowly approaches Rennie from behind as she drops the anchor. Another example happens as Sean, Rennie, Charles, and Miss Van Deusen escape in the lifeboat. As they are floating away, an apparent eye/camera at water level moves steadily toward the lifeboat. As it approaches, there is a reverse shot inside the lifeboat, and from the previous shot's eye/camera position, Julius leaps suddenly from the water and into the boat.

These shots contrast directly with victim eye/camera shots. We can see this through Suzy's eye/camera as Jason hits her with her guitar, or Tamara's eye/camera as she looks through the crack in the bathroom door, watching as Jason wanders the corridor in search of her. Eva's eye/camera provides another example as she stands on the dance floor looking around and seeing Jason almost everywhere she looks, intercutting her eye/camera with reverse shots of her looking around the room in panic. These are a few of the very typical examples of us seeing through a victim's eyes in this movie.

Once the remaining group arrives in New York City, Rennie's perspective is dominant, including the eye/camera. Exceptions include the junkies watching the group before attacking them. This is an overtly aggressive look from secondary characters, which is consistent with the alternation between the eye/camera of victims and aggressive eye/camera shots of characters who are not the killer. One of the most notable experiments with the eye/camera in a movie littered with them occurs during Julius's decapitation. We see through his eye as his head spins through the air and lands in a dumpster.[7]

After Julius's death scene, all but one significant eye/camera shot originates within the movie's "final girl," Rennie. We see Rennie's eye/camera as she is walking down the alley after escaping from the junkies, images in the frame blurred to indicate the effect of the drugs forcefully administered to her, as well as Rennie's eye/camera as she drives toward Jason, verified by the fact that the previous and following shots show her in the driver's seat. The spectator sees through Rennie's eye as she looks into a flaming puddle, which turns into a flashback from her childhood, further situating the film's perspective within Rennie. We later see her eye/camera as she is running through the sewers in an attempt to escape Jason, but there is an eye/camera shift to Jason, as Rennie

---

7. The eye/camera shot from Julius's decapitated head can be identified as a form of spectacle within a film with a premise that hinges on spectacle: displacing a familiar, iconic character (Jason) to a familiar iconic location (Manhattan).

throws toxic waste at Jason, showing his perspective only as a victim at this point. One further eye/camera shot from Rennie places her as a victim as Jason leaps from the flood of toxic waste in order to grab her, an attempt that is unsuccessful.

A final eye/camera shot, however, continues the perspective game established early in the movie. The eye/camera comes from a low-angle shot moving quickly towards Rennie and Sean as they stand on the sidewalk looking around. They turn and look at the camera, and in a reverse shot, we see Toby the dog leaping towards Rennie in a friendly manner, undercutting the previously built tension. This final shot reverts to the playfulness of the use of aggressive, non-killer perspective.

These examples demonstrate that *Jason Takes Manhattan*, with few exceptions, positions the audience within and adopts the perspective of victim. The only eye/camera shots within Jason occur when he is watching or looking, and at the very end, as the victim, but not performing aggressive action against a victim.

And, as a congealing agent for the victim perspective, *Jason Takes Manhattan* introduces one shot not seen before in this series: the victim-camera. As Wayne searches for Jason in the engine room, he is trying to film the events with his video camera. As he moves ahead, steam comes out of a nearby valve and knocks off his glasses. Then we see a blurry eye/camera shot which recreates his faulty vision. To compensate for this, he looks through his camera. We then see through the victim-camera, black-and-white, with crosshairs and timestamp. Wayne uses the camera to identify one of his fellow students who he has just shot with a gun, due to his bad eyesight. The camera tilts up and Jason appears in the frame (figure 2.4), smashing the camera, which is where the victim-camera shot ends.

The use of the victim-camera in *Jason Takes Manhattan* is a device not frequently seen in the slasher film at the time this film premiered. Although films like *Peeping Tom* (1960) and *Cannibal Holocaust* had used it before this point, *Jason Takes Manhattan* precedes *The Blair Witch Project* by ten years. Therefore, *Jason Takes Manhattan* acts as a significant precursor to the later victim-camera trends. This is especially notable for its use of, for that time, more accessible home video recording equipment instead of the film cameras used for *Peeping Tom* and *Cannibal Holocaust*. Affordable cameras also bring this home video aesthetic to a mainstream film that appears in a much more shocking scene three years earlier in the independent horror film *Henry: Portrait of a Serial Killer*.

Both *Friday the 13th Part III 3-D* and *Friday the 13th Part VIII: Jason Takes Manhattan* foreground victim perspective alongside playfulness and spectacle. The knowing poking of poles toward our eyes, or the showing of a threatening point-of-view from a friendly dog, render our position vulnerable, playing on our fear of threat and proximity. More importantly, it shows us what it feels like

Figure 2.4. *Friday the 13th Part VIII: Jason Takes Manhattan*—Wayne's victim-camera. (Paramount Pictures / Horror, 1989)

to see something attacking us, or worse, not seeing our attacker until it is too late. The victim eye/camera shots clearly and unambiguously give us the scares we go to slasher films for. However, while the perspective of the victim dominates in *Jason Takes Manhattan*, we see how the movies in the series, after the peak of the first slasher cycle begin to explore inconsistencies in eye/camera use.

Eyeball soup

With *Jason Takes Manhattan* depicting both aggressive and passive points of view, we still have an overriding sense of a victim's perspective. Most other films in the series, however, do not align clearly with neither one nor the other. These films alternate seemingly indiscriminately between the two, with an occasional sense of intent behind these shifts. This tendency appears, most significantly, during the peak of the second slasher cycle in the mid-1980s. This timing is especially important as this is the point where slashers are more playful in an effort to distance themselves from the hackneyed, predictable tropes of yore.[8]

In fact, by the time we get to *Jason Goes to Hell*, eye/camera use appears practically unwieldy. The eye/camera, at different points, inhabits most of the characters central to the narrative. Not only that, but the film attaches the eye/camera to other minor characters as well, without clear consistency. The eye/

---

8. "Yore" being two or three years earlier.

camera works through people as they watch events from a distance, people who are the victims of violent action, and those who are the perpetrators of violent action. There is no clear standard for the use of the eye/camera, and at this point, slashers were desperate to regain a successful formula. I like to think of what ensues in *Jason Goes to Hell* as joyous chaos.

One demonstration of the variety of first-person experience in *Jason Goes to Hell* is apparent in one of the earliest eye/camera shots in the movie. After Jason is blown up, the security officers close off the site for examination. We see this in an extreme long shot from an eye/camera. In reverse shot, we see Duke, the bounty hunter, watching from this position. This shot cuts to an (initially) unidentified eye/camera shot wandering through the crime scene. The eye/camera approaches an officer talking in a relaxed manner to the woman used as bait in the investigation.

This shot highlights the characters on-screen as potentially vulnerable. The relaxed postures of the characters reveal their lack of concern to a threat, and the noisy, crowded surroundings become a potential camouflage for a character with sinister intent. However, the officer then turns to address the eye/camera saying, "Good shooting Mahoney, now clean up all this shit, huh?" The film does not introduce Mahoney to us as a character until this point, and whoever Mahoney is, they never reappear in the film. This sequence demonstrates just one way *Jason Goes to Hell* creates disorientation around the identity of the looker. In other words, we experience ambiguity around who we are seeing through, to the point where we are entirely unsure of our relationship to the characters, who "we" are supposed to be, and whether the subject of our look is friend or foe.

Jason X on the other hand, contains a more consistent eye/camera design, and as a result works in a dissimilar way to *Jason Goes to Hell*. With one significant exception, the eye/camera does not inhabit characters as violent action occurs. Instead, *Jason X* alters eye/camera shots between those of stalking or searching and vulnerable passivity. Like *Jason Goes to Hell*, though, the movie divides perspectives evenly between Jason and other characters.

The opening credits appear over images representing the inside of Jason's brain, both in physical and abstract ways. We see extreme close-ups of brain matter and blood vessels, sparks of electricity, fire, as well as images of people and events. The image tracks backwards, blending into a representation of Jason's cognitive thought, and moves outwards to show his eye. The movie then returns to his cognitive thought, which includes eye/camera shots of doctors examining Jason. These images then become a reflection in Jason's eye. By doing this, we get to experience the world as Jason, while also seeing into Jason. The movie shows that it is, in fact, Jason we see in and through at the end of the sequence.

The image cuts to bloody medical instruments, and then cuts between an eye/camera shot and a reflection of Jason's eye/camera in his eye as a doctor with a harness moves larger into the frame. The doctor leaves the harness when he steps backwards, and the movie intercuts this with images of chains attached to the harness. After this sequence ends, we witness Jason suspended by a harness and chains in the middle of a warehouse-sized room. This holds similarities to scenes later in the movie where Jason is passive. In this opening scene, we see through his eye/camera as the guard approaches him with a tarpaulin saying, "Why don't you stare at this a little while, you bastard?" before throwing the tarpaulin over his head. After this, we only see Jason's eye/camera as he walks up behind Crutch without killing him, and then as he wanders the corridors of the spaceship before Geko's death. The final eye/camera shot from Jason occurs as Kay-Em 14 fires a small rocket at his head, decapitating him before he regenerates as "Uber-Jason."

The eye/camera shots from other characters are very similar to those of Jason. We see Kay-Em 14's eye/camera as the group initially finds the cryogenic facility, and they are looking around the room. As Brodski is searching the ship for Jason, we see him examining the area as he tries to track Jason. We also see Crutch's eye/camera as he and Ray look at the severed limbs of a crewmember on the bridge of the ship. In more active sequences, the viewer is shown the eye/camera of Condor and one of the two VR Teen Girls[9] as Jason stands over them about to attack. The reviving of Rowan is another instance of the eye/camera highlighting vulnerability. We see her eye/camera as she looks at the people standing around observing her, her naked body covered only by a sheet and disoriented.

A significant break from this tendency to situate the eye/camera within a vulnerable or relatively passive position occurs as Kay-Em 14 kills Jason before he regenerates. She appears holding several guns, firing them at Jason for an extended period, shown through multiple angles cut at a rapid pace. Many of these shots are from Kay-Em 14's eye/camera, including one showing her hands holding guns on the left and right sides of the frame. She extends her arms and fires the guns toward Jason. This is the only scene involving the eye/camera inhabiting a character during immediately aggressive violent action.

Furthermore, these eye/camera shots from Kay-Em 14's point-of-view are strongly reminiscent of first-person shooter video games (figure 2.5).

Interestingly, *Friday the 13th: The Game* contains no such first-person shooting or hacking. There *is*, however, some handy first-person stalking in the aptly named "stalk" mode.

---

9. "VR" is, of course, Virtual Reality—they appear as parts of a program on the holodeck. They are credited as "VR Teen Girl #1" and "VR Teen Girl #2."

Figure 2.5. *Jason X*—Kay-Em 14 watches herself shoot Jason, framed like a first-person shooter game. (Crystal Lake Entertainment / Friday X Productions / New Line Cinema, 2001)

Jason X here gives us the catharsis of the experience of killing Jason. It also maintains elements of the science fiction genre by incorporating this modern video game aesthetic to create a sense of interactivity. Ultimately, *Jason X* incorporates few eye/camera shots in comparison with most others in the franchise, and reveals, as in *Jason Goes to Hell*, inconsistency in aesthetic design.

To complicate these examples of movies in the series that wildly fail in creating a clear intent behind using the eye/camera (besides saying, "This is a horror movie, see?"), we also have a movie that filters elements of eye/camera stylistic design into the general, non-eye/camera camerawork. This film, *Friday the 13th* (2009), becomes problematic to an eye/camera reading. While eye/camera shots are often identified through the use of handheld camera and relatable height, the majority of that film is shot in this way without being located within the eye of a fictional character. This helps me demonstrate how this use of the camera has come to signify the genre without needing to be an actual eye/camera shot. Objects in the foreground still often obscure mounted, steady shots, which is an unusual composition for a Hollywood film from the 1980s.

This is apparent in the scene where Whitney and Mike are exploring Jason's house, which inhabits a voyeuristic position. While this stylistic use of the camera creates an overall visceral impact and kinetic drive to the narrative, it can also communicate a simultaneous sense of vulnerability and aggressiveness. As Mike and Whitney run through the forest away from Jason's house and head for their own campsite, the handheld camera from approximately Jason's height

Figure 2.6. *Friday the 13th: The Game*—Searching for people as Jason in "stalk" mode. (Illfonic / Gun Media, 2017)

is intercut, moving at their pace both in front of and behind them. The shot in front reveals that there is nobody immediately behind them, and the shot behind them could appear to be chasing them, but is also close enough to appear to be escaping with them. This ambiguity creates difficulty in defining the perspective relationship between film and spectator, as it can vary from one viewer to another. In this way, spectator reading of *Friday the 13th* (2009) can be that of voyeur, victim, or aggressor—or shifting from all three at different points. The frequent use of the camera to create an ambiguity between eye/camera shots and objective shots is a reflection of the evolution of the genre's aesthetic; these remakes borrow a visual style without the meaning behind it.

In spite of this, we can detect eye/camera shots through defining the position of space and character outside of eye/camera locations. For instance, after hearing someone outside and assuming it is Wade watching her have sex, Amanda tells Richie to make Wade leave. Once Richie exits the tent, Amanda waits a few moments and then looks out of the tent flap for Richie. From her position, we see her eye/camera, partially framed by the edge of the tent opening.

Later in the movie, Chelsea sees Jason on the shore of the lake watching her. She goes underwater and swims under the dock, waiting for him to leave. We see a medium shot from her, and long shots of Jason's location where they are in relation to each other, and Chelsea's eye/camera reflects this position, revealing it is, in fact, a true eye/camera shot. There are also many eye/camera shots from Jason's position. One such example involves Donnie the mechanic as he looks around the attic of the barn where he works at the different artefacts. The camera approaches him from behind, moving very close to him. Then, in reverse shot, we see Jason from this position just before he attacks. We also see Jason's eye/camera as he walks up to Trent's house and looks into the window where Trent and Bree are having sex. As the camera draws closer, the light from inside the window reflects off the hockey mask which, in turn, reflects off the window, revealing Jason's position and informing us that we are witnessing an eye/camera shot.

Although *Friday the 13th* (2009) contains more victim eye/camera shots than Jason eye/camera shots, the numeric difference is small. Ultimately, the nearly equal appearance of both enhances the sense of perspective ambiguity. This ambiguity can either exploit the perspective of each of us as individual viewers (if you are predisposed to seeing the world as a victim, then that's the way you read the film; ditto aggressor, ditto neutral) or create disorientation. The aim of the visual style can be attributed to an attempt to create visceral impact and the filmmaker's desire for a kinetic design, in line with director Marcus Nispel's earlier films, *The Texas Chainsaw Massacre* and *Frankenstein* (2004). This is a potential response to the rising popularity of the victim-camera movement by using a similar style without limiting what a camera can capture within the diegesis (a word meaning the "world" of the film). We also experience the visceral aesthetic of the victim-camera without being held back by a pesky fictional camera to boot—even if it looks like a victim-camera, we can still see it as the experience of a character, not just an image-grabbing machine.

"Is that you, John Wayne? Is this me?"

Whether there is a clear overarching thematic connection to an aggressor or victim perspective, or even just chaotic, indiscriminate eye/camera use, direct eye/camera shots, with some of the exceptions I've identified, tend to clearly identify that the shot is coming from the eye position of a character within the film. When it is not, a film can at least imply that we are seeing through a character not yet introduced in the movie. However, the specifics of eye/camera style and framing can create the same visceral impact of a direct eye/camera shot. Simultaneously, this coding—the elements of style that inform us that we are viewing an eye/camera shot—disorients or creates suspense without the need of another character. In some cases, movies leave it ambiguous whether or not a shot is, in fact, an eye/camera shot. In other cases, it is apparent that the device cannot be trusted to inform us that we are seeing through a character. A movie can use eye/camera coding, but will alter it from a direct character perspective in order to either distort or clarify the experience of the character.

The most complex use of the eye/camera in *Friday the 13th Part 2* are shots that create a distinct advantage over the audience. The movie accomplishes this through keeping us unsure of the character we are looking through, or even if we are witnessing an eye/camera shot at all. The example given by Humphries of the eye/camera coded shot preceding Marcie's death sequence in *Friday the 13th* can serve as an example of this. It also proves that *Friday the 13th Part 2* is not the first film to engage in this sort of trickery.

This is what I call a *"mimic"* eye/camera, and it appears frequently in *Friday the 13th Part 2*. In the opening sequence, Alice, the final girl from *Friday the 13th*, wakes up from a dream which shows us the events of the previous film.[10] She then walks about her house as the camera follows her, coded very much like an eye/camera shot. It is shot at head-height, handheld, and largely positioned within shadow. At one point, Alice goes into her bedroom, closes the door all but a crack, and removes her clothes before putting on a bathrobe. We do not see this undressing and dressing process, but the camera watches through the crack in the door as she throws her clothes one at a time onto her bed, and Alice emerges in a bathrobe. As she walks to the shower, she moves toward the camera and even looks at it. If the audience were viewing an eye/camera, Alice would reasonably be expected to see the character the audience is seeing through due to direct eye contact with the camera and the close proximity. However, the movie maintains this pretense as Alice goes into the shower, and the camera keeps its distance. It enters the bathroom only after the shower starts. The camera moves slowly toward the shower, still very reminiscent of an eye/camera shot. The lights are very bright in the room, and as the camera reaches the shower curtain, it is suddenly pulled aside to show Alice in close-up looking straight at the camera. This sudden encounter has no apparent effect on the events, as the image cuts to similar camera movement following Alice as she walks to pick up the ringing telephone. We are clearly nobody, even if Alice confronts us.

This misleading use of eye/camera coding serves three purposes in *Friday the 13th Part 2*. Initially, it creates a sense of Alice being watched, even if the shot is not from the point-of-view of a specific character who is actually watching her. Secondly, the continued use of eye/camera coding, even after it becomes apparent that it is not an eye/camera shot, puts us at ease. It informs us that we are no threat to the character we are watching. In fact, because we do not watch Alice undress or see her in the shower, she maintains a sense of modesty, and we maintain a sense of propriety and respectability. The audience does not see

---

10. This informs the audience of the narrative up to this point, a topic I will address in chapter 4.

Alice's nudity, and her lack of apparent physical vulnerability guards her against the viewer being a threat. This sense of ease the mimic eye/camera provides places the audience in a vulnerable position, as the viewer becomes unable to tell when they are a threat or benign. In this way, eye/camera coding in *Friday the 13th Part 2* puts the movie in a position of power over the audience.

In *Friday the 13th Part III 3-D*, Miner repeats, although less frequently, mimic eye/camera shots like those in *Friday the 13th Part 2*. One notable example is the sequence in which Debbie is in the shower. As she bathes, an eye/camera-coded shot moves toward the shower, and we can see her outline through the shower curtain. In reverse shot, from inside the shower, Debbie opens the curtain and it turns out to be Andy, walking on his hands. Although this is the perspective of a character, it is not that of the character's eyeline, but of the character's footline.

This shot, eye/camera moving toward the shower, is repeated a few moments later after Andy's death, but as Debbie opens the curtain, nobody is there. The shot repeats again in direct eye/camera as Chris comes back to the cabin to investigate the tap running in the bathtub. There is no silhouette of a person behind the shower curtain as Chris approaches, but we see the same movement and positioning. *Friday the 13th Part III 3-D* is an example of Miner's continued experimentation with, and unique usage of, eye/camera coding. With mimic eye/camera shots appearing briefly in *Friday the 13th*, and with their continued use in the following two sequels, we can deduce that mimic eye/camera shots, at this point in film history, had become a new generic convention for the slasher. The mimic eye/camera acknowledges that we as viewers both recognize this as a common shot and perhaps even expect it.

There are two significant mimic eye/camera shots in *The Final Chapter*. The first is Jason's attack on the nurse in the hospital. In this sequence, a handheld camera approaches the nurse, first moving around a set of shelves containing medical equipment. It then slowly moves straight towards her. She quickly turns around and Jason appears from the right of the frame and attacks her within the shot, which shocks the audience due to the unexpected direction of attack. The second of these significant mimic eye/camera shots takes place during Terri's death. We see her in the rain getting her bicycle. The camera steadily moves in her direction, but instead of going straight towards her, the camera moves behind her. At this point, the shot could still conceivably be an eye/camera shot as it is out of her line of sight, and the camera tracks in to a window of the house, potentially in an attempt to view the goings-on inside. The camera stops and lightning flashes, revealing in shadow Jason stabbing Terri with a long object. We hear the deathblow and her scream. The position of Jason in relation to the shadow and the camera location reveals that the image is in no way connected to his sight. This causes a disorienting shock derived simultaneously from the discovery that the viewer is not seeing an eye/camera shot and the unexpected stabbing of Terri, who we assume is relatively safe once the camera has passed her.

The significance of these shots stems from the play on expectation based on previous uses of the eye/camera and mimic eye/camera shots. Both eye/camera and mimic eye/camera shots create the same form of tension and suspense. And while an eye/camera shot can be verified as an eye/camera shot as it plays out,[11] the nature of a mimic eye/camera shot is not revealed until the end of the shot or after, crucial to sustaining the tension created.

The primary difference in *The Final Chapter* is one of timing. The mimic eye/camera shots in the previous films in the series climax in the revelation that there is no threat from the location of the camera. This allows the viewer the opportunity to process this information before an attack occurs or before the film shifts to another sequence. *The Final Chapter* creates mimic eye/camera shots that climax in violence, but the violence is shocking since it occurs from an unexpected direction. As a result, there is no time for the viewer to process the fact that the camera is no threat. As such, the movie has the double advantage of employing eye/camera aesthetics and framing, supplying the tension and suspense that comes with such camera usage while also reaping the benefits of the shock generated from a shot that records a sudden, violent action from a third-person perspective.

Both *A New Beginning*[12] and *Jason Lives!*[13] feature minimal usage of the mimic eye/camera shot. *Jason Lives!* also contains few direct eye/camera shots

---

11. One example of this is the appearance of Mrs. Voorhees's hand in frame to remove a branch during an eye/camera shot in *Friday the 13th*.

12. In *A New Beginning*, there is brief shot moving behind Ethel before she is attacked from the front, and a shot following Pete. In this shot, before Pete turns around, he looks at the camera briefly before looking at other areas off-screen, indicating that the camera is not inhabiting a character. This sort of manipulation of the eye/camera model is not unusual for the series, and can be seen in earlier films.

13. *Jason Lives* contains two mimic eye/camera shots. One occurs outside the camper van where Cort and Nikki are having sex. The camera establishes the camper van, and the frame conspicuously swish tilts up slightly and then to the left, looking like a handheld image. After this, Jason steps into the frame in profile from the right, and the shot remains completely still until it cuts to the next shot. Later, as the police officers are looking around the camp for Jason, a shot using eye/camera coding appears behind a police officer moving slowly towards him, just before a little girl runs into the frame and grabs him. At that point, if it were an eye/camera shot, both characters in the frame would see the seer, but they are not.

in comparison to other films in the franchise released during the Paramount years. Although there are different approaches to the eye/camera, few shots apply the direct eye/camera.[14] These eye/camera shots seem to have little design in the form of development and progression, aside from the fact that earlier ones are linked to victimized characters. After this, we see characters that are observing and searching, and these shots end with Jason's eye/camera.

However, *Jason Lives!* introduces one unique eye/camera use that I will call the "*off-model*" eye/camera shot. In off-model eye/camera shots, we witness a shot very close to the eye of a character. However, based on the other shots within the sequence, we know that the camera does not inhabit the exact space or position of the character's eye. In these cases, usually the camera is only shifted a couple of inches, shown from eye/positioning when the character is not looking, or rotated.

During Lizabeth's death, for example, Jason apparently stabs her in the mouth with a long pole. In the off-model eye/camera shot, Jason appears in the top of the frame as she is lying down, but when he thrusts the pole downwards, the end disappears above the frame. If it were a direct eye/camera shot, the pole would have gone from the top of the frame, with the end disappearing in the bottom of the frame. In this case, the positioning of the camera is just below Lizabeth's mouth.

In the scene showing the business executives' paintball game, Katie jumps out of the brush and shoots Stan and then Larry with paintball pellets. A seeming eye/camera shot shows Katie aiming and shooting at the camera, cutting as the paintball hits the top of the frame. However, there is a cut to a reverse shot, where it is clearly shown that the paintball pellet strikes Stan's chest, placing the off-model eye/camera shot also on his chest (figures 2.7 and 2.8).

As Tommy and Megan are running away from the police in a car chase, Megan thrusts Tommy's head into her lap so that they will not see him in the car. We see an off-model shot of Megan's crotch from Tommy's position.

---

14. The first direct eye/camera shot is of Lizabeth after she falls out of the car and reaches into her wallet to give Jason money as he approaches her. After she looks up, he has disappeared and we see through her eye as she looks around the area for him. Secondly, we see from Roy's eye/camera as Jason throws him roughly into a tree. Next, we see an eye/camera shot of unknown origin as Jason slashes a machete through three executives at once. The seer is unidentified, though this sequence creates no suspense, as the view is essentially the same for any of the three characters. Fourth, there is an eye/camera shot of a police officer as he looks at Roy's severed limbs, and another eye/camera shot from a police officer as he looks around the camp for Jason. The final eye/camera shot is from Jason in the movie's climax, as he walks through the lake while approaching Tommy in the boat.

Figures 2.7 and 2.8. *Jason Lives! Friday the 13th Part VI*—The mimic eye/camera. Katie shoots, the paintball hits the top of the lens, with Stan and Larry clearly shot in the chest. (Paramount Pictures / Terror Films, 1986)

However, whereas Tommy's eyes are perpendicular to the seat of the car, the off-model eye/camera shot is rotated ninety degrees, parallel with the seat. Megan's crotch is shown upright, instead of sideways as a direct eye/camera shot would indicate. The most interesting off-model eye/camera shot precedes Cort's death.[15] After Jason kills Nikki in the camper's bathroom, he moves toward Cort who is driving. There are two shots showing Jason approaching in the rearview mirror from what would be Cort's eye/camera, if he were looking. When he does

---

15. This is a striking and inventive death sequence, as I'll discuss further in the next chapter.

look, he screams, but director Tom McLoughlin does not cut to a direct eye/camera shot in that moment. McLoughlin creates a visceral effect or proximity fear (or excitement, in the case of Tommy) by positioning the camera close to the victim's eye. He adjusts it slightly to maximize its effect, allowing the viewer to process the typically swift events without the problem of disorientation.

As used in *Jason Lives!*, the off-model eye/camera shot serves a range of purposes. In the cases of Lizabeth's death and Tommy looking at Megan's crotch, the off-model shot is designed to decrease the disorientation that would occur by showing the same images from a direct eye/camera. For Lizabeth, the pole that stabs her would appear at the bottom of the frame, and for Tommy, Megan's crotch would appear with her thighs parallel with the top and bottom of the frame.[16] By having the pole end above the frame for Lizabeth rotating the camera 90 degrees for Tommy, each shot frames the subject in a way that makes it easier for the viewer to process the visual information. The off-model eye/camera shot looking at Katie repositions the camera to provide the visceral shock of an object moving directly toward the camera lens. The paintball hitting a foot below the camera lens diminishes the visceral impact. For Cort's attack, the off-model eye/camera shot creates the tension of an eye/camera shot. However, it intensifies the suspense of the impending attack by establishing his ignorance of Jason's presence. *Jason Lives!* frequently applies the off-model eye/camera with the purpose of either clarifying visual information or enhancing emotional impact.

The hunted becomes the hunter and back again

For all of its many virtues—and each chapter will address some of these—*A New Beginning* proves a significant turning point in the use and development of the eye/camera within the series. The film begins with an eye/camera shot moving through a forest trail in the rain at night. We do not know who we are seeing through, nor are we aware of the location or intent of the character. The shot clearly establishes genre components from the outset: eye/camera, forest, night, and rain are all elements frequently used in horror films. These images, common to horror, accompany the music familiar to the franchise and provide a grounding in the genre for the viewer.

The source of the eye/camera turns out to be young Tommy Jarvis, played by Corey Feldman (reprising his role from *The Final Chapter*). Young

---

16. While a direct eye/cameras shot of Megan's crotch would likely maximize the 1.85:1 frame, it would certainly be disorienting.

Tommy walks through the forest and looks from the trees into a clearing with a tombstone, which reads, "Jason Voorhees." He sees two men digging up the coffin below, before Jason rises from the grave, killing the two men, and advancing on young Tommy. As Jason strikes, there is a cut to a young man in the back of a car, who we discover is Tommy.

He sits up swiftly and opens his eyes, indicating that the previous sequence was a dream. This positioning within Tommy's dream initially establishes the perspective as belonging to Tommy. The subsequent eye/camera shots belonging to Tommy verify this, including the shot in which he looks out of the window from the van on his way to a halfway house (where most of the film takes place) and the later shot showing him watching from his bedroom window while Joey is killed. Even though the film's style indicates Tommy's perspective, the mechanical and silent movements of John Shepard's performance as Tommy, coupled with traditional perceptions of the eye/camera inhabiting the stalker,[17] leads us to suspect Tommy of either being, or eventually becoming, a killer.

Subsequent eye/camera shots complicate this assumption. The eye/camera later moves away from Tommy, and we next see it from Pete's perspective. We experience Pete's eye/camera as he looks around, suspects that someone is behind him, and instead sees a rabbit hopping in the woods. While he is actively searching during this shot, this is the point where the eye/camera begins firmly inhabiting the victims—although he is not killed immediately. The next sequence depicts Vinnie's death; we see from his eye/camera as the killer shoves a road flare into his mouth.

Until the climax of the film, all of the eye/camera shots are based in the victim. Lana's eye/camera appears first as she sees the killer's feet appear behind the car door, and again as a hatchet swings toward her. We see the eye/camera of Raymond as he watches Tina and Eddie having sex in the forest before he is killed. We see Tina's eye/camera as she looks at the trees while lying on the blanket, and again as the garden shears are plunged into her eyes. Eddie's eye/camera follows this as he approaches Tina's nude body, thinking she is resting, before he is killed. The deaths of Junior and Ethel are both shown through eye/camera shots. We experience Robin's eye/camera as she turns over in bed to find Jake's dead body before she is herself killed. These eye/camera shots of the victims provide a direct contrast in technique to the same effect as those in *Friday the 13th*. The eye/camera inhabits the victims instead of the killer, but in both instances, they perform the function of hiding the killer's identity. The eye/camera shots of victims in *A New Beginning* focus on the impending

---

17. The popular examples of *Halloween* and *Friday the 13th* intrinsically suggest this.

deathblow instead of the identity of the attacker. The immediacy and close proximity of whatever weapon is used also creates a directly visceral interaction between the movie and the viewer.

The final two eye/camera shots that take place in the climax move away from the film's tendency to use the eye/camera of the victims. After "Jason" (who is actually Roy the paramedic in a noticeably different hockey mask) begins attacking Pam and Reggie in the barn, Pam discovers and advances on him with a chain saw. We see her eye/camera during the attack and although she is the victim, Pam is actively pursuing "Jason" (Roy) with violent intent. In this case, the eye/camera shifts from victim being attacked to retaliating victim. We next see the eye/camera of "Jason" (Roy) after Pam and Reggie hide as he looks around the barn. This eye/camera shot takes the position of a violent attacker who has less knowledge of his victims' whereabouts than we do. In a sense, this makes him weaker than the people he is stalking, especially when we compare it to the aggressive positioning of the victim in the previous eye/camera shot and in contrast to other established uses of the eye/camera.

Although the perspective created by the eye/camera varies, there is a consistency to its gradual adjustment. We are initially positioned closely to Tommy as the movie indicates he is a potential suspect. And as the killing begins, the viewer is subjected to the immediacy of the deathblows inflicted on the victims. This gives way to creating first the perspective of an aggressive victim followed by that of a weakened attacker. This progression of positioning and perspective within the eye/camera is more varied than earlier films in the franchise, and is not repeated or replicated in the following sequels or even the remake.

Much like *A New Beginning*, *The New Blood* frequently uses clearly identified direct eye/camera shots. These shots also shift perspectives, numerically favoring the protagonist, Tina, and Jason. The seer is almost consistently a character in a position of power over the vulnerable object of his/her[18] sight. This movie, though, is overflowing with eye/camera shots. But unlike the wonderful random chaos of *Jason Goes to Hell*, or *Jason X*, there is an apparent design behind it.[19]

In most of the eye/camera shots in *The New Blood*, director John Carl Buechler identifies the character the eye/camera inhabits during the sequences

---

18. Gender in these films to date is strictly binary.

19. There are so many eye/camera shots that describing them all would be positively superfluous, like an uninformative modifier, such as the word "positively." I'm limiting myself to the few relevant examples that really help explain the overarching design.

that contain them, usually in shot/reverse shot.[20] The use of eye/camera within the narrative structure of the film fluidly moves mostly between Tina, who is the final girl of the film, and Jason. The focus of the eye/camera on these two characters clearly links them visually and stylistically. Although the core of the film favors Jason eye/camera shots, the movie initially shows us Tina's perspective before experiencing Jason's perspective extensively. In this way, Buechler develops the movie in order to attach the viewer to the protagonist at the outset before witnessing the atrocities committed by the antagonist from his perspective. The climax, in which Tina and Jason meet in a series of battles, alternates frequently between Tina and Jason's eye/camera, creating a confrontation, a showdown, between perspectives. Not only do we witness the face-off between the two characters, the movie also attempts to develop a struggle between two opposing perspectives. This concludes as we see the eye/camera of Tina's dead father as he sneaks up on Jason from behind and drags him into the water.

As with its two immediate predecessors, *Freddy vs. Jason* also appears to be indiscriminate in selecting the characters the eye/camera inhabits. Freddy is initially in control of Jason, who is far more powerful than the people he stalks and kills. But Freddy has a direct connection to us, the audience, often subjectively talking to us in voice-over, and driving the narrative forward. There are multiple eye/camera shots from other characters, primarily the central group of girls: Lori, Kia, and Gibb. Most of these consist of walking, searching, and exploring, such as when Lori, in her dream at the police station, walks through the corridor and approaches a door labeled "Authorized Entrance Only." The eye/camera shots that break from previous franchise films occur as we see two different characters facing each other in eye/camera shot/reverse

---

20. After the opening flashback sequence in which the film shows Tina as a young girl and the death of her father, we see her wake up in the passenger's seat of a car, riding down the road. Next, we see an eye/camera shot from the passenger's seat of a car riding down the road, clearly identifying this as Tina's positioning. During a few sequences in which Jason is chasing victims, among them Michael, Maddy, Dr. Crewes, and Mrs. Shepard, we experience both Jason's eye/camera as he follows them *and* a reverse shot showing Jason following the victim, usually repeated two or three times. During Eddie's death, we see Jason's eye/camera walking up on him, and within the shot, we see his shadow firmly identifying the shot as direct eye/camera positioning. Even eye/camera shots from the position of the victim clearly identify the seer. Kate's death, for instance, climaxes with an eye/camera shot as Jason kills her by shoving a party horn into her left eye. We see in her eye/camera as Jason forces the horn toward the camera, so not only can we identify the character whose eye/camera is seen, but we can precisely locate the eye that is seen through Kate's left eye.

shot situations. One primary example is a scene where Lori confronts her father about the truth of her mother's death. We see through Lori, who is standing on a staircase above her father who is talking to her. In reverse shot, Lori's response is captured through her father's eye/camera.

More significantly, *Freddy vs. Jason* uses an off-model eye/camera shot at an important point in the story. In a sequence similar to the eye/camera shot/reverse shot conversation between Lori and her father, Gibb, in the dream-world boiler room, hides from Freddy in a locker. After a few moments, the locker door opens and Freddy is in front of her, suspended upside down in the air. Gibb screams, prompting Freddy to laugh, which we first see over Gibb's shoulder. Then, as Jason stabs her in the real world, we see through Freddy's off-model eye/camera as Gibb's chest shoots blood. Gibb appears with her head at the top of the frame, body below,[21] instead of her head at the bottom, body above,[22] as would be seen from Freddy's direct perspective. Gibb still looks at the camera and screams, shot from the position of Freddy's eye (figures 2.9 and 2.10).

This shot, along with an eye/camera shot at the beginning of the movie from Freddy looking at a young girl victim in flashback, are the only eye/camera shots from Freddy's position. And, in the flashback shot, we see from Freddy's shadow that he *steps into* his eye/camera from the left side, although the girl looks at the camera the entire time, so it is at least in part off-model. The fact that the eye/camera shot at the beginning occurs before Freddy's first death and that both this and the one involving Gibb is off-model is significant. The "Dream Master" Freddy's direct eye/camera is being excluded from the film's aesthetic whereas Jason's and the central characters' eye/cameras appear frequently. This isolates Freddy and identifies him as the film's ultimate antagonist by victimizing not only the teenagers in the films but Jason, too.

Director Ronny Yu attempts to foreground visceral impact as in his earlier films *Bride of Chucky* (1998) and *Formula 51* (2001), with the eye/camera playing an important role in this effort. Theorist David Bordwell identified an increased inclination towards a visceral aesthetic in Hollywood in general. He claims this came to prominence particularly in the 1980s. Bordwell calls this visceral and heightened approach to storytelling "intensified continuity" (121–38). The general qualities he attributes to intensified continuity are "rapid editing, bipolar extremes of lens lengths, reliance on close shots, and wide-ranging camera movements" (121). Yu's style strongly foregrounds intensified continuity, and in *Freddy vs. Jason*, the director tailors his style to identify the absolute antagonist, presenting him as an outsider.

---

21. Laypeople would call this "right-side up."
22. "Upside down."

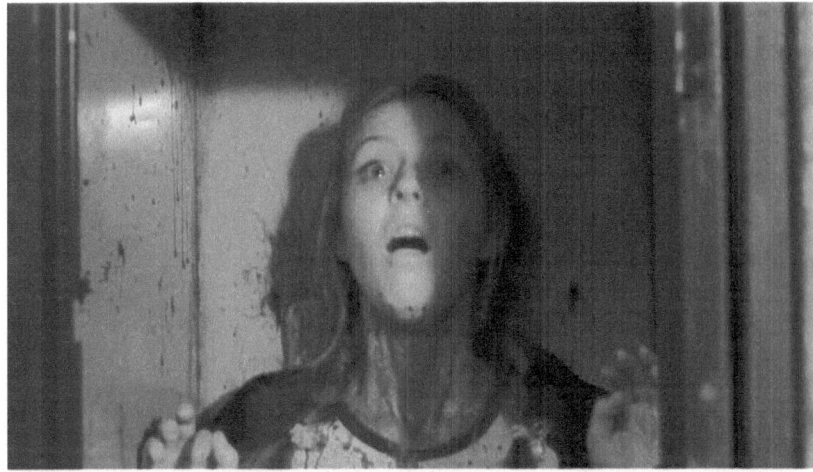

Figures 2.9 and 2.10. *Freddy vs. Jason*—The off-model eye/camera. Freddy and Gibb lock eye/cameras, but Freddy is the only one upside down. (New Line Cinema / Cecchi Gori Group Tiger Cinematografica / Avery Pix / Sean S. Cunningham Films / WTC Productions / Yannix Technology Corporation, 2003)

Jason, by contrast, becomes not quite a protagonist, but certainly a central focus of the story. As a mute character, Jason is the visual narrative drive. We see this through many eye/camera shots based within Jason. Yu establishes Jason's visual perspective early, after Freddy tells us he will resurrect Jason. There is a shot of Jason's hockey mask, and the camera pushes into the left eye of the mask. Here we see a teenage girl standing on a dock, undressing to go into the water. She turns and sees nothing, revealing this to be a mimic eye/camera shot. However, the use of eye/camera coding, combined with the fact that this shot appeared in the eye of the hockey mask, demonstrates this sequence as inhabiting Jason's perspective. We see the girl undress fully in long shot from an eye/camera framed through branches on the edge of the forest before she dives in. Even though we see the girl's eye/camera from the water, looking back at the dock, the camera stays close to Jason as he chases her. The movie returns to his eye/camera once he has killed her and pinned her to a tree.

We see through his eye/camera as she lifts her head and says, "I should have been watching them. Not drinking. Not meeting a boy at the lake." In the same shot, the girl transforms into a dead boy, who continues talking: "I deserve to be punished." Then the boy turns into a different girl, saying, "We all deserve to be punished." Although this girl did not actually transform, this indicates Jason's perspective, explaining his justification for murder, without him speaking. As in the opening credits sequence of *Jason X*, this becomes a representation of Jason's cognitive thought, his "mind's eye"/camera, as opposed to direct vision. While more extensive than the eye/camera, this, along with the early narrative establishment of Freddy's control over Jason, demonstrates how *Freddy vs. Jason* creates some identification and sympathy with Jason. The eye/camera works to reinforce our preferred alignment with Jason and invites us to view Freddy as the baddest of the bad guys.

The eye in time

Eye/camera usage in the first three films in the *Friday the 13th* series sets the franchise apart from other slasher films released between 1980 and 1982. Other films such as *Hell Night*, *My Bloody Valentine*, *Terror Train*, and *Happy Birthday to Me* all make use of the eye/camera and strict character perspective in ways that take cues from *Halloween*. However, the dominant eye/camera positioning is clearly that of the aggressor, with slight shifts to the victim. The opening of *Terror Train*, as described by Dika, is a useful example, wherein a group of girls, including the protagonist, humiliates a boy. This boy is the film's eventual antagonist, and the girls humiliate him for initiation into a sororal organization. Dika writes, "We watch from the heroine's point of view as the boy bashfully undresses near a bed surrounded by veils" (1990, 94–95). We cannot entirely see the subsequent humiliation through this shot. However, the movie places the eye/camera within a character with power over a victim, even if that dynamic shifts later in the film. We still experience these shots through the eyes of an aggressor.

Steve Miner's subsequent entries in the franchise, *Friday the 13th Part 2* and *Friday the 13th Part III 3-D*, developed a more challenging approach to the eye/camera, particularly in regards to audience positioning and perspective. Additionally, the two films use the eye/camera in very different ways.

The notable exception to this victim positioning is the eye/camera of Chris in the climax. At one point, we see through her eye/camera as she advances and slashes at Jason in the hallway of the cabin, and as she swings the hatchet into his head. This final act immediately precedes Jason extending his arms and slowly lumbering toward her, turning Chris from aggressor to victim and allowing us to experience this shift.

Also, *Friday the 13th Part 2* and *Friday the 13th Part III 3-D* both contain a large number of eye/camera and mimic eye/camera shots unique to their contemporaries. Shots like the mimic eye/camera in *Friday the 13th Part III 3-D*—in which the eye/camera moves towards Debbie in the shower but it is soon revealed that nobody is there when she opens the curtain—are a staple of slasher film misdirection.[23] However, sequences like the opening of *Friday the 13th Part 2*, in which a mimic eye/camera follows Alice around her house at length even after it is clear nobody is there, are extremely rare. Even slasher films from that period such as *Fade to Black* (1980) sometimes contain no more than two or three eye/camera shots in the entire film. This may explain the more economical, if still occasionally inventive approach to eye/camera coded shots in subsequent *Friday the 13th* films.

While there is not a decrease in the number of eye/camera shots in *Parts VI, VII,* and *VIII*, the approach to them tends to be more streamlined and direct with less ambiguity. The ultimate aim of the shots in the final three Paramount-produced *Friday the 13th* films appears to be generic orientation and confirming the overarching perspective at the service of the narrative. This, however, diminishes suspense caused by distortion and uncertainty of perspective. There is certainly playfulness within *The New Blood* and *Jason Takes Manhattan*, and a lot of shifting points of view from shot to shot, but all three are generally less groundbreaking and subversive than the earlier films.

Jason Takes Manhattan has a more consistent eye/camera design than its predecessor. This indicates that any sense of standardization in stylistic design is very tenuous at this point. The use of eye/camera between *The New Blood* and *Jason Takes Manhattan* is different to the extent that it appears to be less evolutionary and more reactionary. The design of *Jason Takes Manhattan* appears to be less of a development of the design of *The New Blood* but rather an attempt to create a design distinct from it, where the eye/camera is concerned.

---

23. Isolated mimic eye/camera shots within different contexts from the period can be found in *My Bloody Valentine, Halloween,* and *When a Stranger Calls,* among others.

A significant commonality between *Parts VI*, *VII*, and *VIII* is the early introduction of, and consistent attachment to, a protagonist that drives the narrative development: Tommy in *Jason Lives!*, Tina in *The New Blood*, and Rennie in *Jason Takes Manhattan*. The eye/camera in these movies establishes the centralization of these characters and of Jason as antagonist, which differs from *A New Beginning*. In this movie, Tommy, though the central character, is not clearly identified as protagonist or antagonist until the end. The following three films, however, use the eye/camera in very different ways in order to highlight the protagonist/antagonist relationship. On the other hand, the eye/camera shots in *Jason Takes Manhattan* only use generic orientation as part of the way the use of eye/camera develops over the course of the movie. *Jason Takes Manhattan* presents the viewer with eye/camera shots initially to create generic orientation and visceral shock by moving between victim and aggressor positioning. However, it gradually aligns the movie with Rennie's perspective, with a few exceptions.[24] And, following on from this, the eye/camera shots in *Jason Goes to Hell* do not contribute to the overall perspective of the film, but instead present a variety of perspective experiences from moment to moment and ultimately define generic orientation while providing momentary visceral shock.

In *Jason X*'s sparing use of the eye/camera, it specifically defines the genre(s) it works in, which is significant to the story which is by its nature a hybrid of science fiction and horror. The film largely uses aesthetics from the science fiction genre, only using the eye/camera sequences when a horror aesthetic is appropriate to the narrative. This is the case when Jason sneaks up on Crutch, which reminds the viewer of the potential threat Jason represents, both to individuals and to the entire ship, as Crutch is the pilot. It is therefore significant that, aside from the overt iconography of the series,[25] the eye/camera is the primary stylistic device used to situate the viewer's expectations and understanding within the horror genre while the dominant aesthetic belongs to the science fiction genre. These eye/camera shots provide an extreme sense of contrast to the science fiction sequences of the film, which are strictly shot from an omniscient third-person perspective.[26] The movie sets the horror and

---

24. These exceptions, as discussed, include the junkies watching the group and Julius's decapitation.

25. It is important to note that the iconographic elements of the *Friday the 13th* franchise are filtered through the science fiction genre in this movie: Jason's hockey mask is made of metal with a design reminiscent of Futurism, and the Camp Crystal Lake sequence is placed within the context of a virtual reality hologram.

26. One example of third-person perspective in *Jason X* can be seen in the sequence involving his DNA reconstruction, which is shot through a series of tripod mounted close-ups and medium shots, along with smooth tilts and tracking shots.

science fiction sequences apart primarily by the use of the eye/camera in *Jason X*. Therefore, the movie intensifies the vulnerable eye/camera positionings through this contrast as well as the relative paucity of eye/camera usage.

Eye/camera use in these films becomes a primary example of design based on monetary and business consideration, as initially pointed out by Sean S. Cunningham. Based on the success of the first film, which adapted a style with the aim of recreating the financial success of *Halloween*, the eye/camera became a prominent method of establishing perspective. We can attribute the similarity of eye/camera use in the first two sequels to the key creators behind the original film maintaining creative control. The third sequel adapted the initial style along with a more direct and less ambiguous eye/camera usage, although influence from the first three films is apparent. The final four Paramount films in the franchise reveal a repeated attempt at experimentation for different narrative purposes. This reflects the desire to develop a successful formula in light of declining box-office receipts. Experimentation continued through the first two "Jason" films released by New Line Cinema, with *Freddy vs. Jason* and *Friday the 13th* (2009) simultaneously employing generic trends at the time but in a distinctly auteurist fashion.[27] In other words, we can see that the filmmakers for the New Line films are trying new things while also sticking to the elements we have come to expect from these films, but Ronny Yu and Marcus Nispel bring their own personal, recognizable style to their entries in the series.

Ultimately, we can infer a couple of significant points. First, the overall effect of the eye/camera in the individual films indicates a specific design that often reflects the development of a cycle of intent and effect. We can observe this cycle—in which a filmmaker uses the eye/camera in one way and the next filmmaker builds upon this with changes based on personal style—by looking at the way film style and aesthetics developed over time within the franchise as a whole. Secondly, the range of approaches and alternate framing of eye/camera aesthetics within this film series alone problematizes a sociocultural or psychoanalytical generalization of the device. In other words, we can't reduce the pleasure we get from it to "voyeurism" or "scopophilia." Since these films have used the eye/camera in so many different and complex ways, such an assertion is simply myopic.

In the first instance, an observation of the overall approach to the eye/camera in each individual film demonstrates a precise progression of development.

---

27. As discussed, a comparison of Ronny Yu's films to *Freddy vs. Jason* and Marcus Nispel's films to *Friday the 13th* (2009) reveal similar visual aesthetic trends in camerawork across the films of each director.

Significantly, *A New Beginning* acts as an important pivotal text. Although I have just used the term "cycle" to describe the progression of intent, this is not wholly accurate. This continuum more closely resembles a spiral, where the return or repetition of a tendency of a previous group of films undergoes a specific mutation that replicates these previous tendencies with a stylistic alteration, not unlike throwing purple dye into a running washing machine full of white clothes. Sure, they come out clean, but your clothes are more fun, or at the very least just a little different.

I'd also like to return once more, and only briefly, to negative criticism of the eye/camera. While three of the first four films favor perspectives of aggression and power, there still exist examples of victim perspective. Furthermore, the frequent use of mimic eye/camera challenges our reading of perspective, inviting us to actively engage with the film. This works contrary to arguments for the eye/camera as invitations to passive sadistic pleasure. As mentioned, the following films attempt to create generic orientation or develop an overarching visceral aesthetic. They frequently alter the perspective between victim and aggressor, and include the perspectives of passive witnesses. This undermines such arguments again, since we can only experience voyeuristic or sadistic pleasure through the perspective of an aggressor. Indeed, the final two films, through their development of an overarching visceral perspective, in a sense victimize us, the viewer, and in so doing establish a design that creates tension, suspense, and disorientation.

Ultimately, the eye/camera proves to be a device that has multiple functions, which can be developed with nuance and provide a design that is integral to the narrative. This is specifically the case within *A New Beginning*, *The New Blood*, *Jason Takes Manhattan*, and *Freddy vs. Jason*. When the eye/camera is applied to the characters within the *Friday the 13th* films, whether to Jason[28] or the victims, it can act as a signifier of power or vulnerability. However, the eye/camera shots from any of these characters can indicate power or vulnerability, such as the passive eye/camera shots from Jason in *Jason X* or the eye/camera of Deputy Winslow as he pursues Jason in *Friday the 13th Part 2*. And although eye/camera use can suggest an overarching perspective towards either power or vulnerability in any given movie, these positions can alternate not only within a film but sometimes within a single sequence, as in *The New Blood*.

The examples from the *Friday the 13th* series demonstrate both a cohesive aesthetic continuum as well as the variety provided within films with a wide

---

28. I use Jason here as the predominant antagonist in the series, though this statement includes Mrs. Voorhees in *Friday the 13th*, Roy in *A New Beginning*, any of the people possessed by Jason's spirit in *Jason Goes to Hell*, and even Freddy in *Freddy vs. Jason*.

range of writers and directors. This reflects theories of pleasure through repetition that genre viewing provides which the works of Barry Keith Grant, Edward Buscombe, and Steve Neale indicate. Dika accurately describes this tendency in her writing about *Friday the 13th* as a model for recombining generic elements to a successful end:

> (The) overall tendency in *Friday the 13th Part 2* toward the replication of material while supplying a suitable level of variation serves two purposes for the film-viewing audience. It facilitates the film's game by supplying the known ground rules, while the innovations supply the film's interest and shocks. This technique allows the viewer to feel secure in his knowledge of the formula, distanced by the formulaic predictability of the events, while nonetheless excited by the surprises and variations. (1990, 84)

The evolution of the eye/camera within the *Friday the 13th* movies exemplifies this statement. With the eye/camera established as a generic convention on the release of *Friday the 13th*, the sequels include it as a staple of the genre while altering how the eye/camera is framed, contextualized, and used over the course of the franchise. The eye/camera, however, is only one aspect of the entire visual design of these films, and the image is only one element of the aesthetics of each film.

Chapter 3

Hearing Cutting

In writing about movies, *The Image* holds a mystical power over the way we fundamentally analyze a film. Admittedly, this makes some sense. After all, we don't *see* sound. And editing, by common agreement in Hollywood, should be invisible. Nothing should detract from the story we come to immerse ourselves in. However, this provides a little difficulty to my analysis of perspective. The camera can take on the properties of a specific point-of-view rather easily. But what is the perspective of sound? What is the perspective of the edit? It's harder to define each individually, but when they work together, it is easier to identify through whom the filmmakers want us to experience the events on-screen.

As for sound and editing developments within the *Friday the 13th* series, the death sequences in these movies tell us a lot. Death sequences are useful here as they are frequently recurring and consistent set pieces throughout each film in the series. This is natural, as they elicit the most powerful emotional responses and, indeed, are central features within the genre. For a slasher film, death sequences provide climactic spectacles to punctuate key moments in the narrative. These sequences contribute to defining the genre, and therefore all elements of film style are pointed toward these set pieces, with an aim to effectively elicit the appropriate emotional response within a viewer. Conrich explains that "the relationship that the *Friday the 13th* films has with its audience is also dependent on exploiting a visceral curiosity; a desire to view the body modified and pushed beyond the limits of normality and acceptability" (2010, 183).

This, he argues, bears similarities to Grand Guignol stage shows, serving as essential sequences which define each genre. However, in spite of the significance of death sequences to the slasher, there is little research on them resulting in a surprisingly ignored area of study. Even Vera Dika's analysis centers on the stalking element of the narrative. One exception is Jonathan Lake Crane, who writes detailed analyses of death sequences only to explain what they say about our fears as a culture. However, their significance to the films, and their typically brief screen time, allows for very useful points in these movies for consideration. Concentrated collections of cuts and kills embody the most affective moments of the movies, during which the skill sets of stylistic inventors reside.

Robynn J. Stilwell writes of the way sound in cinema contributes to viewer/character identification, saying:

> Experiencing a strong identification with a character in the film places us in another's subject position, creating an emotionally empathetic response. Film has many ways of coaxing the audience into that position, from character development, narrative discourse and events, to the more "visceral" point-of-view shot compositions and sound design. Because of its intimate relationship to our real, physical bodies, via the vibrating air, sound seems more immediate. (51)

Stilwell powerfully expresses the close link between sound and its impact on the emotional engagement of the viewer. This is extremely useful to consider when establishing perspective.

Little work has been done to date concerning sound in the horror film, even less with respect to the slasher film. Of the work that has been done, Michel Chion identifies the significance of sound in creating off-screen space, occasionally using examples from horror films such as *The Invisible Man* (1933) to illustrate his theories. Chion, in finding an appropriate archaic term to express a specific concept in sound, writes, "Acousmatic, specifies an old dictionary, 'is said of a sound that is heard without its cause or source being seen.' We can never praise Pierre Schaeffer enough for having unearthed this arcane word in the 1950s" (1982, 18). Chion's writing on acousmatic sound highlights occurrences when the sound is diegetic but the original source is not seen. Chion's "acousmêtre" specifically relates to the voice that is heard but whose source is not seen. At the same time, we watch this with the anticipation of expecting to see the source of the voice at any given point in the film. For Chion, this foregrounds the importance of sound in the cinema. Sound informs and enhances its visual counterpart, and acousmatic sound can frustrate, heighten, and complicate the experience of watching a movie.

There has been some renewed interest in the use of sound in horror, and Chion's work is frequently at the forefront of this discussion. K. J. Donnelly addresses Chion's work on cinematic voice (103) before breaking off into an argument regarding the integral use of music to the sound design in the *Saw* films (2004–2017) (103–104).

As Donnelly acknowledges, "Michel Chion points to technological developments in cinema that have had a notable impact on film aesthetics" (104).

Chion's writing on the acousmêtre and specifically acousmatic sound proves a useful tool to understanding sound design in the slasher film. However, I will be using a very specific variation on this concept. To be more precise, I will discuss sounds used to represent something (an action, an event, an object) in the off-screen space of a film. However, as the sound is not visualized, it retains some ambiguity as to the sound's diegetic reliability. In other words, it's a sound that could reasonably exist in the world of the film, but since we don't see it, we are not always certain it does. As this deviates slightly from Chion's interpretation of "acousmatic," I will call this an "unverified diegetic sound."

René Clair, writing on the potential of sound to enhance cinema, details a sequence from *The Broadway Melody* (1929) that articulates unverified diegetic sound:

> For instance, we hear the noise of a door being slammed and a car driving off while we are shown Bessie Love's anguished face watching from a window the departure which we do not see. This short scene in which the whole effect is concentrated on the actress's face, and which the silent cinema would have had to break up in several visual fragments, owes its excellence to the "unity of place" achieved through sound. In another scene we see Bessie Love lying thoughtful and sad; we feel that she is on the verge of tears; but her face disappears in the shadow of a fade-out, and from the screen, now black, emerges a single sob. (94)

Especially relevant to the way sound communicates what we do not see is the way the edit interacts with this. In his brief handbook on editing theory, Roy Thompson states, "An important element of the edit can be the sound. Sound is not only more immediate than visuals but also more abstract. The very experienced editors have a saying, 'You don't have to see what you hear'" (46). This statement effectively stresses the relationship between not only sound and editing, but sound and vision, which Clair also highlights.[1] So, while visual depictions of bodily mutilation can provide spectacular set pieces for slasher films like *Friday the 13th*, by including the death within the film space without visually showing it, we experience the sequence in a completely different way.

Death sequence editing in the *Friday the 13th* franchise displays a distinct development from the inception of the series to the present, with shot framing, shot length and number of cuts being a major determining factor in the tone and pace of a sequence. Chion addresses the connection between a moving, changing image and sound design:

---

1. Also addressed by David Bowie.

> Sound and image are not to be confused with the ear and the eye. We find proof of this in filmmakers who infuse their images with what may be called the auditive impulse. What does this mean? Cinema can give us much more than Rimbaudian correspondences ("Black A, white E, red I"); it can create a veritable intersensory reciprocity. Into the image of a film you can inject a sense of the auditory, as Orson Welles or Ridley Scott have. And you can infuse the soundtrack with visuality, as Godard has. (1994, 134) [parenthesis in original]

He continues:

> I have said elsewhere that the ear's temporal resolving power is comparably finer than that of the eye; and film demonstrates this especially clearly in action scenes. While the lazy sphere thinks it sees continuity at twenty-four images per second, the ear demands a much higher rate of sampling. And the eye is soon outdone when the image shows it a very brief motion; as if dazed, the eye is content to notice merely that something is moving, without being able to analyze the phenomenon. In this same time, the ear is able to recognize and to etch clearly onto the perceptual screen a complex series of auditory trajectories or verbal phonemes. (134–35)

This discussion relates directly to a largely indecipherable image accompanied by a complex sound design that can be seen. For instance, in many of the boxing sequences in *Raging Bull* (1980), we can apply this same theory to a sequence where fast, disorienting editing is accompanied by a series of clearly designed or distinguished sounds.[2] In a boxing film (and, particularly, in *Raging Bull*), the moments of spectacle hinge on the key set pieces of boxing. Similarly, this is true of the murder sequences in slashers, which climax with the deathblow.

John Belton explains another dimension of this argument, saying, "Though off-screen diegetic sound—whether dialogue or sound effects—will, with few exceptions, ultimately be tied to the seen (or unseen) sources and thus be 'explained' or 'identified,' we experience that sound *through* what we see on the screen" (65) [emphasis in original]. Belton, in opposition to Chion, argues that sound design entirely relies upon the image. However, his statement points toward a situation in which a movie juxtaposes an image that implies an event with a sound clearly reflecting an occurrence, which creates a precise understanding of the unseen event.

So when we analyze these sequences, we ask: What do we hear? Is the sound of the deathblow on- or off-screen? How closely does the sound resemble the action it is meant to represent? (In other words, does it seem like a sound

---

2. Todd Berliner (2005) creates a wonderful and thorough analysis of the stylistic components of this movie.

constructed to directly resemble its realistic counterpart, or is the deathblow represented by a noticeably artificial sound effect created to elicit a specific response from the viewer?)[3] Is this deathblow accompanied by other sounds? Ambient noise? Voices? Nondiegetic sounds standing in place of other apparent noises? Does the sequence have a musical accompaniment?

These questions are supported by a series of peripheral questions: How many shots does the sequence contain? How long does the sequence last? Does the sequence favor a certain camera positioning, either specific or general? If so, what? Using the answers to these questions, we can determine whether the deathblows are either on- or off-screen, and further examine whether editing stands as a visual equivalent of the deathblows.

Sound design plays a crucial role in *Friday the 13th* and the subsequent installments in the franchise. Writing of a different franchise, Donnelly says, "*Saw* evinces a unified and complex field of music and sound effects. This inspires a certain sonic (and audiovisual) complexity, while the more self-contained nature of the soundtrack inspires less in the way of extended passages of synchronization" (106). Donnelly's argument is strong and convincing, and while *Saw* demonstrates this use of sound design in a manner rarely approached in preceding films, elements of this method appear in *Friday the 13th*. "The convergence of music with ambient sound and sound effects," writes Donnelly, "contravenes the film tradition of solid demarcation between such elements" (107). *Friday the 13th* does not achieve this as fully as *Saw*, but the integration of sound elements still appears within the composition of the score. Composer Harry Manfredini describes the unusual methods taken in recording the score: "I was also not a big fan or user of electronic instruments at the time. I wanted to stay orchestral. So things that you might think were synthesized were just me making sounds. I spent a lot of time scraping and hammering on the piano of the poor studio owner, and playing screeching sounds on an Irish tin whistle" (quoted in Bracke, 39).

The unconventional sounds serve to blur the lines between ambient noise, sound effects, and score in much the same way as Donnelly describes the use of soundscape in *Saw*. James Wierzbicki laments the fact that Hollywood remakes

---

3. We can see an example of a noticeably artificial sound effect in Stanley Kubrick's *A Clockwork Orange* (1971) as Alex delivers the blow that kills the Cat Lady. In the scene, the Cat Lady is lying on the ground, and Alex stands over her, poised to strike her with a giant sculpture of a penis.[a] Music is loud on the soundtrack, the Cat Lady screams, and Alex thrusts the ceramic dick toward her head. At the moment he strikes her, there is a quickly edited montage of paintings, and on the soundtrack we hear the loud crash of cymbals instead of a sound that would communicate something solid hitting flesh, meat, and bone.

[a]Trust me, the symbolism is not lost on me.

of Japanese horror films have removed the context for the use of specific sounds on the soundtrack leading to a less cohesive narrative. Sarah Reichardt writes about the way Dmitri Tiomkin's score for *Mad Love* (1935) brings added layers of narrative to the film, making it useful in terms of emotional resonance while it simultaneously contributes to the development of plot and characters. This represents a renewed interest in the stylistic use of sound in horror and the depth of significance that contemporary critics attribute to sound in film.

The killer's theme, which was first heard in *Friday the 13th*, turned into an iconic trademark of the film, continuing throughout the series. It is recognizable as a repeated time delay voice that sounds like a whisper of "ch-ch-ch-ch, ha-ha-ha-ha." This sound signifies the presence of the killer. "Harry [Manfredini] is an equipment junkie, and he has something called an echo reverb machine," says Sean S. Cunningham (quoted in Bracke, 39). "I don't know what Harry was saying, but it is like guttural sounds, hard sounds. The two words that he used were 'kill' and 'mother.' 'Ki, ki, ki. Ma, ma, ma'" (ibid.).[4] These words specifically reference the climactic revelation that Mrs. Voorhees feels compelled and possessed by Jason to kill the counselors. This is not immediately apparent upon first hearing it, yet it is still exemplary of how the score's design blurs the lines between sound effects and score. This example also demonstrates the slippage between inner monologue (or dialogue) and score, showing a distinct blend of narrative and emotional resonance and impact.

Friday the 13th, unlike the mainstream American slasher films preceding it, features brief but explicit sequences of graphic bodily mutilation to punctuate its death sequences. Although in-shot bodily mutilation was not new,[5] key death sequences generally combine sound and editing in a way suggestive of a violent attack. The shower scene in *Psycho* combines frequent fast cuts with Bernard Herrmann's harsh, dissonant score of high strings, and with sounds of the knife swishing through the air, the knife penetrating the skin, the water from the shower falling, the rings of the shower curtain grating on its support bar, and Marion Crane's screams. Both the knife and Marion appear in two or three shots together. The shot most indicative of violence is a medium shot of her naked torso, with Mother's hand holding the knife stabbing downwards, just in front of her body without touching it.

The opening sequence of *Halloween* culminates with Michael stabbing Judith, which Carpenter shoots in a single take. However, the surrounding clown mask

---

4. Verified by Manfredini (Grove, 39).

5. The death scene of Detective Arbogast in *Psycho* is one earlier instance. The camera shows Arbogast in medium shot as he stumbles backwards down the stairs, beginning with a nonfatal knife slash at his face, which Van Sant turns into multiple slashes in the remake. And let's not forget the infamous eyeball-slicing shot from *Un Chien Andalou* (1929).

Michael wears blacks out much of the edges of the frame. All we see is the flash of the knife, Judith recoiling, and a simultaneous pan right and tilt up to the knife stabbing without Judith in shot; high, dissonant keyboard sounds accompany the sequence, along with the sounds of Judith screaming and the knife penetrating flesh. After this, the camera simultaneously pans left and tilts down to Judith, bloody, falling to the floor but we see no visible body penetration.

This tendency of unseen bodily penetration recurs throughout all the death sequences in *Halloween*, with the exception of the climax as Michael revives after collapsing behind the sofa. He stabs at Laurie, and the knife rips her sleeve and scratches her arm, accompanied by an instrumental sting and the sound of Laurie screaming and her sleeve ripping. *The Texas Chain Saw Massacre* also combines editing and sound to imply violent bodily penetration, while showing very little. The seminal sequence of Leatherface placing Pam on a meat hook is a clear example. This sequence begins from behind the meat hook, large on the right of the frame with Leatherface carrying Pam toward it, beginning in long shot. As he moves into close-up, he places her back to the camera and lifts her. The only sounds we hear are Leatherface's breathing and Pam's screams. The image cuts to a reverse long shot, as Leatherface lets go of Pam and she apparently catches on the hook. There is no sound of the hook going into flesh. There is a shot of the blood-splattered wall behind Pam followed by a close-up of her moaning in shock; her mouth is open as she reaches for the meat hook (figures 3.1–3.5).

Tom Savini, recognized for his work with director George A. Romero and particularly for his special makeup effects in *Dawn of the Dead*, was hired to do special makeup effects for *Friday the 13th*. Savini applied his skill to create in-shot effects infusing *Friday the 13th* with an aesthetic similar to Romero's zombie films, but more importantly, connecting *Friday the 13th* to the stylistic tradition of much Italian horror, including the giallo film.[6] *Suspiria* (1977), as an Italian horror film by Dario Argento, a filmmaker with strong giallo ties, contains a close-up of a girl's heart being stabbed. In *Deep Red*, Professor

---

6. Mikel Koven directly connects *Friday the 13th* to the narrative tradition of what he calls "the terror tale" in folklore. Koven includes *Friday the 13th* along with *Halloween* and *The Burning* in a set of examples "in which the killer was *always* the killer and the action was motivated largely by trying to avoid this monster" (2006, 163). However, he argues that *Friday the 13th* is amongst the slashers that do not share similarities with the giallo film, unlike *Terror Train*, *My Bloody Valentine*, and *Prom Night*. Koven makes this claim based on specific narrative intricacies, validated through his overarching argument towards generic identification. My argument is that the *Friday the 13th* series links to the giallo tradition by the already demonstrated formal and stylistic similarities, as well as through the overt acknowledgment by the filmmakers (especially Cunningham) of the influence giallo had on the films.

Figures 3.1, 3.2, 3.3, 3.4, and 3.5. *The Texas Chain Saw Massacre*—Pam placed on the meat hook. The hook is never shown entering her back. (Vortex 1974)

Giordani is killed after we see a close-up his face being smashed and ground onto a solid desk.

These visual interpretations of death and mutilation became a featured element and a spectacular draw from a marketing standpoint. This can be seen in Annie's death in *Friday the 13th*, as she is backed against the tree by the killer; the score is tense but also quiet and subdued. In a medium shot, the killer steps between the camera and Annie while he slashes the knife across her throat; this is accompanied by a relevant sound effect and a sudden increase in the volume of the music. As the killer steps away, we see the wound in her throat open and blood stream down her front.

Similarly, during Jack's death sequence, we see bodily penetration from two angles. He is laying on the bed smoking, and Ned's blood drips on his forehead from the bunk above him. He wipes the blood off and looks at it. As he begins to sit up, a hand comes from underneath the bed and holds his head down. The image cuts to a close-up of Jack in profile, with a hand on his head as the point of an arrowhead stretches the skin underneath, then breaks through the skin, and blood flows onto his throat and chest. This shot cuts to a high-angle shot looking down on him as more blood comes out and the arrow emerges even more. This is shown while high, loud strings are heard on the score at the moment the hand comes from underneath the bed; audible, too, is the rustling of the bedclothes and Jack gurgling through the blood.

Finally, Mrs. Voorhees's death is not only shown in-shot, but also in slow-motion. Alice is seen in long shot and slow-motion with a machete moving to strike Mrs. Voorhees. There is a cut to Mrs. Voorhees's mouth dropping in surprise, and then a cut to Alice in close-up as she swings the machete. There is then a reverse shot as the machete passes through Mrs. Voorhees's neck in slow-motion, and the head comes off rotating in the air and blood shoots out of the neck wound (figure 3.6). There is the sound of the machete swishing through the air, and the score contains strings holding a tremulous high note. The slow-motion and the tremulous note on the score highlight the violent action, while the swish of the machete punctuates the point of mutilation.

Although these images become central features of the film, the other deaths use comparatively simple methods of implication in order to convey violence. The deaths of the girl counselor in the pre-credit sequence, as well as those of Ned, Brenda, and Bill, are not shown at all. We see Ned dead with his throat slashed, in the top bunk where Jack and Marcie are having sex. Brenda's mutilated body is thrown through a window to scare Alice. Bill is shown with multiple arrows piercing his body, going into a wooden door, leaving his body suspended in the air.[7] The girl counselor is not shown in death at all; the image freezes and dissolves to white on her screaming face in close-up.

---

7. The reveal of Bill's body echoes the death of Bob in *Halloween*. Bob (a very generic name not dissimilar to "Bill")[a] is stabbed through the mid-section, the knife pinning him to a door, leaving him suspended off the floor in contravention of all laws of physics while Michael stares curiously at his lifeless body. I share this in the event you still need more evidence that *Friday the 13th* borrows from *Halloween*.

[a] Please keep in mind, this statement is made by somebody improbably named "Wickham."

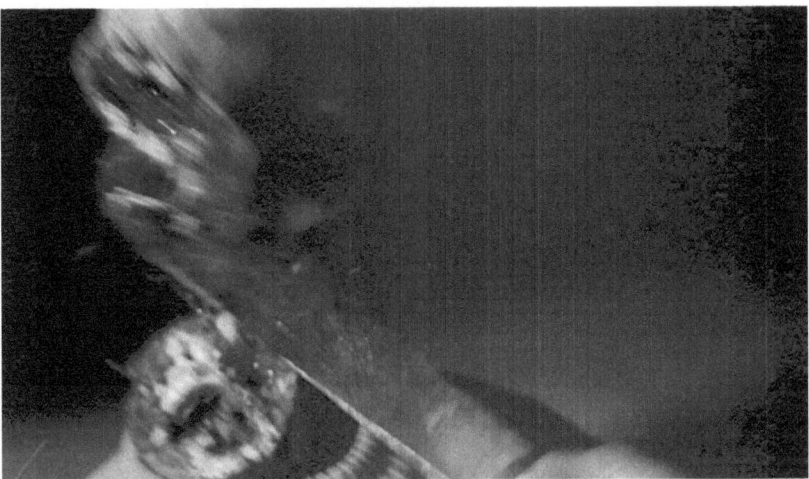

Figure 3.6. *Friday the 13th*—Mrs. Voorhees's head is chopped off in-camera. (Paramount Pictures / Georgetown Productions Inc. / Sean S. Cunningham Films, 1980)

The remaining deaths—the boy counselor, Steve, and Marcie—are all shown either just outside the frame or through implied editing and sound. Béla Balázs writes of "Sound-Explaining Pictures," commenting, "The close-up of a listener's face can explain the sound he hears. We might perhaps not have noticed the significance of some sound or noise if we had not seen its effect in the mirror of a human face" (119). The sequences depicting the deaths of Steve and the boy counselor illustrate this idea.

The boy counselor's death is shown through three shots. The eye/camera moves toward him, as he retains eye(/camera) contact trying to explain what he was doing. As the boy appears in close-up, the eye/camera lunges forward accompanied by a sound effect indicating a knife penetrating flesh and an orchestral sting. The boy doubles over, as there is a cut to a long shot of him falling over, holding his stomach and bleeding. The image then cuts back to the eye/camera shot as it begins to pursue the girl counselor.

We see Steve's death through a single eye/camera shot. The killer shines a flashlight in his face, and Steve walks toward the camera saying, "Oh, it's you! What are you doing out here?" His voice and the rain are the only sounds heard, but as he moves into close-up, as with the boy counselor, there is an orchestral sting and a sound of knife penetrating flesh as he is apparently stabbed just below the frame. He doubles over as the image cuts to the next sequence.

Marcie's death is more structurally complex. In the bathroom, she hears a sound over by a row of showers. She opens one curtain that she has seen moving, with nothing inside. From inside the shower, we see Marcie in medium shot as the shadow of a hatchet appears on the wall behind her, rising into the air. We hear her talking to herself as the score grows in intensity. As she turns around, there is a cut to a slightly high-angle medium shot while she looks at the hatchet above her. The score continues to increase in volume, and there is a cut to a low-angle shot of the hatchet raising. There is another cut to the same high-angle shot of Marcie, her face contorted into a cry, which we hear, and another cut back to the hatchet as it swings downward, grazing the hanging light. This causes the light to swing, and as a result, the shadows on the wall move. In this shot, we hear the clink of the hatchet against the bulb followed by a thud, implying the hatchet striking Marcie over the music's gradual swell. The music climaxes at the impact of the hatchet onto Marcie's head. After this sound, there is a cut to Marcie, slumping to the ground, dead with a hatchet buried in her face. Here, Cunningham creates a fluid exchange of perspectives between the killer and Marcie in this sequence.

The three categories I have listed—on-screen mutilation, out-of-frame mutilation, and unseen death—each establish perspective in the way they employ sound and editing. The on-screen mutilation sequences all use sound and editing to highlight victim perspective. For example, after running away from an apparent threat, Annie is finally pinned against a tree, and the fact that the frame holds without editing echoes Annie's immobile position. The slash sound the knife makes against her throat, while strictly an unverified diegetic sound, precedes the opening of the wound in her throat. This creates a visceral identification with the viewer: although the victim would not see the wound, the viewer imagines the sensation of this mutilation, creating a direct connection with the victim.[8] The deaths of Jack and Mrs. Voorhees use sounds of mutilation that have a visual counterpart to attain a similar visceral effect, while editing reflects the unique position in which each character is placed.

The attack on Jack, in timing and in source, is sudden and unexpected for both the viewer and the character. As he is pinned down, his facial expression communicates shock, and different shots of varying durations, ranging from

---

8. This is an example in which I would agree with Shaviro's claim that "in horror films, our primary excitement and involvement is with the victims, not with the monsters or murderers. Our 'identification' or investment is with the very bodies being dismembered, rather than with the agents of their destruction" (60–61). In this instance, the visual depiction of bodily mutilation creates a visceral connection with the viewer. My argument, the one at the heart of this book, deviates from Shaviro, which is, simply, that viewer attachment or "identification" depends largely on how each sequence is framed. However, I do admire Shaviro's aim to defend horror films against the kind of thoughtless reflex that negative sociopolitical criticism of the genre is rooted in, as he later claims (61).

long shot to close-up, echo Jack's mental panic as he tries to understand what is happening. By contrast, Mrs. Voorhees's death is shot in slow-motion, using shots of roughly the same length, without much variation in positioning. Mrs. Voorhees is in the same place during each shot of her, as Alice moves toward the stationary camera. This timed steadiness of editing and camera positioning echoes Mrs. Voorhees's expression of shock as she sees the attack coming but is too stunned to do anything about it. This communicates her sense of unavoidable impending death. Although Cunningham includes the slow-motion and protracted shots focusing on the act and gory aftermath of Mrs. Voorhees's decapitation for the purposes of spectacle, they are still stylistic decisions that contribute to the creation and establishment of perspective in the sequence.

The unseen deaths function in different ways where perspective is concerned. Ned and Bill are both unaware that they are in danger. Furthermore, the last time we see them alive, Ned is walking by the lake when he notices someone walking into a cabin and begins to walk toward it, while Bill is trying to repair the generator. Brenda, however, is following distant cries for help and walks onto the archery range where the arc lights turn on unexpectedly and she is unable to see anything but the lights. In Ned's case, there is a character who appears far in the distance, and Brenda is following the source of what might be considered an acousmêtre. However, they are both the primary figures of viewer attachment in their respective sequences. Also, the last time we see Bill alive, he is the only character that we see or hear, so there is no indication of the presence of a killer, either in or out of frame.

The deaths of Bill and Brenda, however, are necessary, postmortem, to contribute to Alice's perspective during the climax. Alice discovers Bill's dead body as she is looking for him, and we see Brenda's body thrown through the cabin window in order to frighten Alice. This increases the sense of danger experienced by both Alice and the audience.

Ned's body, however, is never discovered by any characters in the film. As Jack and Marcie have sex, we see them in medium profile, arguably an omniscient or at least perspective-free shot. There is no musical score accompanying the sequence—just the sound of the rain and thunder outside the cabin, heavy breathing, and Marcie's high-pitched moans. The camera then cranes upward to the bunk above them, revealing a close-up of a bloodied Ned with his throat slashed, without any changes to the sound of the sequence. No character discovers Ned's body at any point, and his corpse is shown solely for the benefit of the viewer, for both grotesque spectacle as well as to create tension surrounding Jack and Marcie's lack of knowledge of the danger they are in.

The absence of music also foregrounds the fact that this sequence lacks character perspective and directly engages our experience in the narrative, making it particularly unique within the context of the film. The girl counselor's death, in contrast to the other unseen death sequences, communicates the perspective of the aggressor. There is only the continuous eye/camera shot capturing the action once she becomes the focus of the aggressor. The volume of her voice increases based on her proximity to the eye/camera, producing an aural connection to the aggressor as well. The sequence ends with a freeze-frame and enlargement of the girl counselor's face focusing on the fear, as opposed to the bodily mutilation, of the victim.

Visually, the sequence preceding the girl counselor's death is similar to that of the deaths of the boy counselor and Steve. All of these sequences are shot using the eye/camera. The killer stabs the boy counselor and Steve below the frame, but it is implied that these are fatal blows. Although we do not see the fatal blow strike Marcie, the editing and sound create an understandable rendering of the violent act, even before the viewer sees Marcie with the hatchet buried in her face.

The compared quotes between Chion and Belton here become important to the reading of these sequences. Though we do not see on-screen bodily mutilation in the case of the boy counselor and Steve, Cunningham shows their faces as it occurs. They both lurch forward as a sound effect and an orchestral sting indicate the bodily penetration aurally. Belton would likely claim the sound is tied visually to the motion and expressions of the characters, creating a complete meaning. However, the sound establishes a more complete sense of the action happening off-screen, prompting a visceral response in us. Chion's argument is that the inability to see the source of the sound creates a tension in us, and as viewers, we are predisposed to desire a visualization of what we hear.[9]

We can apply this argument to the experience of viewing these sequences. Generic expectation allows the viewer to anticipate the forthcoming deaths, a knowledge we share with the killer whose eye/camera we experience as the boy counselor and Steve are each killed. The visual is not necessary in eye/camera because the perspective of the aggressor is apparent, and this shared knowledge of the event occurring off-screen solidifies the aggressor perspective. The fact that we see these events in single takes with no edits echoes the steady gaze of the attacker. The sounds indicating the stabbings solidify our knowledge of the unseen events, even if the viewer experiences tension caused by the

---

9. Chion's argument specifically applies to the acousmêtre, supporting his claim for the importance of the voice in cinema. However, in the case of horror films, death becomes the central focus of the genre. Therefore, the sound of someone being physically penetrated achieves an importance close to, if not equal to, that of the voice due to the spectator's relationship to generic expectation. In a slasher film, characters are brutally killed, so it doesn't matter whether we see it or hear it; either way, we are expecting it.

desire to see the sources of the sounds. However, the sudden cut to the next sequence, coming after the killer stabs Steve, complicates his death. While we anticipate Steve's death through generic codes (i.e., eye/camera, dark and rainy night, flashlight limiting the victim's eyesight), the sudden change of scene echoes the surprise Steve experiences while he is being killed. This causes a double perspective, beginning with the aggressor up through the moment of the stabbing, and immediately followed by a victim perspective created through the shock and visceral impact of the edit. The edit between eye/camera and omniscience during the boy counselor's death only briefly changes the visual point-of-view, while retaining the time continuity within the sequence. The boy counselor's death is not completely removed from the perspective of the aggressor, and the edit merely contributes to the visceral impact. The sound design compounds this without changing character perspective.

The structure of Marcie's death sequence works differently from those of Steve and the boy counselor. Three primary elements alter the sound. Firstly, the music gradually crescendos throughout the sequence, climaxing as the hatchet strikes Marcie in the face. This is different from the music accompanied by a sharp orchestral sting, which plays over the stabbings of Steve and the boy counselor. Secondly, as Marcie senses her impending death, she lets out a high-pitched cry before she is killed, and this contributes to the music's gradual swell. Finally, the change of weapon, from knife to hatchet, leads to the sound of a deathblow of a different timbre to that of the stabbings of Steve and the boy counselor. As the hatchet strikes, there is a low heavy thud with a slight crunch and squish, as opposed to the high swish and squish sounds indicating a stabbing.

This sequence also contains a greater number of shots of short length than the death sequences of Steve and the boy counselor. This results in a change in perspective from the experience of viewing Steve's death. The first thing we see in Marcie's death sequence is the shadow of the hatchet being raised on the wall behind her as she, unaware, is looking into the shower cubicle. Thus, the viewer shares the knowledge of her impending death with the aggressor, in a steady unwavering shot. As Marcie turns around and sees the hatchet above her, the cuts occur more frequently, and the music proportionally increases to hear dread of the occurrence, mingled with her cry.

The frequent cuts reflect Marcie's surprise and disorientation, focusing more upon the hatchet than the person controlling it. As such, the sequence begins briefly establishing aggressor perspective and changing quickly to victim perspective, playing out this key sequence from that positioning. These are examples of the recognized potential for aesthetic, or stylistic, complexity in the use of sound and editing at the outset of the *Friday the 13th* series. Furthermore, these demonstrate the use of fluid perspective shifts that would further develop over the next thirty years. We can see these developments more clearly through the way each kind of perspective is constructed in their relevant films.

Killing by ear

The perspective of an aggressor shows up more frequently in the earlier films where eye/camera is concerned. However, apart from the fluctuations that occur in the first movie, aggressor perspective appears most frequently in *The Final Chapter* in death sequences using unverified diegetic sound and editing. The technique of rapid editing in *The Final Chapter*, as it appears in death sequences in the rest of the film, contains shots of a weapon entering the body, maximizing the visceral impact of the sequences. The remainder of the sequences employing unverified diegetic sound for deathblows contain fewer shots of longer length, indicating aggressor perspective.

The shots leading up to and including Samantha's death are comparatively long, with a steady, deliberate editing pace. After the movie establishes Samantha's perspective through her eye/camera shot approaching the raft, the image cuts to an extreme long shot of her climbing into the raft and lying down on her stomach. Heard on the score is quiet, suspenseful music, and the sounds of her body against the water as she swims and leaps into the raft are very hushed and distant. The shot holds long enough for her to settle into the raft, squirming to get comfortable and gradually relaxing. With the shot still holding, we hear the sound of a twig snapping and leaves rustling, which are slightly louder than Samantha's movements. She calls, "Paul! I know you're out there!" Despite projecting her voice for Paul's benefit, her voice sounds as though it is far away from us.

The shot then cuts to a close-up of Samantha looking out over the lake, with the music still soft, but she then calls for Paul again, this time, her voice louder and clearer. After a long pause, she splashes the water with her hand and says, "Screw you, Paul." This statement, along with the splash, retains the volume of her previous line in the shot. She settles back onto the raft, and after a few moments, the sudden sound of movement in the water, along with a sting from the score, punctuate a sudden cut to a full shot of Jason leaping out of the water beside Samantha in the raft and placing his hand on her back.

At the moment he touches her, she screams with the music on the score loud and tense. There is then a cut to a medium shot of Samantha. Her head is lying screen left, Jason's hand on her shoulder in the middle of the frame. The music and her scream are sustained, but there is a ripping and a wet slicing sound, just before a spearhead emerges from Samantha's lower back at the right of the frame. This shot remains steady, holding for about four seconds, before cutting to a close-up of Samantha from the front, shaking and jerking in response to the action. Her scream retains the same volume, but the volume of the score increases with this shot. The length of the shots and the deliberate pacing of the editing, combined with an increase in the volume of sounds based on visual proximity to Samantha, echo Jason's positioning. Although his exact location is ambiguous until his appearance, visually and aurally the movie provides us information reflecting a stalker and aggressor's perspective. We watch steadily, and the sounds she makes increases based on our proximity to the victim.

Another significant sequence is the mimic eye/camera shot depicting Terri's death (discussed in the last chapter). Director Joseph Zito captures this sequence with this one shot, so editing is not used to communicate the mutilation. Instead, the sounds of the sequence work together with the mimic eye/camera to establish atmosphere and mood, as well as to communicate the events and perspective. There is a soft dissonant chord produced by the violins on the score, sustained and wavering slightly. The sound of rain on the ground punctuated by the sound of thunder creates the ambience of the sequence.

We can see Jason's shadow stabbing Terri with a spear, and since lightning reveals this event through silhouette, there is a crack of thunder accompanying this. There is also a loud orchestral sting as well as a loud, wet crunch to indicate the bodily penetration. Terri's scream immediately follows this, which is comparatively quieter than the penetration sound effect; this choice emphasizes the mutilation as opposed to her reaction. In relation to Jason, this would be spatially accurate, though perhaps not to the extent presented. Once this has occurred, the shot does not cut away immediately, but continues to push in to the window of the cabin for a few additional moments (figures 3.7–3.9). The relationship of the sounds to the two characters in this sequence, as well as the continuation of camera movement after Terri is killed, all indicate, in spite of presenting a mimic eye/camera shot, that the sequence is presented from Jason's perspective. While other sequences in *The Final Chapter* also use unverified diegetic sound and editing to communicate death and mutilation, their design is similar to these discussed as well as others in previous films.[10]

Sensing the Attack

As we have seen, these movies frequently use the perspective of a victim of violent action to create a visceral response from the viewer. We can extend Stillwell's statement, linking sound to response and empathy, to this

---

10. For example, Sara's death is aesthetically executed in a similar way to the final sequence in *Friday the 13th Part III 3-D*, which I will discuss.

Figures 3.7, 3.8, and 3.9. *Friday the 13th: The Final Chapter*—The camera stalks Terri, but passes by her, showing her death in silhouette, before stalking toward the window. (Paramount Pictures / Georgetown Productions, 1984)

understanding of victim perspective. Stillwell's statement also relates to how central victim perspective is to the reading of slasher films.

Friday the 13th Part 2 only contains one death sequence rendered through unverified diegetic sound and editing. Vickie, looking around the main cabin, comes into a room where a white sheet is covering something on the bed. As she comes close, the sheet is pulled down, revealing Jason, who then sits up and looks at her. Vickie begins to back away, and becomes trapped in a corner. There is a long take of the knife in Jason's hand in sharp focus, while Vickie is out of focus in the background. The camera moves with the knife steadily toward Vickie.

As the knife and camera stop advancing, a rack focus—a device in which the camera's focus is changed from one object in the frame to another—to Vickie occurs within the shot. She appears in a slightly high-angle close-up, the knife out of focus in the foreground. The music maintains a consistent volume during this shot, with discordant strings playing in tremolo throughout. We can also hear the sound of thunder outside, as well as Vickie's breathing and occasional cries of "no." At the end of this shot, there is a cut to a low-angle close-up of Jason lasting no more than a second, as he stabs downwards. As we witness this, there is an orchestral sting that carries over to the next shot of Vickie in close-up, as the knife swings downwards below the frame. As this happens, there is a slight ripping sound and a thud that accompanies her cry, indicating the deathblow.

The tremulous strings continue, and the shot holds for a few seconds longer as blood begins to appear on her lower lip and her eyes glaze over. This sequence retains Vickie's perspective throughout. We experience this killing from the point-of-view of the victim, with the visual focus on the knife leading up to the stabbing, the swiftness of the two cuts as she is stabbed echoing her surprise, the sound of her voice and the penetration of the knife as she is stabbed punctuating the suspenseful music, and the long hold on the shot as she dies capturing the pain registering on her face.[11]

---

11. I have excluded the sequence in *Part 2* containing the double pinioning of Sandra and Jeff, as every sound used has an on-screen source. The editing between three shots—the spear held aloft, Sandra screaming, and the spear emerging from the mattress and hitting the floor—appears swift due to the brevity of the second shot but still provides an opportunity to show where all the sounds are coming from. There is nondiegetic music, but aside from that, all that is heard is the moaning of the couple as they have sex, Sandra's scream, which is shown in the second shot, the spear ripping through the mattress at the beginning of the third shot, immediately followed by the thud of the spearhead hitting the wooden floor underneath. There is no sound used to render the unseen violent bodily penetration.

Friday the 13th Part III 3-D stands apart from Vickie's death sequence in its use of an increased number of shots of shorter length. We can see this during Chili's death sequence, which also incorporates unverified diegetic sound. After watching Shelly die in the doorway, she runs upstairs to check on the others in the house. Chili finds them dead, and in a single full shot, comes down the winding staircase, and moves toward a closed door which is blown open by a gust of wind. She backs away from it moving closer to the camera, turns around, and registers an expression of shock in close-up as Jason's hand grabs her shoulder. Throughout, the score dominates the soundscape of the entire sequence. In the background, we hear Chili muttering to herself and whimpering. We hear the sound of the wind that blows the door open, followed by a scream from Chili just before a loud bang as the door hits the wall, and she squeals as Jason grabs her shoulder. After Chili squeals, there is a brief pause and the image cuts to a close-up of a red-hot poker held by Jason as he thrusts it toward the camera (in 3-D). The dominant score accompanies this shot, along with an increasing hiss as the poker moves closer to the camera, signifying distance from us as well as the heat of the weapon.

This is an example of an observation made by Bordwell and Thompson: "One characteristic of diegetic sound is the possibility of suggesting the *distance* of its source. Volume is one simple way to give an impression of distance. A loud sound tends to seem near; a soft one, more distant" (194) [emphasis in original]. The image cuts back to the close-up of Chili, looking downward and screaming. Chili is thrust backwards slightly when the poker stabs her. She screams and the hissing grows even louder with the penetration. The image then cuts to a close-up of the poker, held by Jason's hand on the left side of the frame, running through Chili's midriff at the right of the frame. The red tip emerges from the other side of Chili. Smoke emerges from the wound and the hissing becomes suddenly louder.

The image then cuts back to the close-up of Chili looking downward, with smoke rising in front of her face as she sinks below the frame. Her scream and the music both fade to a lower volume at the end of the shot. The source of tension in this sequence is the overbearing music, functioning in a way similar to the music in *Suspiria*. This, in combination with the editing of multiple short shots, and with the changes in sound volume based on relative locations in the film space (the way the hissing grows louder as the poker comes closer to Chili), all indicate Chili's perspective throughout the sequence.

Another relevant sequence in terms of creating the perspective of victims in *Friday the 13th Part III 3-D* occurs at the end of the climactic confrontation between Chris and Jason. After a surprise attack by Ali, Jason cuts off his arm and hacks at him with a machete. Miner frames Jason from behind in medium shot. He is hacking at Ali below the frame, with each sound of Jason's machete entering Ali's body being entirely unverified diegetic. In a reverse medium shot, Chris, holding a hatchet she picked up off the ground, slowly stands. She moves toward Jason with the nondiegetic score playing steadily and rhythmically, creating a slow crescendo, while Jason's hacking continues. There is a cut to the reverse shot of Jason from behind, the camera keeping Jason in medium shot as he stands up and turns to face the camera, looking at Chris. He pauses, and the shot cuts to a close-up of Chris as she swings the hatchet toward the camera. During this shot, she grunts, starting low, increasing in both pitch and volume.

This grunt and the music carry over to the next shot, positioned over Jason's shoulder, showing Chris in medium shot as the hatchet moves toward Jason's head. There is a crunch as Jason's head jolts backward, but the camera *does not capture* the actual point of penetration.[12] At this point, the strings on the score hit a high, sustained, wavering note. And as Jason's head swings forward in compensation for the backward motion, there is a cut to him in close-up. The hatchet is sticking out of his head as he snaps his head upright, pauses and reaches his arms forward. This sequence is notable for alternating between two perspectives at two different points. During the first part of the attack, Chris's perspective is predominant as she approaches Jason. He is unaware of her approach, but as he turns around, the pace of editing quickens, and her grunt increases with volume placing the viewer in his spatial position. The editing indicates and reflects his surprise. The final shot, as he reaches out to Chris, returns the editing pace to longer shot lengths. And, doubled with Chris's eye/camera, this shift returns the film to her perspective.

The Final Chapter continues the stylistic tendency of using faster-paced editing and unverified diegetic sound in order to simultaneously communicate perspective and to manipulate the cognitive reading of the viewer. Through this, the film creates the visualization of the death sequences and bodily penetration without explicitly showing it. The first and most concise example of this is in the first death to appear in the film, Axel the orderly. We see Axel in a medium shot watching television in a dark room. He takes a sip of coffee, spills a bit on himself, and leans forward to set the cup on a table in front of him. We hear nothing on the soundtrack, until he whispers "shit" after spilling

---

12. This functions, or works, as an unverified diegetic sound in very much the same way as the first appearance of Marcellus Wallace in *Pulp Fiction* (1994) can be considered acousmêtre. Although we see Marcellus from behind in close-up and we can hear his voice, the source of the sound, his moving mouth, is just out of sight. As in *Friday the 13th Part III 3-D*, though we see Jason react to the blow from the hatchet, and the sound informs the viewer that it has occurred, the actual penetration remains unseen.

the coffee. The camera follows his movements in a single shot. As he leans back, Jason's hand grabs his forehead from screen right accompanied by loud, high strings on the nondiegetic score as well as the sound of Axel's struggles and grunts, as the rest of Jason's body moves behind Axel.

Once he is in position, the other hand at screen left brings a hacksaw up to Axel's throat. The image cuts to a darkly lit high-angle eye/camera shot from Jason, the light and camera focus drawing out the shining hacksaw. The music continues as Jason pulls the saw from left to right from this new vantage point, and this is accompanied by a grating and gurgling sound combined. The silhouette of Axel's head prevents the viewer from seeing the details of this first motion of the saw. The movie cuts back to the medium shot of Axel, now with the saw in his throat and blood running from the wound. The grating, gurgling, grunting, and music continue as his head and the saw both turn to the right. This shot quickly cuts to a close-up of the television in front of Axel, showing a close-up of the sexy aerobics instructor while she looks at the camera. This shot holds for longer than the length of the previous two shots combined, the editing of the three together coinciding with the rhythm of the score.

The volume of the diegetic sounds remains consistent. This shot then cuts to the close-up of Axel, his throat mangled and bloody, with Jason's hands on both sides of his head. The shot, lasting less than one second, ends as Jason twists Axel's head to the right, accompanied by a crunch, gurgle, and grunt. This leads to a match-on-action cut—an editing technique where the cut joins images of an action so the motion becomes a distraction from the edit—to a medium shot from behind Axel. The cut leads to a shot of Jason as he finishes twisting Axel's head around 180 degrees, with all sounds continuing in tone and volume. This final shot is still less than a second long, but lasts slightly longer than the previous shot. The consistent volume of the sounds in the sequence and the fast pace of the editing reinforce the victim's perspective.[13] In addition, the match-on-action cut shifts between the first stroke of the saw and the twisting of Axel's head, and the clarity of the sound effects give us a clear conceptual understanding of the actions taking place. This allows us to understand what is happening without it being seen, resulting in a sequence which creates a strong visceral response in the viewer.

One significant sequence in *Jason Lives!* actually shows the bodily penetration that accompanies the sound, but frustrates the viewer's visual connection to the sound through the extremely short shot length showing the mutilation. Cort's death is comprised of several shots shown through a rapid

---

13. This includes the deceptively irrelevant shot of what Axel is watching on the television as the event occurs. This shot further solidifies Axel's perspective.

series of cuts, starting from the moment he sees Jason in the rearview mirror. The primary sounds we hear are the rock music playing on the radio, as he sings along, and his occasional calls to the now-deceased Nikki. In medium shot, he looks into the rearview mirror, and his expression falls. Jason grabs his hair and pulls his head back. We see a low-angle shot behind Cort, who is shown out of focus in the background. Jason's hand is holding a knife as he thrusts it toward Cort, moving from the top of the frame to the middle background. This shot, which lasts six frames, is accompanied by a whooshing sound of the knife speeding through the air. This is followed by a return to the medium shot of Cort, with Jason's knife moving from the left of the frame to the right and entering Cort's temple (figures 3.10–3.13).

This shot, however, is only six frames long, and appears on-screen for one-quarter of a second. The actual penetration only appears in two of those frames before the image cuts to a close-up of Jason. We hear a crunching sound that accompanies this visual penetration, but due to the brevity of its screen time, its visual impact is imperceptible. Instead, the impact of the sequence hinges on the editing cuts and the sound used to indicate the stabbing, which appears to occur at the same time as the cut to the final shot. However, the stabbing sound begins simultaneously with its visual counterpart and drowns out the loud music, making it the focal point of the soundtrack for that moment. Use of these elements in this particular way not only contribute to our experience of Cort's perspective, but also render the visual of penetration secondary to the way sound and editing communicate this moment.

The attack on Michael in *The New Blood* is the only sequence that clearly uses unverified diegetic sound and editing to create perspective in an unusual way. As Jason follows him through the woods, the score is loud as each instrument creates its own steady pulse. The shots cut between Jason's eye/camera following Michael through the forest, and a low-angle shot of Jason pursuing Michael. The sounds alternate between what we see on-screen. In Jason's eye/camera, we can hear the crunching of leaves in time with Michael's footfalls at a distance. In the low-angle shots of Jason, we hear *his* footfalls in close proximity along with the jingling of the chains around his neck.

These shots and sounds all indicate a close alignment with Jason's perspective. Jason's attack on Michael uses a technique that we have seen in the previous film (as well as others in the series). Jason, in one shot, throws a tent peg. There is a swish pan, and we hear a whooshing sound followed by the sound of the tent peg entering Michael's back. A moment later the swish pan ends, showing the tent peg lodged in Michael's back. However, in this sequence, we see Jason throw the knife in a close-up low-angle shot of his face. There is then a cut to a long shot of Jason out of focus in the background as the tent

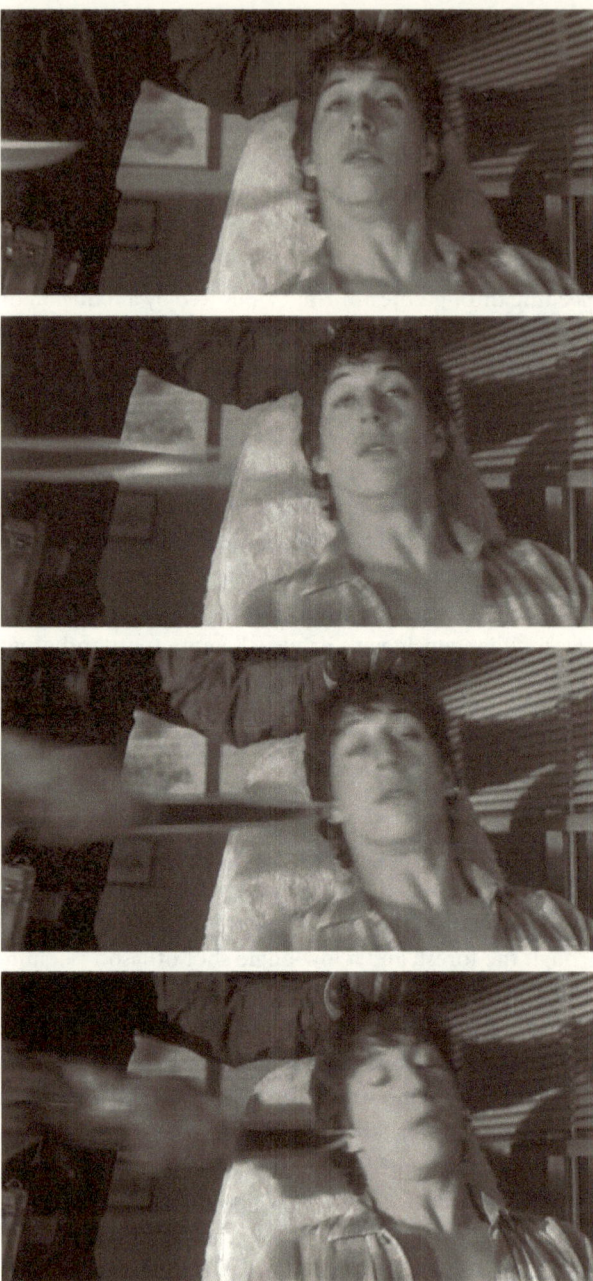

Figures 3.10, 3.11, 3.12, and 3.13. *Jason Lives!: Friday the 13th Part VI*—Four of the six frames of the knife penetrating Cort's head. The screen time is nearly imperceptible. (Paramount Pictures / Terror Films, 1986)

peg comes toward the camera from the middle background swiftly toward the middle lower frame, moving below the frame. The whooshing sound grows louder based on the distance from the tent peg to the camera. The film then cuts to a shot in the middle of the swish pan, so the camera is moving the moment the shot begins.

During this swish pan, the crunch is heard as the tent peg enters Michael's back, the loudest sound on the soundtrack. This appears spatially close to the listener, despite the fact that when the camera stops showing the tent peg in Michael's back, he is seen in full shot from behind. The sequence then returns the camera and sound in close proximity to Jason. Over the course of these two shots, the visual and the soundtrack indicate Michael's perspective in order to heighten the visceral impact on the viewer by aligning them with the victim. However, it also provides visceral impact by creating the unexpected and brief shock of changing perspectives, before moving back to the initial perspective alignment.

Friday the 13th (2009), while more frequently showing on-screen mutilation, prioritizes editing in a manner resembling the scene in *Jason Lives!* showing Cort's death. Because of this, Nispel uses unverified diegetic sound only occasionally. Therefore, the most significant stylistic advance is the continued increase in the number of shots that comprise death sequences. During Donnie's death, the moment of the deathblow includes four cuts linking five shots in less than two seconds.

One sequence within *Friday the 13th* (2009) that provides a key distinction from the other films in the franchise is the death of Wade. The sequence cuts between two shot setups: Wade's eye/camera as Jason attacks him, and a tracking shot set up in front and to the left of Wade following him as he backs away from Jason stopping against a tree. The percussion-heavy score is dominant on the soundtrack. Wade's voice, just underneath it, is heard yelling as he tells Jason to stop. There are three cuts between these shots, and the final shot, consisting of a darkly lit close-up of Jason swinging his machete toward the camera, coincides with the final note and beat on the score. Immediately after that final note and beat, we hear a swish sound of the machete cutting through the air, then a metallic grind immediately followed by a splattering sound, which precedes the image dissolving to black. All of these noises are heard very loud on the soundtrack, and after this, the only remaining sound is the resonance of the final note of the score.

This sequence demonstrates not only the use of unverified diegetic sound, but all other sounds stopping for a sound that creates the moment of climax. Additionally, this sound precedes the fading resonance of the score. Along with the dissolve to black, this indicates the victim's perspective. This recreates the experiential positioning of someone who hears the sound of their deathblow before slipping into unconsciousness. With the evolution of genre aesthetics, *Friday the 13th* (2009) becomes a key example of the increased sophistication in the use of sound and editing to align perspective with a victim.

Being an earwitness

As the series progressed, filmmakers began incorporating sequences involving omniscient third-person (witnessing the events in a godlike manner) and diegetic third-person (a character who watches someone else being murdered) witnesses to events. This appears to be both integral to fluid perspective shifts within sequences as well as isolated instances of third-person viewing. Although I have considered some sequences in which perspectives shift between characters, these are not isolated one-offs. They do indicate a much more experimental approach to communicating perspective which is present throughout the entire series.

The strangest usage of unverified diegetic sound and editing in a death sequence in *Jason Lives!* is Paula's murder. In the lead up to her actual death, we see her in medium shots and close-up shots as she moves around her cabin toward open windows and doors, bracing herself for something or someone to scare her. We are invited to share in this suspense, and the low, steady music from the score helps facilitate this. The editing is steady and even, keeping pace with her deliberate steps through the cabin. When she sees nothing at the window, she moves to the door, which suddenly slams shut. A loud sound effect accompanies this along with a swift, unexpected series of edits.

She relaxes as she realizes the wind blew the door shut, but as she reaches to open it, Jason appears just outside, steps in, and slams the door as she screams. The score begins to combine loud, pulsating low notes with fast, sharp high notes. At the moment the door slams, the image cuts to a full shot of the cabin door from the outside. The score decreases in volume, and Paula's screams are slightly muffled by the cabin wall which separates us from Paula. We hear sounds of nondescript items thrown and torn, as well as glass breaking. There is then a cut to an extreme long shot of the cabin from the outside, and all the sounds that appear in the previous shot decrease in volume. This shot holds for four seconds before cutting to a close-up of one of the cabin windows from the outside. The sounds raise slightly in volume, and we hear a sudden loud splattering sound that accompanies a splash of blood that sprays on the window, before the shot cuts to the next sequence. Every one of these shots is steady and tripod-mounted, and in the case of the doorway and the window, aside from some shifts in lighting, symmetrical. This distancing position, both in terms of camera positioning and sound positioning, as well as the length of the shots, all indicate a rare occurrence of an omniscient perspective used during a death sequence.

While an omniscient perspective, in this case, shares certain points of contact with the perspective of an aggressor, they are distinct perspectives that are important for us to differentiate. In both cases, the editing generally involves longer takes and fewer cuts, and the sound is more subdued and consistent. The key difference between omniscience and the perspective of an aggressor is the distance from the action both in terms of visual and aural space. If the visual and aural space retains close proximity to the killing taking place, then we can identify it as the aggressor's perspective. However, if the action is removed from us, either in terms of distance, as is the case of the previous example, or in terms of actual separation in the following example, we can interpret this as an omniscient perspective.

The difference is subtle but important to the way we understand the stylistic creation of perspective. Clarifying the distinction between the two allows us to consider the effect of each film. The use of omniscience, and the removal of the viewer from the action, frustrates expectation. The slasher traditionally engages the viewer in the events on-screen, typically using a stolid aggressor in these movies. As a result, omniscience deliberately removes the viewer from the primary action of the sequence, creating a tension between providing sufficient information and lack of complete emotional engagement.

While *Jason Takes Manhattan* favors visual depiction of mutilation as opposed to evoking it through implication, two sequences stand out. These adapt death sequences shown in previous films in a more economical manner, relying heavily on unverified diegetic sound over editing to communicate perspective. The death of Tamara occurs within a single take, despite the fact that it follows several shots cutting between her in medium shot, cowering in the shower, and Jason walking up to her in full shot and close-up. The nondiegetic score plays steadily at a moderate volume, while her screams and cries overwhelm it slightly on the soundtrack. Once Jason walks into a slightly low-angle three-quarter close-up shot, he raises a sharp shard of broken mirror above his head, and in a single take, plunges it from the top right of the frame to the bottom left and then below the frame. We hear a slashing sound to indicate the penetration, followed by a louder scream from Tamara. The image cuts after the slashing sound and coincides with the transition from her final scream to a shot of the boat's horn, sounding, blending in with her scream and drowning out the score. The shot lasts four seconds, making Jason the primary focal point of the death sequence without tying the visual element directly to Tamara.

Through this, director Rob Hedden ambiguously places the perspective of that moment between Jason's point-of-view and an omniscient position.

Following this is the death of Mr. Carlson, the first mate on the ship. In a single shot, Hedden positions the camera outside the bridge, looking into the front windows. The rain and thunder are the only things heard on the score. The camera pushes in slowly, keeping Mr. Carlson in the right of the frame. Jason comes up the stairs on the left of the frame, the score playing the hushed "ch-ch" theme indicating his presence. He then uses a harpoon to stab Mr. Carlson in the back, an event obscured by a structural separation between two of the windows as well as the rain dripping down the glass. This is accompanied by a crunching sound, as a sustained orchestral sting coincides with the death. The rain and thunder still dominate the soundtrack, and the windows consistently separate us from the event. This creates a distancing effect from the event, providing another instance of omniscient perspective.

Despite its extensive use of unverified diegetic sound and editing for death sequences, *Jason Goes to Hell* largely recycles the structural elements of sequences from the previous films in the franchise. One exception is the death of Officer Ryan, which adapts the technique used in the death of Mr. Carlson. At the left of the frame, Sheriff Landis talks on the telephone in close-up. The shot is in deep focus, and we clearly see Officer Ryan trying to comfort Jessica in the background at the right of the frame, through the window of Sheriff Landis's office. The focus of the soundtrack is on Sheriff Landis's voice as he says, "You find her and you find her quick! Yeah, well, I will hear from you." The fast, steady dissonant music of the score plays softly below it, and we hear, muffled in the background, the voices of Jessica and Officer Ryan yelling and screaming as Robert, who is now possessed by Jason, approaches. Robert grabs Jessica with one arm, using the other to struggle with Officer Ryan. He takes Officer Ryan's head in one hand and pushes her toward a metal locker.

We hear a hollow metallic thud that links the cut between this shot and the following one, with Robert covering Jessica's mouth in close-up at the left of the frame. In the center of the frame, we see Officer Ryan behind Robert, her back to the camera and her face against a locker, splattered with blood before falling to the ground. The metallic thud increases in volume once the shot changes from Landis's office to the room behind, and the second shot also introduces a splattering, squishing sound to indicate her face being crushed and the blood splattering. The first shot, while in close proximity to Sheriff Landis, depicts an event he does not see by using a split-focus diopter lens—which can show deep focus—giving us awareness of the occurrence. This indicates omniscience, but the second shot is closely aligned with Jessica's proximity to the action, placing perspective with a witness of an event rather than with a

Figure 3.14. *Jason Goes to Hell: The Final Friday*—We sit close to Sheriff Landis, who is completely unaware of the violence in the background. (New Line Cinema / Sean S. Cunningham Films, 1993)

victim or an aggressor (figure 3.14). Here, the perspective of the sequence is not fully attached to the violent act, but moves closer in proximity based on sound and character alignment.

In the same vein as *Jason Takes Manhattan*, *Jason X* favors a combination of the explicit depiction of violent bodily penetration and off-screen deaths. Of the death sequences that do make use of editing and unverified diegetic sound, none demonstrate an evolution in style, aside from the general tendency to use a faster pace of editing. For example, Janessa's death sequence, which lasts approximately two and a half seconds, consists of merely five shots cut together. The only significant difference in depiction is through off-screen deaths, where the sound can be heard in the space we see on-screen. In one such sequence, Jason approaches Condor and draws back his machete before the shot cuts to the other characters listening to the communication of the security team on a loudspeaker. This sequence ends with the sound of Condor's scream through the speaker with no sound effect indicating bodily mutilation. However, we can trace this technique at least as far back as the death of Dallas in *Alien* (1979). In that film, Dallas shines the flashlight on the Alien (or Xenomorph, if you're a nerd like me ['Kane's Son' if you want a debate with your more pedantic friends]) reaching for him in one shot, before cutting to the crew listening to the hiss of white noise from the broken communication link between them. This connection between *Jason X* and *Alien* is understandable considering the narrative similarities (an outside threat, introduced by scientific and economic profiteers, terrorizes a crew on board an expansive spaceship) between the two films.

Freddy vs. Jason uses unverified diegetic sound and editing more frequently than *Jason X* in death sequences, balancing this method with on-screen mutilation and off-screen death. There is also a notable decrease in the length of shots, resulting in a higher number of shots per second in these death sequences. The death of the skinny-dipping girl at the beginning of the film, for instance, contains eight shots over the course of three seconds, an increase from the five shots in two-and-a-half seconds used to depict Janessa's death in *Jason X*. This increase in the pace of editing continues to replicate the visceral shock and surprise of either the victim or a victimized witness, such as the death of Officer Ryan in *Jason Goes to Hell*. This sequence contains a cut between two shots, which attaches perspective to Jessica who is also being attacked by Robert.

The death of Linderman in *Freddy vs. Jason* uses the perspective of a victimized witness, in this case, Kia. However, it also withholds the unverified diegetic sound of penetration to make both Linderman's death and the source of Linderman's death a surprise to both her and the viewer. Linderman, attacking Jason with a flagpole to no avail, keeps stabbing him. The score is intense and fast-paced, just below the volume of the crackling flames that consume the cabin around them. Underneath the score, we hear Linderman's screams of attack, and above all the other sounds, including the wet crunch of Linderman repeatedly stabbing Jason. During this confrontation, we see Kia in a low-canted, or diagonal, angle sitting on the floor, watching them.

This cuts to a high-angle shot over Jason's right shoulder of Linderman in full shot, still attacking and stabbing Jason with the flagpole. There are no changes in sound design up to this point. Jason then grabs the flagpole, pulls Linderman towards him, and the image cuts to a continuation of this action from a low-canted angle in medium shot, showing Jason over Linderman's left shoulder. Jason then grabs Linderman and throws him to the right of the frame. The image then cuts to a medium shot of Linderman thrown toward the wall behind him. The movie cuts to a shot of Linderman flying rapidly through the air from the right of the frame in medium shot into the wall farther back and to the left of the frame. This places Linderman in long shot. As he hits the wall, there is a thud indicating his body simply hitting the wall, with no bodily mutilation implied by the sound. This cuts to a close-up of Linderman's stomach as he bounces off the wall, but in his movement toward the camera and down below the frame, a squishing sound can be heard. As Linderman disappears below the frame, we see a jagged metal wall fixture dripping with blood in the spot where Linderman was. The camera pushes in to show this in extreme close-up, before cutting to a long shot of Linderman falling on the floor from the left to the right of the frame. The movie cuts back to the blood dripping off the fixture.

These eight shots last nine seconds in total, with the length of the shots gradually decreasing toward the climax of the sequence. This fast editing, again, recreates the shock of a victimized character in the sequence, but the low-angle shot of Kia indicates a perspective alignment with her, as opposed to Linderman or Jason. In this way, the sequence depicts Kia's surprise at witnessing the death of Linderman. Furthermore, by reserving the sound indicating bodily mutilation until the point where the metal fixture leaves Linderman's body (as opposed to presenting it when the fixture enters the body), the film shocks us with the same surprise. Here, *Freddy vs. Jason* represents a simultaneous culmination and innovative development of the *Friday the 13th* franchise's sound and editing style where third-person perspective is concerned. The death sequences not only shock in terms of visceral impact, but also unsettle the viewer by creating no basis for expectation. This results in suspense and tension—we never know who we will experience the next sequence through.

The ear evolves: *A New Beginning* and beyond

A New Beginning uses both editing and unverified diegetic sound, working together, for the majority of its death sequences. This differs in part from the previous films in the franchise, most of which attempt a balance between this approach, explicitly shown penetration and mutilation, and off-screen deaths. Although production documents[14] indicate the film was originally designed with more explicit depictions of bodily mutilation, the final product, which has never been released in an "uncut" or "director's cut" format, displays this balance of approaches. This movie, however, incorporates shorter shot lengths, more densely layered soundtracks, and an increased use of eye/camera and off-model eye/camera positioning, as well as distinctive approaches to camera movement.

A New Beginning proves an illustrative example of how not only unverified diegetic sound and editing work together to establish perspective, but how these elements, along with the eye/camera, can do this in an effective and innovative manner. As discussed in the previous chapter, three deaths occur during an eye/

---

14. A letter to the production team from the Motion Picture Association of America dated February 8, 1985, contains the results of an initial screening of an early cut. This document lists sixteen requested cuts, nine of which are highlighted because they would lead to an X rating. Bracke writes that "the film would ultimately require nine trips to the board before it would be granted an R rating" (MPAA letter and quote, 134). I should point out that in the US, most mainstream cinemas will only screen films with an R rating or less, therefore an X rating would result in less exhibition and a lower box-office take.

camera or off-model eye/camera shot. Tina's off-model eye/camera shot shows garden shears plunging toward the camera disappearing out of the top of the frame, ending with a sound to indicate bodily mutilation. After this sound, there is a cut to a high-angle shot of the garden shears moving out of frame, with Tina lying on the ground, eyes missing from their bloody sockets.

We see Junior's eye/camera as he rides his motorbike around the yard, the loud buzz of the engine, and his screaming dominating the soundtrack, until a butcher knife swings from behind a tree from the right of the frame, disappearing below the frame. The appearance of the knife comes with the swish sound of the knife cutting through the air and, the moment it disappears below frame, a wet crunch. This is followed by a cut to a shot of the motorbike's wheels moving from right to left, the sound of the engine following its on-screen position and Junior's severed head dropping from the top of the frame, with a crunching sound as his head hits the leaves.

The most elaborately structured of these is Ethel's death, which starts with a close-up of her face and cuts to her eye/camera, which shows the shattering of the window in front of her by a quickly moving blurred arm. We hear a loud orchestral sting accompanying the sound of the glass shattering, and there is a cut to the knife's point-of-view, demonstrated by the previous close-up shot. Ethel looks at the camera, which snap-zooms into an extreme close-up of her widening eyes, accompanied by her gasp. This shot lasts only a moment before cutting back to her eye/camera, which shows the butcher knife stopping just above the frame. This is accompanied by a wet crunching sound, and blood flowing and dripping from the top of the frame all the way to the bottom. The image cuts to a shot of her hand, as a muscle reflex, squeezing a tomato, also indicated by a squishing sound. This is followed by a return to her eye/camera as the butcher knife is withdrawn with a similar sound to that of penetrating her head. There is then a cut to her head falling into the pot of stew from the upper left of the frame into the middle of the frame, accompanied by a splash.

All of these sequences make use of camera positioning and sound to indicate victim perspective. The sequence with Ethel incorporates editing, too, but also uniquely includes an omniscient visual epilogue. The medium shot of Tina's mangled face as Roy walks away, the full shot of Junior's head dropping after his decapitation, and the close-up just behind Ethel's right shoulder as her mostly obscured face falls into the stew all are framed indifferently to the on-screen characters. In the cases of Tina and Ethel, these shots appear after the killer has moved on, a style which is replicated later in the series but largely unused to this point. By using concentrated forms of perspective as foundational to the movie's style, *A New Beginning* not only stands out as unique within the series, but also becomes a template for future installments.

Pete's death uses a snap-zoom as an alternative to editing to indicate his perspective. We see him in profile facing left trying to start the car. Once the engine starts, as indicated by the soundtrack, a hand reaches between him and us, grabs his forehead, pulls it back, and places a knife in front of his throat. This cuts to a medium shot of Pete from the front, the knife in position, and as the arm begins to drag the knife across his throat, there is a snap-zoom[15] to an extreme close-up of his eyes. This occurs while the score plays a sustained high note, and we hear a slicing and squirting sound. Although the score has foreshadowed Pete's death, we have seen the knife placed at his throat, the actual mutilation remains unseen, the sound acting in lieu of the visual (figures 3.15–3.16). There is then a cut back to the profile shot of Pete, as the knife moves away from his now bloody throat and the hand lets go of his forehead. Despite the steady pace of the editing of this sequence, the snap-zoom is an unexpected visual occurrence that moves contrary to the steady pace of the editing. This creates a shock in the spectator, reflecting Pete's surprise at this sudden attack in addition to satisfying the MPAA requirements for removing graphic bodily mutilation since the zoom masks the graphic violence.

Robin's death sequence contains an image of a machete penetrating something that is *not* her, as a kind of surrogate for penetration before showing her bodily mutilation. In terms of perspective, the movie aligns with Robin using close-ups on her and the erratic editing pace of shots of varied lengths. Significantly, the shot preceding the deathblow is a medium shot of the underside of her mattress. She is lying on the top of a set of bunk beds, and a hand moving from the left of the frame, holding a machete upright, places the tip of the machete against the bottom of the mattress. The hand then pushes up as the machete cuts through the fabric. We hear the sound of cloth ripping and the singing of the metal as it grates against something solid.

The image then cuts to a medium shot of Robin, resting on her back, her head at the left of the frame, her midriff at the right. We hear a wet slicing sound as she screams, before the machete eventually emerges from her chest. Although we see the source of the wet slice through the exit wound, the point of entry remains unseen. However, the previous shot of the machete tearing through the mattress enhances the implied visual, which is completed through the exit wound. The mattress acts as surrogate for her back being penetrated by the weapon. This differs from the death of Jack in *Friday the 13th*, as the arrow

---

15. His shot is technically not a snap-zoom, but a frame enlargement created to resemble a snap-zoom, much like the closing shot of *The 400 Blows* (*Les Quatre Cents Coups*) (1959), which also includes a freeze-frame. However, the enlargement begins at the moment Pete's throat is cut, giving the sensation of consistent motion.

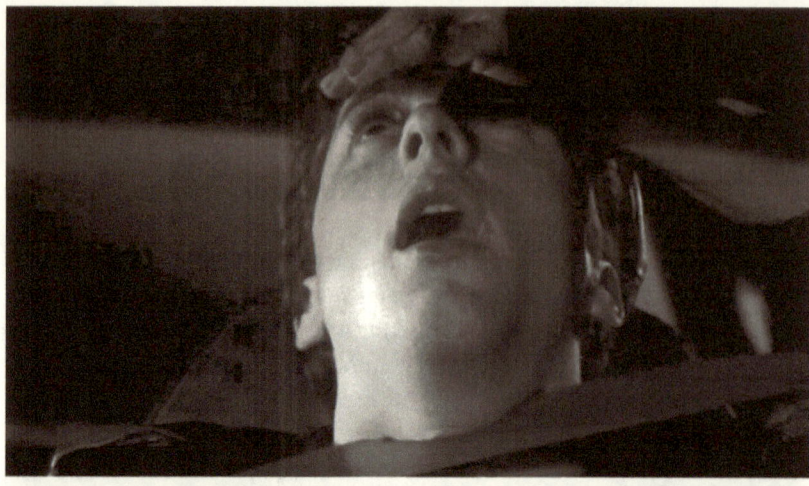

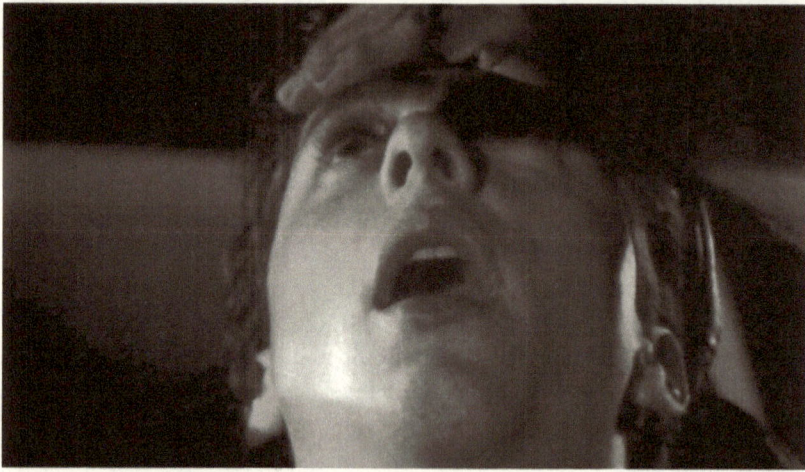

Figure 3.15 and 3.16. *Friday the 13th Part V: A New Beginning*—Pete's throat sliced in two frames from the image enlargement, recreating a zoom effect. (Georgetown Productions Inc. / Paramount Pictures / Terror Inc., 1985)

emerging from his throat is a surprise to us, since the entry point is neither seen nor implied beforehand. Furthermore, the double pinioning of Jeff and Sandra works in reverse, as it shows the spear emerging from the mattress, without us seeing their bodies during the entry or exit of the weapon.

Jason Lives! retains *A New Beginning*'s tendency to favor the depiction of death sequences through unverified diegetic sound and editing, and is shot with eye/camera and off-model eye/camera shots. We see this in Lizabeth's death sequence as well as in the triple beheading of the paintballers Stan, Katie, and Larry. Lizabeth's death sequence is similar to Terri's death in *The Final*

Chapter, and the sequence involving Stan, Katie, and Larry is similar to Jake's death sequence in *A New Beginning*.

Following the stylistic shift discussed earlier with *Jason Lives!*, the three succeeding films do little to advance the structure of death sequences using unverified diegetic sound and editing. However, they each use this method to varying degrees. While *The New Blood* balances this method equally with on-screen mutilation and off-screen deaths, *Jason Takes Manhattan* uses it sparingly, favoring physical special effects to show bodily penetration on-screen. *Jason Goes to Hell* primarily uses unverified diegetic sound and editing to convey the death sequences in the film.

The *Friday the 13th* movies occasionally use sound and editing to align perspective with the aggressor. However, the stylistic evolution of faster editing during these sequences, and the increased reliance on unverified diegetic sounds to create the deathblow, point toward a tendency to favor victim positioning and the visceral impact this perspective provides. Even the later films that begin to align perspective with a victim-witness still place the viewer in a vulnerable position. While it relies on a different stylistic method, it still creates a similar visceral impact. Ultimately, this victim perspective places us in a precarious position of alternating sensations of power, vulnerability, and frustrated distancing. This complicates and confuses what we expect from the genre in order to facilitate shock and surprise.

Although I have hopefully made this clear, I should still note that these films do not solely rely upon the graphic display of bodily mutilation. Dika's analysis of the genre rests on the assertion that these films hinge on the process of stalking, which is why she calls them "stalker" films, not slashers (1990, 13–14). However, the death sequences are spectacular set pieces. By their extreme nature, they attract focus and attention, even if they only consist of a fraction of the running time of a given film, and are consistent narrative elements present in all of the films in the series. As these sequences draw focus, an analysis of their aesthetics is important to understand the way these films attract and engage us.

As for unverified diegetic sound and editing, these sequences demonstrate a more complex stylistic construction of horror, which is designed to generate a range of emotional responses. Alongside other stylistic developments in these movies, the way that sound and editing are used together has developed over time. This reveals that sound and editing are significant elements in creating emotional affect within these films and are useful tools for creating perspective. However, the perspective created in a film, the position through which we experience the events, is only one part of the viewing experience of a movie. The perspective of we as viewers, and how our experience influences the overall effect of the film, is also important to understanding the style and construction of the *Friday the 13th* movies.

Chapter 4

Have You Met Jason?

Assuming you're a fan of slasher films—and, if you aren't, it's impressive you've made it to chapter 4—amongst the fun of watching these movies, we tend to forget how it feels to watch these films as non-fans. In analyzing franchise films, it is important that we remove each from its context to understand how it functions as an individual film. Although the narratives develop as part of a continuous story, each movie is created as an individual film text. And by nature, each individual piece has its own aesthetic design and selective attachment to the other films in the series. The title *Halloween 5: The Revenge of Michael Myers* firmly situates the film it belongs to within a serial continuity. On the other hand, *Halloween: Resurrection* evokes plot points established in previous films.

The experience and perspective of the individual viewer before watching a film has a significant effect on the way each viewer reads the narrative and aesthetics of a film. This is particularly true of watching a sequel or remake within a larger franchise. The opening sequences of the *Friday the 13th* films typically introduce us to the ongoing story, and these tell us how they interact with the experiences of two types of viewers. First, there is what I will call franchise viewers: the group of audiences who have seen at least enough of the preceding films in the series in order to have a contextual grounding for the characters and narrative of the overarching storyline. Anant Zanger writes of these types of viewers, saying, "The act of repetition is performed by both the sender (the cinematic institution) and by the receiver (the audience)—who is ready to consume the same or a similar product again and again—and it is anchored in the selection of the texts being repeated" (15). Secondly, I will address these sequences from the perspective of new viewers—that is, viewers who are screening the individual installment as their introduction to the *Friday the 13th* series. While there are greater and subtler divisions of viewers, these two extremes most clearly illustrate the significance of individual perspective on viewing a film within the franchise.

Jason Mittell writes of the ways in which serialized television stories play with memory when they link to earlier plot lines. Mittell argues that "complex serials strategically trigger, confound, and play with viewers' memories, considering how television storytelling strategies fit with our understanding of the cognitive mechanics of memory..." (n.p.) Following this, Mittell identifies different ways in which series address and adjust elements of the overarching narrative in order to make a connection for individual installments. In his conclusion, he justifies his method of analysis: "The significance of this poetic catalog of techniques is to highlight the importance of underlying cognitive processes in the seemingly simple act of narrative comprehension" (ibid.). In other words, it is handy to look at the way style and information helps us remember what has already happened in the ongoing story.

It proves useful to show the relationship between different kinds of viewers and the narratives of the films placed within the context of serialization. Also, there are benefits to considering how filmmakers use style to present this, but even viewers who have never seen a *Friday the 13th* film, or say a *Harry Potter* film have likely heard of each series. Familiarity with the slasher subgenre was at one point, if not still, widespread. This was particularly the case beginning in the mid-1980s, based on the financial success of the films as well as merchandising relating to the franchise. Ian Conrich has addressed these elements of marketing in his writing on *A Nightmare on Elm Street*[1] and *Friday the 13th*.[2] The iconography of the key franchises reached mainstream consciousness, and the age range of consumers was much wider than the MPAA ratings would suggest.[3]

---

1. "Spin-offs from the *Nightmare* films were the number one selling merchandise of 1987..." (2000, 232).

2. "The iconic status of Jason led to *Friday the 13th* related merchandise which began in the mid-1980s with poster images of the hockey-masked killer" (2010, 183).

3. Conrich (2000) writes of the fact that a large amount of the marketing materials centering on *A Nightmare on Elm Street* were aimed at children, and some mainstream horror films were marketed toward families, with ratings from the MPAA suitable for children, at the discretion of parents, including *Poltergeist* (1982).

According to Rick Altman, "To accept the premises of a genre is to agree to play within a special set of rules, and thus participate in a community precisely *not* coterminous with society at large. Choosing to view a film of a particular genre involves more than just an agreement to purchase, consume and construe in a particular manner" (158) [emphasis in original]. Genre film viewing has its own boundaries, eschewing, scuttling, chucking out not only expectations of other movies, but of the way we interact with the world. This is a striking assertion, but at the very least viewers need to acknowledge these boundaries just to engage in the process of sense-making. Furthermore, multiple genre theorists all assert that expectation, repetition, and novelty are central to the experience of viewing genre.[4]

The pleasures of generic repetition are a major focus of Steve Neale's[5] writing, a concept he succinctly summarizes. Neale (1980) writes, "It is founded in the difference between on the one hand the initial experience and of pleasure, the mark established by that experience and which functions as its signifier(s), and on the other, future attempts to repeat the experience, future repetitions of the signifier(s)" (48). These "signifiers" not only refer to elements of story and iconography, but also to film form. We have observed how the aesthetics of the series rely upon both repetition and innovation in order to develop style and storytelling over time. However, we can also apply this observation to the pleasures and appeal of film sequels. The pleasures of repetition in genre films is amplified when we consider films within the same franchise.

Neale writes at length on narrative elements of the genres, and is thorough in his overview of the horror film (20–25). I am fully aware that the veneer of narrative continuity may seem thin. This is particularly apparent after repeated attempts at sequelization, following a film text created with little forethought as to the specifics of the narrative of films that follow. However, there is a specific narrative continuity between films, and it's useful for us to consider how this continuity is constructed (even if it doesn't seem to make much sense).

Robert B. Ray writes, "While Classic Hollywood had relegated outright sequels to the B-movie ranks . . . the New Hollywood appeared far less flexible, depending to an extraordinary extent on "continuations" of successful films. Thus, between 1967 and 1977, nearly one-third of the 220 leading money-makers were either sequels themselves or films that prompted sequels" (262). Although

---

4. See Cherry (2009, 19–36) for a comprehensive summary and analysis of genre theory as applied to the slasher.

5. Neale typically publishes as Steve Neale, though this early book on Genre is published under the name Stephen Neale.

Friday the 13th appears after this period Ray identifies as the advent of "New Hollywood" it remains the origin of a franchise that continued to regenerate itself. This regeneration is clearly an effort to increase profits, and develop an established property more likely to attract viewers.

Paul Budra, rather presumptuously, explains, "Though financial argument obviously justified the first sequels to *Halloween*, *A Nightmare on Elm Street*, *The Howling*, and even *Friday the 13th*, by the time these films reached their seventh installments many film-goers were simply baffled at their persistence. And we must remember that only a handful of horror films have ever been big office draws" (190).[6]

By contrast, some critics identify sequelization as a tendency of the genre. Sheldon Hall writes, "One can even argue that the sequel, once more common among Poverty Row 'programmers' than major-studio A-movies, has itself become definable as a genre in its own right. Repeatable story formulae are certainly a mainstay of blockbuster production with their guaranteed pre-selling of a 'high concept'" (23). Similarly, Andrew Tudor asserts:

> While it is true that the horror movie has always worked with clearly marked cycles (consider, most obviously, the Frankenstein, Dracula, werewolf and mummy cycles which have recurred throughout the genre's history), the recent reliance on rapid sequences of sequels which, in their marketing, are offered as precisely that, does appear to be a genuinely distinctive feature of 1980s and 1990s horror. It is as if the concept of a "sequel"—or, if you like, the process of "sequelling"—has itself become a major convention of the genre, a phenomenon fully understood and, more important, expected and embraced by a generically competent horror audience. (106–107)

---

6. Budra provides no research to support his first point of audiences being baffled by later franchise films, and I have been unable to find any concrete evidence of this. Box-office receipts, both net and gross, can be found in the appendix of Bracke's *Crystal Lake Memories: The Complete History of Friday the 13th*. This appendix demonstrates a cycle of alternating incline and decline of profits, as opposed to a steady decline. In fairness to Budra, however, this was written in 1998, which, at least with regards to *Friday the 13th*, marks a point of low interest based on box office, between the releases of *Jason Goes to Hell* and *Jason X*.

Budra provides no research for his second point, "that only a handful of horror films have ever been big box office draws." Again, see Bracke's appendix which indicates substantial box-office success for at least five *Friday the 13th* films, see Kevin Heffernan's work on box-office patterns of horror and science fiction films from 1953–68; and see Richard Nowell's work on the marketing and finances of the early teen slasher film (2011).

Whatever the basis of or motivation for these film sequels, they also exist as individual films that can be rented,[7] streamed,[8] sold, or even, upon cinematic release, consumed individually. Because of this, these films have the potential to be analyzed on their own merits, and as individual narratives existing within the overarching framework of a film series.

Despite its close emulation of the generic formula made popular by *Halloween*, and its strong ties to the giallo film, *Friday the 13th* does little to link itself to other films. Dika writes, "*Friday the 13th* has no artistic pretensions, no film-school 'allusions' or 'homages'; instead, its elements have been unambiguously combined for their maximum impact and profitability" (1990, 64). There are two significant exceptions, however. Firstly, as Dika notes, "The title *Friday the 13th* again specifies, if not quite a holiday, as did *Halloween*, at least a recurring occasion of sinister significance" (1990, 66). Secondly, contrary to Dika's claim about the lack of allusions or homages, *Friday the 13th* and its first sequel are heavily influenced by *Twitch of the Death Nerve*. With *Halloween*'s financial success in 1978, the title itself became a major factor in raising the production budget for the film. According to Sean Cunningham:

> I took out this ad in Variety over the Fourth of July weekend of 1979. A full-page ad that said "Friday the 13th" in great big block letters, crashing through a mirror. And underneath it read, "The Most Terrifying Film Ever Made! Available December 1979." I started getting all of these telexes from different foreign distributors all around the world, who said they'd love to see this picture. (quoted in Bracke 18)

David Grove writes, "Fundamentally, *Friday the 13th* began with its title and no more" (16). He later writes, "In truth, the ad in *Variety* was necessitated by the fact that Cunningham was terrified that someone else would take the name *Friday the 13th*, or indeed might have taken it already" (ibid.). As Dika explains, we can attribute the resulting excitement over the title itself to the similarity in title to *Halloween*.

David Grove also discusses *Friday the 13th*'s relationship to *Twitch of the Death Nerve*. "No one at that time, certainly not Cunningham, knew that *Twitch*

---

7. I was renting movies well into 2013. Perhaps this is a little dated.

8. At the time of the most recent rewrite, of the UK streaming services Netflix has none of these movies, and Amazon Prime offers parts 2-8 free to subscribers, with the rest (including the original) behind a paywall. Shudder offers none. I find this disappointingly (yet appropriately) sadistic.

of the Death Nerve was destined to become an acknowledged classic, or that the film was destined to be identified as a major influence upon *Friday the 13th*" (11). Cunningham confirms this, stating, "I think Bava certainly inspired me. His films were shocking and really visually-stunning and they made you jump out of your seat, which was what I wanted *Friday* to be all about" (quoted in Grove, 11–12). Grove further explains:

> The similarities between *Friday the 13th* and *Twitch of the Death Nerve* are obvious, although Bava's film could be described as a black comedy-horror film with its phantasmagoric story of greedy couples meeting their grisly ends while trying to steal a piece of lakefront property. The death scenes in both films rely on throat-cuttings, stabbings and sundry other "in your face" type shocks for their visceral impact. *Twitch of the Death Nerve* was not just a prototype slasher film: it used its kills to punctuate the flow of the story at carefully-timed intervals, amazing the audience with a flurry of shocking images, much as *Friday the 13th* would do a decade later. Is the violence contained in *Friday the 13th* or *Twitch of the Death Nerve* grounded in reality? No. The violence in these films is the stuff of pure fantasy. But does it really matter as long as the audience screams? (12)

This final sentiment is echoed by Bob Martin during his interview with Sean Cunningham while promoting the release of *Friday the 13th*:

> Whatever influences and inspirations are detectable in *Friday the 13th*, it is apparent that Paramount Studios agrees with Cunningham about the film's commercial potential—Paramount's decision-makers have decided to release the film nationwide, in over 700 theaters, this May, a distribution plan that requires a major investment in the production of film prints. (64)

Martin's contemporary anticipation for the release of *Friday the 13th* demonstrates, from its appearance in *Fangoria*, a horror genre fanatic's expectation. Through the information he gathers in an interview with the director and a summary of the film, Martin creates an expectation based upon genre tropes, the previous work of the talent involved, and the declared influence of the filmmaker(s). If this article is to be taken as a representative example, we can deduce that these elements hold great import for establishing expectations in a viewer interested in the horror genre.

Keeping in mind these connections, as well as the opening eye/camera shot, however, there is little else to intentionally connect *Friday the 13th* to an existing work or body of work. Richard Nowell argues for the film's significance as the primary genesis of the slasher film as a profitable genre. He argues that "industry and audience responses to *Friday the 13th* indicated that teen slasher films offered independent filmmakers a low-risk opportunity to realise their commercial objective." (9). Dika describes it best, calling it "the first film to reproduce the success of *Halloween* by copying its intrinsic elements" (1990, 64). *Friday the 13th*, then, was thought of at the time less as a groundbreaking original film, and more as a fun hodgepodge of all the best bits of recent horror movies.

Pieces of the past

Dika describes *Friday the 13th Part 2* as a "recombination" of the successful elements of *Friday the 13th*: "As Miner's directing debut, *Friday the 13th Part 2* is not so much a sequel as a replica, or remake, of *Friday the 13th*. He and screenwriter Ron Kurz copied the Victor Miller script so closely that not only is the story structure identical, but most of the formal, narrative, and visual elements have also been repeated" (78). Constantine Verevis succinctly echoes this through Tom Pulleine's reviews of *Friday the 13th* and *Friday the 13th Part 2*: "*Friday the 13th* was described as a 'bare-faced duplication of *Halloween*,' and the sequel *Friday the 13th Part 2* was seen as 'a virtual remake of the earlier movie'" (64).

Pulleine's comment seems to refer to *Friday the 13th Part 2*'s close attention to an established style for a genre, which was partially created due to the success and influence of *Friday the 13th*. *Evil Dead 2* is an example of a sequel which functions as a remake, as it uses the same broad "situation" as the original. *Evil Dead 2* also contains some of the same characters, including the use of actor Bruce Campbell to play the role of Ash in both films. These characters perform similar functions with no awareness or acknowledgment of the events of *The Evil Dead*, and the film tells a similar, if deviated, story to the previous film. However, the slasher is developed around a very strict formula, but an analysis of a sequel can result in disparate readings. Some see the replication of elements as a form of "remaking" an earlier film, and others merely see this as sticking with generic codes and tropes. *Evil Dead 2* is a unique case, though, as a sequel which demonstrates an ignorance of all previous events in the series.[9] While *Friday the 13th Part 2* retains this highly generic form

---

9. I have phrased it this way, because later *Friday the 13th* installments sometimes ignore selective elements of previous films. In *Jason X*, for example, there is no mention of the fact that Jason went to Hell, nor that his soul can possess the body of others. However, there is still an acknowledgment of previous narrative strands and therefore, according to my definition, acts as a sequel.

proven successful by its predecessor, it still attempts to provide a "way in" for viewers who have either seen *Friday the 13th* or are viewing *Friday the 13th Part 2* without having seen the first film, indicating a continued narrative. This is achieved through the incorporation of clips from the previous movie, framed as narrative exposition, which is a method used to inform the viewer that the rest of the film is a segment of a larger, ongoing narrative.

After the production and distribution credits and logos, the film begins with a close-up tracking shot of a child's feet splashing in puddles along the curb of a suburban neighborhood street. We hear a child's voice singing "Itsy Bitsy Spider"[10] along with the splashing, and the child stops as their mother calls them inside. The camera remains stationary, focusing on a puddle, as the child runs off. Adult feet wearing black boots step into the puddle after the child leaves, an action accompanied by an ominous music cue.

The camera tracks the adult feet walking along the street, intercut with an eye/camera shot from this character looking at the facade of one of the suburban houses as he approaches it. The eye/camera shot serves as a generic cue, eventually focusing and holding on a lit window. This shot dissolves to an interior of the house, where Alice, the "Final Girl" from *Friday the 13th*, is seen asleep on a bed in a lit room while apparently having a bad dream, based on her moans and unsettled movement. Her appearance is the first reference point in this film for viewers who have seen the previous film. For those who have not seen it, her appearance would have little meaning, aside from her being the first character whose face we see. This applies significance to this character. The image goes to soft focus and dissolves to clips from the end of *Friday the 13th* (figures 4.1–4.3).

These clips show Alice's confrontation with Mrs. Voorhees, Mrs. Voorhees revealing herself as the killer, Alice decapitating Mrs. Voorhees, Alice being pulled out of the boat by young Jason, and her discovery, in the hospital, that no boy was found in the lake where she was retrieved. This series of clips simultaneously provides sufficient background information to explain who this central character is, while retaining an awkwardly inconsistent aesthetic to the few previous shots and generally looking different to the rest of the film. The aesthetics of this expositional montage, specifically regarding editing, have more in common with the style of film trailers than narrative film aesthetics. The color hues and general visual template provide a contrast to the rest of the film. This scene, then, stands out significantly, informing the viewer, intentionally or not, that this comes from a different film altogether.

---

10. Here in the UK, where I have lived for twelve years, they sing the song as "Incy Wincy Spider." I'm still not used to it.

Figures 4.1, 4.2, and 4.3. *Friday the 13th Part 2*—Alice sleeps, the image dissolves to clips from *Friday the 13th*. (Georgetown Productions, 1981)

At the conclusion of this montage, the viewer of *Friday the 13th* is reminded of a previously formed attachment to Alice, solidifying their perspective on the forthcoming film. Viewers who have not been previously introduced to Alice or the events of *Friday the 13th* are given sufficient information to attach themselves to the plot and characters of *Friday the 13th Part 2*. At the very least, all viewers are able to attach significance to Alice by virtue of hers being the first face seen. However, we can expect new viewers—that is, those who have not seen the previous film—to retain less attachment to Alice. However, new viewers are placed on (near) even ground with franchise viewers once Alice is killed and the new characters are introduced. Franchise viewers will hold a higher significance to the appearance and killing of Crazy Ralph later in the movie since he also appears in the previous film. By contrast, new viewers will likely only register his function as the "prophet of doom" and victim.

Friday the 13th Part III 3-D also uses footage from the previous film to indicate narrative continuity, but discards the framing device used in *Friday the 13th Part 2*. The film begins *in medias res*, with final girl Ginny on the run from Jason, and discovering his shack. This is followed by her confrontation with him and the appearance of Paul, which helps Ginny ultimately dispatch Jason. The editing of this sequence is designed less as a clip montage and more as a fluid narrative progression. Even though the sequence is shortened, the sound and cinematography retain consistency so that the shots in the sequence cut together smoothly. As a result, we see the climactic encounter between Ginny and Jason, but not the final sequences showing Ginny and Paul returning to their cabin, Jason leaping through a window and grabbing Ginny, and Ginny being removed from the camp the next morning on a stretcher. Since the reappearance of Jason is significant to the plot of *Friday the 13th Part III 3-D*, a shot with a similar visual style shows Jason, shot from the chest down standing up from where he was left for dead and taking his machete from the ground. The sequence ends with the final shot from *Friday the 13th Part 2* of Jason's shrine to his mother: Mrs. Voorhees's rotting, dismembered head sitting on a table surrounded by candles.

The added shot of Jason getting up off the ground serves two functions. First, it reduces the amount of time necessary to set up the significant narrative plot points for the understanding of the rest of the film. This creates a more manageable preface that contributes to the narrative flow instead of interrupting it. Secondly, this eliminates the facial reveal, to which Conrich attributes great significance: "I would argue that in the slasher film, more frightening than the mask is the concealed face, which is often revealed in the climactic conflict (and sometimes in the prelude)—the 'face shot' that audiences expect. The *Friday the 13th* series is no exception with the mask never able to impart the ultimate horror of what lies beneath" (2010, 180) [parenthesis in original]. Through this method, *Friday the 13th Part III 3-D* retains the shock value of not revealing the concealed face until the climax.

This sequence is also set distinctly apart from the rest of the film. *Friday the 13th Part III 3-D*, being the film's original theatrical release title, hinges the film's aesthetic on a 3-D visual design. The sequence applied from *Friday the 13th Part 2*, while cropped to fit the 2.35:1 aspect ratio from its original 1.85:1 aspect ratio, is not adjusted to 3-D, retaining 2-D cinematography. The 3-D dramatically stands out against this when the opening title of "*Friday the 13th*" comes out of Mrs. Voorhees's eye socket toward the viewer on the left of the screen; "*Part III*" comes out of the socket at the right of the screen, as illustrated in chapter 2 (see figures 2.1–2.3).

The characters directly identified in the opening sequence are Ginny, Jason, and Mrs. Voorhees, who is referred to as "Mother." This is the pivotal point of the viewer's perspective and relationship to *Friday the 13th Part III 3-D*. Franchise viewers have a clear understanding of who these characters are and their relationship to one another, with a certain amount of depth. New viewers, however, only receive a superficial understanding of these elements. Ginny can be understood as a central victim, Jason as the primary antagonist, and "Mother" as Jason's dead mother whom he idolizes. While this information is all that is necessary to understand the remaining film, the sudden appearance of these characters in action, who are depicted as previously established characters, could potentially disorient new viewers. Franchise viewers could view this sequence comfortably from the beginning because of a previously defined relationship with the characters. In this way, the opening of *Friday the 13th Part III 3-D* behaves more as a serial continuation than a loosely attached sequel.

The introduction to *The Final Chapter*, a title which directly alludes to a serial narrative, returns to the framing device used at the beginning of *Friday the 13th Part 2*. This time, the frame is a clip from *Friday the 13th Part 2* in which Paul is telling the other counselors the story of Jason as they sit around a campfire. Relevant clips are shown from *Friday the 13th* through *Friday the 13th Part III 3-D*, including death sequences to punctuate the story. For instance, Steve Christy's death from *Friday the 13th* is shown after Paul says, "Some folks claim they've even seen him right in this area." Following Paul's statement that, after seeing his mother beheaded, "he took his revenge," film clips from the deaths of Vickie, and Sandra and Jeff, as well as the first attack on Ginny are cut into the sequence.

The campfire story framing needs little context, as the story of Jason sounds like the sort of myths and urban legends that are typically passed around the campfire. Famous horror author Stephen King has described this style of storytelling:

> The story of The Hook is a simple, brutal classic of horror. It offers no characterization, no theme, no particular artifice; it does not aspire to symbolic beauty or try to summarize the times, the mind, or the human spirit. To find these things we must go to "literature"—perhaps to Flannery O'Connor's story "A Good Man Is Hard to Find," which is very much like the story of The Hook in its plot and construction. No, the story of The Hook exists for one reason and one reason alone: to scare the shit out of little kids after the sun goes down. (35)

Mikel Koven describes the function of urban legend narration within its oral context as "to connect the audience, hearing about something in the past, with their immediate present" (2008, 126). Where the story of Jason appears as an urban legend in the *Friday the 13th* films, Koven's observation can be attributed to both the listener within the story—the teens around the campfire—and the film viewer. In this particular case, the campfire story is verified through the inclusion of the other film clips. Here, the audience is briefly informed of Jason's backstory, leading up to the point where he is killed at the end of *Friday the 13th Part III 3-D*.

This sequence proves problematic to the narrative pacing, as the beginning of the campfire story comes in the middle of a longer sequence from *Friday the 13th Part 2*. Because of this, and despite the inclusion of a shot of the moon to preface this sequence, the aesthetic build-up to the sequence is lost, creating a discomforting shock, demanding full attention at the outset. At the conclusion of this sequence and the opening titles, however, a crime scene is recreated from the closing sequence of *Friday the 13th Part III 3-D*. As discussed, the camera roams around the crime scene, which is closely reconstructed from the final shots of that film.

As in *Friday the 13th Part 2* and *Friday the 13th Part III 3-D*, new viewers are now provided with enough contextual information to understand the forthcoming narrative, although it is apparent that a significant amount of information has been missed. Franchise viewers, however, may recognize characters and events but will be drawn into the franchise experience more by the crime scene sequence, which creates a reminder of the story and precise location. This is particularly evident where the body of Jason is concerned, despite being performed by a different actor, and this sequence being shot after the completion of the previous film. Jason's dead body lays in precisely the same position as it did at the end of *Friday the 13th Part III 3-D*. Again, the perspective of franchise viewers are rewarded by having seen the previous films, while new viewers are placed in a disorienting position until the narrative pacing demonstrates a fluidity and stylistic equilibrium absent from the pre-credits clip sequence.

Figure 4.4. *Friday the 13th Part VII: The New Blood*—The crane shot created for this film as the framing device to link film clips together. (Friday Four Films / Paramount Pictures, 1988)

The New Blood returns to the use of film clips in order to establish the narrative of the series. The clip sequences used in *Friday the 13th Part 2* and *The Final Chapter* hold similarities to the aesthetics of cinema trailers, and the opening of *The New Blood* more closely adopts this aesthetic than either of these previous films. After the production titles, there is a long high-angle shot of a graveyard seen through a thick sheet of rain, the camera lowering as if on a crane (figure 4.4). This is a shot filmed for *The New Blood*, and is used as a repeated visual to tie the film clips together.

At this point, a voice-over accompanies the image, saying, "There's a legend 'round here. A killer buried, but not dead." It is a deep, slightly gravelly male voice. The second sentence here plays over a cut to a clip of Jason's hand holding a machete as he walks through the woods, and then breaking through a window to grab Tommy in *The Final Chapter*.

The film then cuts back to the lowering crane shot of the graveyard, the spikes of a high iron fence rising up from the bottom of the frame (see again figure 4.4). The voice-over accompanies this shot again, saying, "A curse on Crystal Lake. A death curse." This echoes Crazy Ralph's warning about Camp Crystal Lake from *Friday the 13th*: "It's got a death curse!" The camera continues to lower, showing the graveyard through the bars of the iron fence, then tracks forward through the opening in the fence, into the graveyard, bringing into frame a tombstone marked "Jason Voorhees." The voice-over says, "Jason Voorhees' curse. They say he died as a boy, but he keeps coming back. Few have seen him and lived. Some have even tried to stop him. No one can." These lines of voice-over accompany clips of deaths that occur in *Friday the 13th Part 2*, ending with young Tommy swinging the machete into Jason's head from *The Final Chapter*. After this, the tombstone, still filling the screen, is struck by lightning which causes it to explode. There is then a cut to shots from *Jason Lives!*, where lightning strikes the metal post Tommy has rammed into Jason's body, bringing him back to life.

This starts a series of clips from that film, showing and explaining Jason's return to life, and his violent rampage thereafter. It also shows Tommy struggling with and then sinking Jason to the bottom of Crystal Lake with a large rock attached to a chain and placed around Jason's neck. The shots of Jason sinking are accompanied by a return of the voice-over, saying, "People forget he is down there, waiting." And the final shot of this sequence shows air bubbles disturbing the surface of the water above Jason and then dying out. A series of lights shining into the camera follows this, positioning themselves in the pattern of the holes of Jason's hockey mask. The front of the hockey mask gradually illuminates, until a streak of light cracks the mask from the middle simultaneously upwards and downwards.

The mask breaks apart, and falls aside, with the words "*Friday the 13th*" appearing behind it in red. As the title grows larger in the frame, the subtitle, "*Part VII—The New Blood*," appears underneath. The full title then increases in size more quickly, until it moves around the frame, returning the screen to black. The time it takes for this entire opening sequence to elapse is approximately three and a half minutes, which is not an unusual length for a full theatrical trailer.

Other elements stand out as similar to contemporary film trailers. It was common for voice-over to provide a vague narrative summary in trailers around that time. We can see this in the trailers for *Beetlejuice* (1988) and *Die Hard* (1988), and the voice-over in this opening is very similar to the voice-over in the trailer for *Psycho III* (1986). Also, the graveyard framing shot specifically for this segment is strikingly similar to the specially shot footage we see in teaser trailers of this period especially. The teaser trailers for *Masters of the Universe* (1987), *The Gate* (1986), *The Fly II* (1989), and many other films of the time use footage exclusive to advertising materials, as in this graveyard framing shot. These teaser trailers also use voice-over that is similar—not just in the way it is written, but also to the way the voice sounds—to the voice-over at the beginning of *The New Blood*.

Half of the previous movies—namely, the three immediately preceding *The New Blood*—focused on Tommy as a central character, but this film introduces "new blood" in Tina. This provides a distinct advantage to new viewers as the filmmakers need only communicate the background of Jason and identify him as a primary antagonist. In the most basic terms, this opening successfully communicates this ongoing narrative, in the same way the campfire-framed opening of *The Final Chapter* did. First, the voice-over tells the viewer that the story of Jason is a local legend, and that he is an indestructible killer that has returned from the dead. This legend is used in lieu of explaining Jason's precise background, his relationship with his mother and so on, that franchise viewers would be aware of. Second, the film clips used verify the truth of this legend, demonstrating that it is not an exaggeration. Finally, the clips used from *Jason Lives!* explain why, at the start of *The New Blood*, Jason is chained to a rock underwater. Therefore, the opening provides new viewers with sufficient information to understand and anticipate the narrative to come, in much the same way a trailer would communicate similar information. Franchise viewers will find little of this information illuminating, and the introduction will manage to provide a crude, rudimentary way to establish the mood of the film, by providing mostly dark compositions, visual depictions of violence, and menacing, tense music.

This method of communicating an ongoing storyline using film clips from previous films in the series does prove to be useful and succinct. However, a movie can frame this story information in a variety of ways. Such variations can enhance the movie's aesthetic, as well as articulate some of the film's themes. Alice's nightmare in *Friday the 13th Part 2*, the campfire story in *The Final Chapter*, and even the trailer-like opening of *The New Blood* all establish the sense of the horrifying experiences portrayed in the previous films and Jason's status as legend. Even the truncated climax of *Friday the 13th Part 2* at the beginning of *Part III 3-D* informs the viewer not only of his violent potential but also of his obsession with his mother. This provides, within a single continuous clip, enough character information to create a sense of Jason's motivation and begins to establish the myth surrounding Jason. While this is useful, these sequences stand out stylistically in contrast to the rest of the movie(s). However, other movies in the series created alternatives to this in order to maintain individual stylistic continuity.

Let me show you how I remember it

The New Blood was the last film in the franchise to use clips to establish the running narrative of the *Friday the 13th* movies. An alternative to this is shooting new footage to contextualize new films within the running narrative. *Jason Takes Manhattan* is one movie that foregoes the use of film clips to establish this. The movie begins by showing establishing shots of New York City's evening skyline featuring the World Trade Center. Timely, late 1980s pop/rock music accompanies these shots. Along with this, we hear a voice-over, saying, "It's like this: We live in claustrophobia, a land of steel and concrete, trapped by dark waters. There is no escape, nor do we want it. We've come to thrive on it and each other. You can't get the adrenaline pumping without the terror, good people. I love this town." From the Manhattan skyline, there is a cut to a high-angle shot of Times Square, which then cuts to young punks on the street.

This then cuts to a shot of an alley with an open steaming sewer, and then a close-up of the open sewer. After this, we see a pair of hoodlums mugging a man for his wallet, and as they run away, one of them takes the money and throws the wallet away. There is a match-on-action cut to the wallet falling into a barrel filled with wastewater, causing a rat to crawl out. We then see shots of a busy diner, the subway escalator, inside a subway train, two junkies shooting up in an alley, and finally the ambiguous eye/camera low-angle shot of the Statue of Liberty, ending with the camera sinking under the surface of the water. All of this establishes Manhattan, using the voice-over and the seedy events, such as the mugging, the rat in the waste water barrel, and the junkies, to provide a dark tone to the story we are about to see. This also encapsulates the narrative outline of the film, which moves from the tourist side of New York to the grittier, darker side of the city. The movie presents the opening credits of the film over this sequence.

The following scene opens with the camera emerging from underwater. We see an establishing shot of a houseboat. Inside, a teenage boy and girl are dancing and kissing, accompanied by the same music heard in the credits, which is playing on the radio. The same voice as the voice-over comes on, revealing that the speaker is the disc jockey on the radio station, saying, "You've been listening to WGAZ, the electricity of Manhattan. This request has gone all the way out to Crystal Lake and the Senior Class of Lakeview High." The girl then exclaims, "That's us!" and thus establishing Crystal Lake as the new location after the Manhattan opening. The boy leaves to lower the anchor, which lands near some electrical cables. He then goes in to the bed, where the girl is naked under the covers. She asks what is bothering him, and he says that nearby is the summer camp where "all those murders" took place and that "the guy's dead now, somewhere at the bottom of this lake, if you believe the stories." This provides a similar introduction of Jason as part of the local landscape of myth and urban legend.

There is a cut to the anchor at the bottom of the lake, slowly dragging toward the electrical cables. The boy then explains that Jason was a child who drowned in the lake thirty years ago. He explains that this is because the counselors were not paying attention and the murders started once people had forgotten about it. This is the first time since *The Final Chapter* that a movie introduces Jason's backstory of being a child that drowned at the camp as part of the narrative context. We see Jason drowning, a shot created specifically for this film, instead of using a clip from *Friday the 13th*. It later becomes significant, as Rennie sees the boy Jason while her uncle is teaching her to swim. This event makes Rennie afraid of the water, so extending this far back in Jason's history is important to understanding the story.

The boy then describes the conclusion of *Friday the 13th*, revealing that Jason's mother, seeking vengeance, killed the counselors until one of them decapitated her. There is a cut again to the anchor underwater still dragging closer to the electrical cables, as the boy says, "Legend has it that Jason came back to get even, vowing to kill every teenager in the area, and every now and then the murders just start up." The camera continues past the cables to a piece of the dock that collapsed on Jason at the end of *The New Blood*, with his legs and hand sticking out from underneath it, restaging the crime scene, as also occurs after the film clips in *The Final Chapter*. The boy concludes with: "Forget about it, Suzi, they're just stories." It is at this point that the anchor cuts into the cables, and the electricity produced in the water brings Jason back to life.

As in the previous film, this story provides all the information necessary to understand who Jason is, including the part of being a young boy who drowned, a fact that had been omitted from the beginning of *The New Blood*. Franchise viewers are aware throughout the boy's story that everything he is saying is true within the world of the franchise. Furthermore, this creates the anticipation of *how* Jason will come back to life, as he, a supernatural creature, met a supernatural death at the end of the previous film. Also, providing a new format for telling Jason's story is a method which retains franchise viewers' interest without showing them images they have already seen.

To new viewers, the story provides enough information to understand the narrative, without implying that there is much information lost by not viewing the previous films. It condenses the information from previous installments to support the story for *Jason Takes Manhattan*. The only thing that may create curiosity in new viewers, as in the three previous films, is why Jason is wearing a hockey mask in the first place, but since it is part of the popular contemporary iconography, this may not even be a point of concern.

In contrast, *Jason Goes to Hell* begins without establishing the previous movies. *Jason Lives!*, which we will consider later, gradually places context clues as to the characters and backgrounds of Jason and Tommy, as well as establishing an idea of the relationship between the two. *Jason Goes to Hell* not only does less of this, but in some ways creates an account of events that exists nowhere else in the series.

The film begins with an establishing shot of Crystal Lake at night, and then cuts to a woman driving a convertible through the forest. She passes a sign noting that Crystal Lake is four miles away. This is followed by a sequence involving the woman at the cabin, Jason's chase of her, and the attack by the FBI. In this sequence, and throughout, there is no indication of backstory or context. This is with the exception of the apparent fact that the FBI has sought and tracked Jason all along.

Nobody actually speaks the name "Jason Voorhees" until the shots interspersed throughout the opening credits show parts of the autopsy for the first time. And, in this case, it is spoken into a tape recorder for the coroner's report. After the coroner eats Jason's heart and becomes possessed, killing his assistant and the armed guards, there is a cut to a television show called *American Case File*. This is the first time the movie gives any background on Jason. The voice-over by Robert, the host of the show, reveals Jason to be a known serial killer. Robert reports, "For over twenty years, the mere mention of the name Jason Voorhees has been enough to send a shudder of fear through the hearts of an entire nation. Born in 1946 to Elias and Pamela Voorhees, Jason was believed to have drowned in Camp Crystal Lake at the tender age of eleven. Sadly, he did not. Since then he has been responsible for eighty-three confirmed murders and speculated scores of others." After this, Robert interviews Creighton Duke, who is introduced as a bounty hunter and tells of Jason's ability to move in and out of other people's bodies. This way of establishing Jason is the culmination of the presentation of him as a folk hero, or folk monster, throughout the series.

The only information provided that appears in the previous films are his name, his mother's name, the fact that he drowned at Crystal Lake as a boy, and that he is a serial killer. Aside from that, the other information resembles a precise journalistic report that is not verified in the earlier films. There is also Duke's revelation about Jason changing bodies, which sets up both an explanation for his incessant returns from the dead and a driving plot point to create an alternative to the strict narrative forms developed by the series.

This introduction becomes disadvantageous to both new and franchise viewers. New viewers obtain a thin grasp of the character and significance of Jason. The story of his drowning only sounds peripheral, and the simple fact that he is a killer is all the motivation offered. Although if we are reinventing the mythology, stripping it down to its bare essentials would be the way to go for someone coming in fresh to the story. The possession of the coroner and Duke's description of Jason changing bodies provides new viewers with enough information to glean that Jason kills because he is a supernatural form of evil. This sudden change in lore could potentially disorient franchise viewers. While franchise viewers may be more thoroughly familiar with the character of Jason, the revelation that he can change bodies has the potential to undermine their loyalty by reinventing the lore and the format of the narrative. *Jason X*, however, removes this new mythology established in *Jason Goes to Hell*, returning to the narrative established by previous films.

Aside from establishing mood and setting—namely, a dark mood used to show medical experiments and detainment of Jason—there is no background information provided in the opening credits sequence of *Jason X*. Following the credits, we see Jason on a platform in extreme long shot in chains, in a large, dimly lit, open room. This is followed by a series of close-ups of the chains on his body, finally revealing his masked face. At the bottom left of the frame, words appearing as though typed on the computer screen spell out: "Location, Crystal Lake Research Facility." The text then disappears, replaced by, "Subject, Jason Voorhees," and finally, "Status, Awaiting Cryogenic Suspension." These captions provide us with our only initial information, and the fact that he is restrained using chains and leather straps indicates that he is dangerous.

The following sequence shows Rowan discussing Jason with Dr. Wimmer, who reveals that he is canceling cryogenic suspension in favor of researching his ability to regenerate tissue. This is a piece of information, like that of Jason changing bodies in *Jason Goes to Hell*, new to franchise viewers. However, this does not entirely alter the narrative history of the series, but instead attempts to explain it. After this exchange, the fact that Jason kills all of the armed guards verifies that he is, in fact, a dangerous character. It is not until later, when Jason and Rowan are found in cryogenic hibernation and Rowan is eventually revived, that the film reveals Jason's backstory. This occurs over thirty minutes into the film. The backstory, however, takes place after the events of the previous films.

The professor tries to sell Jason as a specimen, and his potential buyer reveals that he has killed over two hundred people, far greater than the confirmed eighty-three mentioned in the previous film. Later, Rowan says that he was a notorious murderer, executed for the first time in 2008. Rowan says, "We tried everything. Electrocution, gas, firing squad, we even hung him once. Nothing worked. Finally, it was decided that if we couldn't terminate him, we could at least contain him—cryogenic stasis—freeze him until we could figure out what to do." This is all the background information provided, which becomes beneficial to both franchise viewers and new viewers, as it informs all viewers of the unseen previous narrative.

While a familiarity with genre tropes proves beneficial to understanding the humor in *Jason X* for both new and franchise viewers, a familiarity with the series itself becomes a source of humor for the franchise viewer. In one of the climactic sequences, Jason is lured into a holographic projection of Camp Crystal Lake, circa 1980, in order to distract and confuse him. The projection also creates two young girls (the VR Girls mentioned in an earlier footnote) who ask Jason if he wants to "smoke pot" and have "premarital sex," as that is what they enjoy doing. They remove their tops and get into their sleeping bags.

Those familiar with the slasher subgenre after the release of *Halloween* likely know that, as common tropes (particularly post-*Scream*), these things—doing drugs and having sex—tend to result in violent death. By discussing these tropes semi-openly, the film creates a self-referential humor, common to the period. However, Jason's violent response to this proposition sees him swinging a sleeping bag containing one of the girls into another sleeping bag containing the other girl. This crushes their bodies against each other, before finishing by swinging the sleeping bag into a tree (figure 4.5). This is a direct reference to a death sequence in *The New Blood*, in which Jason kills a girl by picking her up wrapped in her sleeping bag and swinging the sleeping bag into a tree, breaking her back (figure 4.6).

This specific form of self-referentiality is referred to by director Jim Isaac as an "homage" to *The New Blood*,[11] but more suitably settles into Frederic Jameson's (64–65) or even Thomas Leitch's (116–19) definition of "parody."[12] This is one example of the ways in which *Jason X* references both the genre and the series for the amusement of both new and franchise viewers.

In crossing *Friday the 13th* with the *A Nightmare on Elm Street* franchise, *Freddy vs. Jason* inherently deals with the challenge of introducing, defining, and combining two serial narrative storylines and their focal characters. As I describe in my own contemporary film review, the film does this with Freddy talking directly to the viewer "through narrative voice-overs, which sound more like the soliloquies of an even more demented and much less intelligent Hamlet"[13] (2003, 2C). Freddy tells us from the outset that the children gave him his power, that he killed them, and that the parents of Springwood killed him out of vengeance. We hear this over a staged sequence depicting predeath Freddy menacing a young girl, looking at children's photographs and newspaper clippings of the murders, and ending with shots of the parents setting him on fire.

---

11. Audio commentary, US DVD of *Jason X*.

12. The sleeping bag scene from *Friday the 13th* (2009), discussed in the previous chapter, links more to what Leitch calls "allusion."

13. Apologies for the self-promotion here. This review is the first film-related thing I ever published after getting my MA. My hometown paper printed it, and I like that it's still out there somewhere on microfilm—specifically, in the Danville, Virginia, public library.

Figure 4.5. *Jason X*—Jason hits two virtual reality teen girls against each other inside their sleeping bags. (Crystal Lake Entertainment / Friday X Productions / New Line Cinema, 2001)

Figure 4.6. *Friday the 13th Part VII: The New Blood*—Jason kills a victim by trapping her inside her sleeping bag and hitting her against a tree. (Friday Four Films / Paramount Pictures, 1988)

There is then a cut to a black screen, panning left to right, and emerging from the right of the frame is Freddy's t-zone. His eyes are the primary focus of the image, in extreme close-up moving past the left edge of the frame, and apparently moving his mouth along with this voice-over. This is significant, because though it is still an acousmêtre, director Ronny Yu suggests that it is not solely Freddy's disembodied voice. By looking directly into the camera while his cheeks appear to form the words we hear, the viewer is aware that

Freddy is speaking directly to the viewer. A series of film clips from the earlier *A Nightmare on Elm Street* movies follows this, demonstrating the extent of Freddy's powers. These clips appear as he explains that he comes to his victims in dreams, and that his powers derive not from being alive but from being remembered and feared, which allows him to return repeatedly.

Freddy explains that the people of Springwood have forgotten him, and he has no way to take revenge. At this point, the film cuts to an extreme close-up of Freddy's mouth, centered in the frame, again speaking directly to the viewer. He says, "But I found someone. Someone who'll make them remember." There is then a cut to Jason's hockey mask lying on the muddy ground, a visual that is accompanied by the *Friday the 13th* theme music. The camera pushes in to its right eyehole, as we hear Freddy say, "He may get the blood, but I'll get the glory," and inside the eye hole we see a dock on Crystal Lake, which eventually fills the frame.

Here, Yu exploits the stylistic conventions of the slasher film. Yu employs expressionistic lighting, mostly dark, with predominately blue moonlight and small splashes of white light coming from the lamps overhanging the dock. A young woman stands on the dock, about to get undressed, and turns around when she hears a noise. Thinking it is somebody named Mike, she turns around and teases him by opening her shirt, and baring her breasts. When nobody responds, she fully undresses, and goes for a swim. Becoming nervous, she returns to the dock and begins to get dressed. Here Jason chases her through the forest, which is shrouded in mist and fog. She backs against a tree to hide, and Jason suddenly appears, running her through with a machete, which also goes into the tree. She dies stuck in a standing position. The entire scene acts as an exaggeration of familiar tropes from previous *Friday the 13th* films, but presented in a more generic way than similar sequences in *Jason X*, which tends to reference specific set pieces in the series.

Next, the girl morphs into various victims, claiming responsibility for not watching the campers, as described in chapter 1. After this, we hear a female voice, saying "Jason." At this, Jason turns around, and his mother stands behind him and says, "My special, special boy. Do you know what your gift is? No matter what they do to you, you cannot die. You can never die. You've just been sleeping, honey. But now, the time has come to wake up. Mommy has something she wants you to do."

The movie cuts to Jason's decomposing body in the mud again, with his heart still beating, indicating that the previous sequence was a fantasy. We still hear Mrs. Voorhees's voice: "I need you to go to Elm Street. The children have been very bad on Elm Street. Rise up, Jason! Your work isn't finished!" There is then a dissolve to Jason's hockey mask, as his mother says, "Hear my voice and live again!" At this point, his eyes open, and we see him climbing up off of the ground and walking away into the forest. There is a dolly-in to Jason's mother after this, and she says, "Make them remember me Jason. Make them remember what fear tastes like!" Here, her face morphs into Freddy's revealing that he has controlled this vision for Jason. Freddy then looks in the camera and says, "I've been away from my children for far too long," before the opening credits begin.

Regarding its relationship to previous films, *Freddy vs. Jason* proves problematic, as the distinction between franchise and new viewers becomes blurred with two separate franchises now funneled into a single film. So it is useful to address the *Nightmare* series in the same way as I have with the *Friday the 13th* series. In other words, I will here assume the viewer is moderately aware of the cultural significance and iconography of the character of Freddy Krueger, an assumption the film appears to make of its viewers.

With the character of Freddy, his background, and his motivation established, the introduction of Jason is directly linked to Freddy's existence as a supernatural being who returns from the dead, explained in the opening. The significance of Jason's rotting corpse shown on the ground with the hockey mask in primary focus may not be directly apparent to new viewers. However, to franchise viewers, we can link Jason's death to the conclusion of *Friday the 13th Part III 3-D*, *The Final Chapter*, *The New Blood*, *Jason Takes Manhattan*, or *Jason Goes to Hell*. This, of course, depends on the individual franchise viewer's memory and their cognitive "go-to" movie. Whether viewed by a franchise or new viewer, the movie clearly establishes the fact that Jason is dead at this point. The fantasy sequence for Jason establishes a generic, however exaggerated, death sequence in the style of the other *Friday the 13th* films. This creates the generic tone for the benefit of new viewers, providing familiarity with the *Friday the 13th* films.

Furthermore, due to the exaggerated elements of the sequence, franchise viewers could potentially see this sequence as a form of self-referential parody. The morphing teenagers claiming responsibility for their inattentiveness to the campers establishes Jason's motivation. Also, the appearance and identification of Jason's mother, and his immediate obedience to her, further develops his character and motivation. For new viewers, this is a succinct way of providing enough information to create a character identification with, and even empathy for Jason. At the same time, franchise viewers receive an artistically rendered summary of familiar backstory elements. At the end of the sequence, Freddy's appearance establishes the premise of the narrative for all viewers.

These films demonstrate how the creation of new footage to place a film within an ongoing narrative provides a unique opportunity to adjust and direct the previous storylines to serve the purposes of the individual film. In addition to providing stylistic cohesion, this method creates a concise reflection of the significant characters and narrative strands as they apply to each film. The films sometimes omit strands of narrative, as when *Jason X* ignores the events of *Jason Goes to Hell*. However, they ultimately retain the primary elements of previous installments in order to sufficiently inform new viewers while also comfortably reminding and connecting with franchise viewers. However, there are films that do not fully explain the ongoing narrative, creating breaks and differences between the experiences of both new and franchise viewers.

No need to explain

A New Beginning breaks from the tendency of providing backstory using clips taken from previous films in the series. The movie begins with a tracking shot following a figure in a yellow raincoat through the forest during a thunderstorm. A reverse shot shows that this character is Tommy Jarvis, the young boy from *Friday the 13th: The Final Chapter*. The character of Tommy is performed by Corey Feldman, who was, by this point, a recognizable child actor due to television appearances and the mainstream success of *The Final Chapter* and *Gremlins* (1984). Tommy walks into a clearing containing a grave with a wooden marker with "Jason Voorhees" written in white paint. Soon after, two young men appear with shovels and torches and begin to dig up Jason's grave, while Tommy runs to hide amongst the trees.

As the young men find and then pry open Jason's coffin, Jason comes to life, kills both of them and emerges from his grave as Tommy watches on. Jason then turns and sees Tommy watching him and walks over to him. Jason raises his machete, with which he was buried, and in slow-motion brings it down towards Tommy. There is a cut to a zoom shot[14] framing Tommy centrally, first in medium shot, moving into close-up, also shown in slow-motion. This shot cuts to Tommy, now older waking up with a gasp in a moving car. Along with this sudden cut, the use of slow-motion imposed on the film during editing indicates that the person waking up is, in fact, Tommy. This suggests the preceding sequence was a dream. There is then a cut to Tommy's eye/camera, where we see that he is in the backseat of a vehicle, with two people sitting in the front seat and a metal mesh separating the front and back seats

---

14. This is quite significant considering the image enlargement replicating a zoom-in during Pete's death. The use of zooming or zoom-like images become a stylistic motif, which actually contributes to a relative cohesive aesthetic in the film. This is especially useful in films that toy with incoherence, as I argue here and elsewhere (2015b).

of the car. After this, there is a cut to the logo on the outside of the vehicle which reads, "Unger Institute of Mental Health," and the camera pulls back as the vehicle, which we can now see is a van, drives away. The shot then dissolves to the opening titles.

The information this sequence provides makes little difference between the new and franchise viewers. However, when it comes to recognition and attachment to a character, the two experiences are worlds apart. The central character of this sequence is young Tommy, who is portrayed by the same actor as the previous film, and will therefore immediately draw the attention of franchise viewers. New viewers, though, even if they do not recognize Corey Feldman by his appearances in other films and on television, are drawn to him visually, because of his bright yellow raincoat.

Franchise viewers, however, are at a disadvantage. The familiarity of the character and context of Tommy would lead them to believe this opening sequence is an actual occurrence within the world of the film, as opposed to a dream, and is occurring at a time contemporary to the original release (1985). The music, dress, and fashion of *Friday the 13th Part III 3-D* and *The Final Chapter* heavily imply that the movies are set around the same time as their release. I have written, and quoted elsewhere, the following:

> *A New Beginning*, on the other hand, leaps forward to the "present" of the film after Tommy awakes. This could potentially disorient the franchise viewer, because of their familiarity with and attachment to Corey Feldman in the role of Tommy. The new viewer lacks this contextual baggage, conceivably understanding the earlier sequence to occur in approximately 1975. The fashion is not time-specific, and the only music playing is the orchestral score. This allows the new viewer to shift from young Tommy to 17-year-old Tommy more easily without being confused by the quantum leap between the two films. (Clayton III 2013, 195, quoted in 2015b, 40)

I revisit my own work here not only out of narcissism[15] but because it extensively explains two points. First, this opening favors and rewards new viewers. Second, it is one of many examples of the unique strength and creative brilliance of *A New Beginning*. The adjustment franchise viewers must make to this temporal disparity is not likely to last long. However, this change—along with the potential for familiarity and attachment to Tommy—demonstrates at least a lack of concern for attachments made by viewers of the previous film. At most, it may place franchise viewers at a disadvantage. Although franchise

---

15. Admittedly, it *is* part narcissism.

viewers have the advantage of knowing Tommy's and Jason's backstories, this knowledge becomes a hindrance in continuity that does not affect new viewers.

Although the pre-titles sequence of *Jason Lives!* contains similarities to *A New Beginning*, it heavily rewards franchise viewers at the risk of isolating new viewers. Like *A New Beginning*, there is no series of clips to explain the background and context of the film. *Jason Lives!* begins with a series of tripod-mounted establishing shots of a cloudy sky with flashes of lightning, Camp Crystal Lake, and the surrounding forest at night shrouded in fog. Then we see an old pickup truck driving down the road in the middle of the woods.

The first cut after this shows Jason's hockey mask in close-up held by someone, as a male voice says, "I don't know how you talked me into this, Tommy." There is then a cut to a three-quarter shot of a young man riding in the passenger's seat of the car, talking. This shot connects the voice we hear in the previous shot to him. The mention of the name "Tommy" will likely be met with recognition in franchise viewers, as Tommy was one of the central characters in the previous two films. The male character on-screen then says, "Hell, I must be crazy. You know, if the institution ever found out about this, they would haul our butts back in straitjackets. Permanent." We hear another voice saying, "You didn't have to come, Hawes." The movie cuts to a three-quarter shot of a blond young man who looks similar to seventeen-year-old Tommy, from *A New Beginning*, driving the truck. He speaks again, connecting the voice from the previous shot to him, saying, "This is between me and Jason." Hawes then says that he does not understand the therapy in what they are about to do, and that seeing Jason's corpse will not destroy the hallucinations. Tommy responds, "Seeing it won't, but destroying it will." Hawes then looks in the back of the truck and sees a canister of gasoline.

This exchange becomes more rich and informed from knowledge of at least the two previous films. The establishing shots begin the film suitably, defining the location of the action, but a combination of action, music, and the speed of the dialogue inside the truck has the momentum of a sequence that could fit into the middle of a film. The words spoken between Tommy and Hawes reveal three things. First, Jason is dead or at least buried. Second, Hawes and Tommy have been living at an institution, likely subjected to psychiatric treatment. Third, Jason plays a significant part in Tommy's background and mental condition. This information follows accurately from the background of the previous two films, and franchise viewers are then comfortably positioned within the overarching narrative of the series.

New viewers, on the other hand, would have a nebulous grasp on at least two of these three elements. First, the indication that Jason is probably dead or at least presumed dead from the outset is suggested in the choice to use *Jason*

Lives! as the film's title. This title indicates that he was either not dead when last seen, or that he will be brought back to life from the dead. Between the two it is uncertain for new viewers as opposed to franchise viewers. Franchise viewers will most likely have seen the machete enter halfway through Jason's head at the end of *The Final Chapter* or even know from *A New Beginning* that somebody had to pretend to be Jason, further verifying the fact that he is dead at the outset.

The second element, Hawes and Tommy coming from a psychiatric institution, has the potential to misinform new viewers. Hawes, a new character to the franchise, appears paranoid and scared to both the new and franchise viewers. However, his paranoia comes with good cause, which makes his exact mental condition ambiguous. Tommy is staring straight ahead as he drives, looking focused and determined. His expression and the delivery of his dialogue draw the viewer to his assuredness, but again his mental condition is dubious. Furthermore, his trustworthiness as a character is called into question. Franchise viewers will be familiar with Tommy, and in spite of the final shot of *A New Beginning*, where it implies that he is the next Jason-style killer, this has apparently not happened. He appears more talkative and stable than the mute seventeen-year-old Tommy from the previous film. Because of this, franchise viewers are more likely to invest trust in Tommy and identify with him more readily.

Finally, both franchise and new viewers are made aware that Jason is a part of Tommy's past, but the latter are not given enough information to know the exact relationship between the two. Franchise viewers will likely be aware that Jason has killed Tommy's mother and has terrorized him and his sister, or that the thought and memory of Jason is closely linked with the killings during the events of *A New Beginning*. New viewers are left with little context as to Tommy's history and motivation, which again hinders identification and understanding.

This lack of defined motivation on Tommy's part is never fully resolved, but identification becomes easier once Tommy brings Jason back to life in the following sequence. New viewers know that Tommy is potentially a victim, and want to destroy the antagonist so that he does not hurt anyone again. However, the fact that he digs up Jason's grave in the first place because he has "gotta be sure," will seem motivated by paranoia to new viewers. This will seem at least somewhat reasonable to franchise viewers, considering Jason's penchant for coming back to life. The only clip from a previous film in the franchise comes as Tommy stares at Jason's decayed corpse in the coffin. The camera is framed tightly on Tommy's face in close-up, and we hear the audio track from the end of *The Final Chapter*, with Tommy hacking at Jason with a machete and screaming "Die! Die! Die!" faintly over this shot. It is at this point that new viewers can experience some empathy for Tommy, even if he immediately stabs the corpse repeatedly with a piece of the metal fence surrounding the cemetery. Hawes notes, "Oh, boy, he must've really messed you over," reinforcing this empathy new viewers experience. Ultimately, the cumulative effect of these contextual clues is not as powerful as foreknowledge of the events of the previous films. The setup heavily relies on awareness of the earlier films.

The examples of *A New Beginning* and *Jason Lives!* reveal how less narrative context creates a strong divide between the perspectives of the franchise and new viewers. *Jason Lives!* begins the story with little indication of the previous characters and plotlines in the franchise. The movie continues from the events of the previous films, and without sufficient context, this creates a challenge for comfortably placing new viewers into the story. *A New Beginning*, however, subverts knowledge of previous films. This can potentially disorient franchise viewers without creating difficulty for new viewers. While establishing an ongoing narrative for both new and franchise viewers, a reboot of the franchise presents the opportunity to create and develop its own orientation for a narrative.

The good ol' days

To this point, each film in the series retains a semblance of selective serial continuity. In other words, these movies behave as though they are segments of a larger story, even if they have taken liberties with that story. However, *Friday the 13th* (2009) does not need such narrative links to the previous series. The point of the film, as a remake, is to reconfigure the original story in anticipation of the possibility that the series will start all over again. The movie, however, does not discard the narrative of the earlier series. It reimagines its origin, presenting specific, selective links to narrative continuity. Where *Friday the 13th* (2009) proves a useful example is in the way the overall stylistic design subtly, but precisely, reminds viewers of the *experience* of viewing the first few films in the series.

Verevis creates a broad theoretical structure for film remakes and suggests a way to understand them. He writes:

> More often, [...] film remakes are understood as (more particular) intertextual structures which are stabilised, or *limited*, through the naming and (usually) legally sanctioned (or copyrighted) use of a particular literary and/or cinematic source which serves as a retrospectively designated point of origin and semantic fixity. In addition, these intertextual structures (unlike those of genre) are highly particular in their repetition of *narrative units*, and these repetitions

most often (though certainly not always) relate to the content ("the order of the message") rather than to form (or "the code") of the film. (21) [emphasis and parenthesis in original]

Verevis is basically saying that remakes are most often thought of as being connected to other movies, and our awareness of the originals creates boundaries around how the stories can be told. Also, Verevis asserts that in remakes, there is a distinct tendency to recreate plot points rather than emulate the style of the original. In the case of *Friday the 13th* (2009), we are given a remake that repeats partial narrative units as well as partial form replication, or, it recreates both story and style elements.

Despite the indication provided by the title[16] and the advertising campaign,[17] the opening sequence contains a re-creation of the climax of the original *Friday the 13th*, shown between title cards. This sequence is shot in black-and-white, showing a young teenage girl in a tight yellow short-sleeved shirt, reminiscent of a 1970s–'80s camp counselor uniform. We can see this sort of uniform in movies like *The Burning*. The girl is crying and runs through the forest in the rain. An older woman suddenly leaps out, attacks her with a knife, and backs her against the shore of Crystal Lake. The woman says, "Come here now. You're the last one. I've killed all the others. It'll be easier for you than it was for Jason." The girl cries, "Why are you doing this?" and the woman responds, "You need to be punished for what you did to him." The girl says, "I didn't do anything," and the woman replies, "You let him drown. Jason was my son. You should have been watching him, every minute!"

The woman draws back to stab the girl, but the girl suddenly brandishes a machete and decapitates her. After a series of shots showing the dead woman and her necklace sitting in the mud, a young boy's arm is shown picking up the necklace and cleaning it off. Over this footage, we hear the voice of the woman saying, "Jason, my special, special boy. They must be punished, Jason, for what they did to you. For what they did to me. Kill for mother." A flash of lightning initiates a cut to the lake with still waters from a high-angle shot, in black-and-white. The camera tilts up and the frame fills with color, showing

---

16. The original lobby film poster and general promotional materials, such as cinema trailers and TV spots, present the title as simply *Friday the 13th*.

17. The tagline on the US release lobby poster is "Welcome to Crystal Lake," indicating an initial introduction. The poster also states, "From the producers of *The Texas Chainsaw Massacre*," a popular remake released in 2003. The word "Chainsaw" makes this apparent, as the original film's title reads: *The Texas Chain Saw Massacre*, and I make a big deal out of this because I'm a pedant. This suggests the intent to promote *Friday the 13th* (2009) as a remake or reboot.

a green shore and trees with a cloudy blue-gray sky and yellow flecks of light shining through, and reflecting off the water. A caption appears over this shot that reads, "Crystal Lake, Present Day."

This opening serves a similar narrative function to the opening clip sequences of *Friday the 13th Part 2* and *The Final Chapter*. These movies establish the story of Jason's mother from *Friday the 13th* as necessary background to launch the story in the rest of the film. The movie resorts to this, instead of developing Jason on his own terms, or providing an alternate extended backstory. We can see the approaches of rewriting the history of the killer in the remake *Halloween* (2007). Here, the way the movie establishes backstory and character motivation closely resembles that of a sequel, as I have addressed through the work of Sarah Wharton. The rest of the film develops a separate narrative to any of the earlier *Friday the 13th* films, excluding, of course, the general focus on Jason, a killer in a hockey mask, terrorizing teenagers. There is part of the film's form, however, that links it to the earliest installments in the franchise.

Verevis, discussing genre in relation to remakes draws attention to both *Chinatown* (1974) and particularly *Body Heat* (1981), writing, "A further connection between *Chinatown* and *Body Heat* can be found in the suggestion that the latter's anachronistic dialogue and ambiguous costumes and setting make it (metonymically) a *nostalgia film*" (117) [emphasis and parenthesis in original]. Frederic Jameson also draws on *Body Heat* when he writes, "The insensible colonization of the present by the nostalgia mode can be observed in Lawrence Kazdan's [sic] elegant film *Body Heat*" (67). After a brief explanation of the narrative, Jameson focuses on the film's aesthetic:

> The word "remake" is, however, anachronistic to the degree to which our awareness of the pre-existence of other versions, previous films of the novel as well as the novel itself, is now a constitutive and essential part of the film's structure: we are now, in other words, in "intertextuality" as a deliberate, built-in feature of the aesthetic effect, and as the operator of a new connotation of "pastness" and pseudo-historical depth, in which the history of aesthetic styles displaces "real" history.
>
> Yet from the outset a whole battery of aesthetic signs begin to distance the officially contemporary image from us in time: the art deco scripting of the credits, for example, serves at once to programme the spectator for the appropriate "nostalgia" mode of reception [. . .] (ibid.)

Dika, considering Jameson's argument, develops her own concept of nostalgia, stating that "what is significant is not just that the nostalgia films return to old stories, but that they also return to old film genres, and to those genres' imagistic and narrative signifying systems. The past thus returns through the composite of an old generic universe" (2003, 10). In other words, Dika claims that nostalgia films remind viewers of old generic conventions, simultaneously establishing and dispelling expectations.

These theories surrounding nostalgia in terms of form and content prove useful when discussing *Friday the 13th* (2009). I have been using the term "aesthetics" to indicate elements of stylistic development that contribute to the manner in which a story is told. These stylistic elements communicate their own set of emotional and informational codes. "Nostalgia," however, I use to denote a sensation of memory for a specific period, or even a specific film, indicating stylistic similarities between movies separated by time and contemporary styles. Combined, I will use the phrase "nostalgia aesthetics" to indicate a stylistic design that differs from contemporary standards in some manner, and replaces them with stylistic conventions from a different period. Or, nostalgia aesthetics could even mean a movie that creates the sensation of a time period or film which in some ways interacts with the more recent movie so that both are feeding off of each other. Certain recent movies borrow elements of the form and structure of past films to create an experiential tension, or slight disorientation, through their juxtaposition. In other words, our experience is stretched between two movies or time periods simply because elements of the older movie are laid over a more recent one. This simultaneously reminds a viewer of a time period or a film while developing other elements according to contemporary standards.

Friday the 13th (2009) initiates an aesthetic game. It swings between subtle speckles of early 1980s form and a fiercely up-to-date form. As an example, in the shot following the establishment of present day Crystal Lake, we see a group of teenagers hiking through the woods. While the events of the previous sequence could have occurred in the early 1980s, a time period supported by the clothes the girl is wearing in that sequence, this group of present-day teens in some cases wear similar clothes. The character of Richie, for example, is wearing a T-shirt with a similar fit to the girl from the introductory sequence, and tighter-fitting blue jeans than his friends. Richie and Mike have longer hairstyles than most of the male characters in *Freddy vs. Jason*, or even some of the closer contemporaries of *Friday the 13th* (2009) (figure 4.7).

The same could be said of Clay and Nolan from the next group of teenagers. These hairstyles, however, have more in common with those of Jack, Ned, Steve, and Bill from *Friday the 13th* and even Paul, Ted, Mark, and Jeff from *Friday the 13th Part 2*.

Fashion aside, moments of lighting and cinematography also create a form of nostalgia aesthetics. In the scene where Nolan and Chelsea take Trent's boat

Figure 4.7. *Friday the 13th* (2009)—Richie (right) in 1980s-esque couture and Mike (center left) shares Richie's penchant for longer hair. (New Line Cinema / Paramount Pictures / Platinum Dunes / Crystal Lake Entertainment, 2009)

out for waterskiing, the brightly sunlit set piece is unusual for a death sequence in a contemporary slasher film. As the scene continues, the sun becomes a prominent part of the framing and composition. The color is not muted or washed-out, as would generally be expected, but it emits a bright golden-yellow hue. The sun itself and its reflection off the water frequently produce lens flares, which, while not unusual,[18] enhance its golden tint (figure 4.8).

This reinforces the unusual color scheme for a sequence in a horror film of this period. This again brings to mind *Friday the 13th* in the scene in which the counselors are sunning themselves on the dock and Ned pretends to drown, which uses similar sunlight coloring and lens flares. Contrast this sequence with the death of Lawrence, which uses shaky camerawork, fast cuts, and Jason's speedy chase, unlike the earlier franchise films.

In one sequence, the music overtly contributes to this nostalgic connection to the early 1980s. Wade, who wears a hairstyle and fashion that shares more with trends of 2009, is in the forest searching for naturally growing marijuana, listening to headphones. The music Wade hears is the loudest element of the soundtrack—the rock song "Sister Christian" by Night Ranger, which was released in 1983. This song is also the only pop song featured to such an extent in the film, creating a very specific auditory link to the early 1980s. We hear a song that was released more than twenty-five years before the film, but we see Wade listening to the song on an mp3 player. This creates a vague tension (or

---

18. See the cinematography of Janusz Kaminski in Steven Spielberg's films, which use harsh lens flares, mostly in washed-out whites—for example, in *Saving Private Ryan* (1998), *Minority Report* (2002), and *Munich* (2006).

Figure 4.8. *Friday the 13th* (2009)—Waterskiing into the sun. (New Line Cinema / Paramount Pictures / Platinum Dunes / Crystal Lake Entertainment, 2009)

at least a slightly jarring juxtaposition), and aids the reading of *Friday the 13th* (2009) as a late 2000s nostalgic film.

Franchise viewers have the opportunity to view the opening sequence as a reminder of Jason's background, immediately making a connection with the previous film. This fosters a comfortable connection to their franchise familiarity. New viewers, however, see a brief background during the opening credits, helping them understand why Jason kills. As a result, the story to come and the character of Jason do not seem motive-less.

Both new and franchise viewers, however, have the tools to make this association with the nostalgia aesthetics of *Friday the 13th* (2009). Franchise viewers, through the introduction, have an immediate reference for connection to this earlier period through *Friday the 13th*. New viewers, based on their familiarity with films from the early 1980s, have the ability to link cinematographic and fashion elements to a period thirty years prior to the making of the film.[19]

Throughout the *Friday the 13th* series, the aesthetic design of the films, particularly the opening sequences, tend to either reward or inhibit the viewing experience based on the specific perspective of the viewer. Each entry in the series appropriates an increasingly selective segment of the mythos and backstory. How each movie presents this opening segment provides distinct

---

19. Assuming, of course, this is not the first film they have seen or they have never seen any 1980s movies. If that is the case, I truly wish these poor souls the best of luck.

advantages and disadvantages for viewers based on their previous awareness and knowledge of the earlier films. This indicates the central significance of aesthetic and formal design in the inclusion of the viewer within an ongoing serial narrative, and how each of us are positioned relative to the movie. But we aren't limited to our experiences simply of slasher movies. The extreme popularity of the slasher, and the *Friday the 13th* movies particularly, meant that they didn't just stay in their little box, developing on their own personal Galápagos. The aesthetics in genres that are more "respectable" and even "highbrow" Hollywood, as well as these dirty little "lowbrow" pictures, fed off of each other, fused, paralleled, and mixed—much like my metaphors.

Chapter 5

The Importance of Being Jason

The *Friday the 13th* films create a serialized narrative where there is an overarching mythology. This mythology, though, occasionally rests upon familiarity with the series for an individual story to hang onto. However, each film has its own style in spite of its attachment to a larger fictional universe or a continuing story. Filmmakers can distill each of these stylistic conceits into a few broad approaches, but it still stands that perspective can be rendered in multiple ways. These combinations of style provide the general aesthetic template for each film. What then remains are two simple questions: what does *Friday the 13th*'s approach to perspective signify, and why is it important?

Experiencing *Friday the 13th*

At its most basic level, perspective creates a framing element that dictates the viewer's experience and understanding of narrative events. This is important within the horror genre, as it is central to eliciting fear from the viewer. It is important as it draws the viewer in. It is important because in the rare case of omniscience, perspective frustratingly separates the viewer from a threatening or traumatic event. However, horror films can elicit subtler textures of this fear, and the specific perspective determines these textures. Individually, the reading of the aesthetic elements could be affected by pure chance. Filmmakers sometimes must choose the best of a series of bad takes, either on film or on the audio track. Sometimes they need to cut short a great take to omit a mistake. And, as anyone who has tried making even a short film knows, other potential unforeseen circumstances can occur in the process of filmmaking. The combination of elements that appear in a film is by nature meticulously designed in order to create a specific response in the viewer. Even films that intentionally remain ambiguous take great pains to organize the elements to fit this aim.

The communication of perspective is essential to genres outside of horror. Although comedies, for instance, don't require a direct incitement of fear, perspective is still useful in making you feel the primary emotions of a film as strongly as possible. Ultimately, perspective works as both the catalyst for and the vessel of emotional affect. Perspective provides and monitors emotional intensity not only from sequence to sequence, but moment to moment.

A filmmaker's awareness of the perspective of the viewer affects the overall design of the film and, in turn, can be used to influence the experience of watching a movie. Here issues can arise surrounding "target audiences" and context. A film like *Triumph des Willens* (*Triumph of the Will*) (1935) was designed to inspire the German people of the late 1930s with hope and confidence in the ruling political party. But watching this movie in another country, or accounting for historical hindsight, greatly alters the meaning of the film to viewers. This is an extreme example admittedly, but it very clearly illustrates the point. We could say the same thing of *Yankee Doodle Dandy* (1942) or—lest we are tempted to think this merely a past tendency—*American Sniper* (2014).[1] For the maker of a film sequel or remake, the filmmakers need to account for a minimum of two viewer perspectives: those familiar with previous entries in the series, and those unfamiliar with earlier films in the series. In some cases, we can factor in perspectives that lie in between the two. There are those of us who have only seen some of the earlier films, or those who have seen none but are aware of the cultural and iconographic significance of the series and so on.

Friday the 13th, its sequels, the cross-franchise film, and the remake—even the video games—incorporate such a wide range and variety of perspectives. They also incorporate such a large range of stylistic developments that we can see how the horror genre and the slasher subgenre work, and how these aesthetic elements function within film. My analysis only reveals a small part

---

1. I would suggest this movie makes efforts at critique that I would speculate were jettisoned following Chris Kyle's death during pre-production. However, without knowing for sure, and staying aware of the response on all sides of the political spectrum, *American Sniper* was taken as both heavily jingoistic and deeply Islamophobic.

of the potential that research on the *Friday the 13th* films can contribute to film studies in general. In order to understand this potential, it is of key significance to understand that the *Friday the 13th* films are not autonomous products. For the most part, they make attempts to engage simultaneously with their cultural, economic, and artistic contexts as well as their viewers.

Paramount's *Friday the 13th* films and New Line Cinema's *Jason* films give to their generic contemporaries as much as they take from them. This exchange results in a group of movies that demonstrate the adaptability of a genre to contemporary trends. But these movies don't just adapt, they also reconfigure these trends in a unique manner which are copied by movies that come after. These films demonstrate the ability for style to develop and evolve while retaining the core generic elements successfully enough to warrant further entries in the franchise and repeated home video releases. The *Friday the 13th* franchise has remained competitive with its generic contemporaries, and has influenced the form of slasher films throughout its now forty-year span.[2] Even the earlier *Friday the 13th* movies make unique adjustments to both popular generic models as well as other movies. The borrowing of stylistic elements of giallo films is a perfect example. And these films make these adaptations and adjustments in order to feed viewer expectation, while advancing the aesthetics of horror.

In general, *Friday the 13th* provides an excellent model for analyzing the trends of an extremely volatile genre, both in terms of financial success as well as formal construction. I assert, in perhaps foolhardy fashion, that we can look at the series as a superior representative sample of the genre. This series allows for examination, analysis, and research at a level not provided by any other franchise. It is also clear, to me at least, that *A New Beginning* also represents the potential for creating a difficult, challenging film within the strictures of a generic formula and continuing storyline.

All of this points to significant (yet fairly obvious) observations about the aesthetic treatment of horror and slasher films. We can make even more valuable observations concerning the reading and analysis of the *Friday the 13th* films, and even the slasher subgenre as a whole. In order to make these observations, perspective proves a useful and potent starting point for spearheading a formalist analysis.

It's clear that critics rarely look favorably upon the *Friday the 13th* movies. Much theoretical writing suggests that *Friday the 13th*, its sequels, and the remake are of little or no value as an artistic artefact. Or, at worst, they are

---

2. And I'm personally hoping that it will continue.

toxic, damaging, socially irresponsible movies.[3] Key theorists like Carol Clover and Robin Wood appear to make this very argument. Writers with a focus on narrative, such as Kim Newman, acknowledge the popularity of the series, but seem to ignore the fact that these films provide anything significant or beneficial. This leaves the franchise as little more than a series of fleeting references or footnotes. While these approaches can yield valuable results, the *Friday the 13th* series can seem deeply insignificant.

However, someone like Vera Dika, looking at these movies through genre theory, breaks it down to a series of successful generic elements. These elements have been used as a model of reproducing previous generic successes, providing enough variety to engage viewers. This mix of replication and change brings us back to these movies repeatedly. Looking at the *Friday the 13th* series in this way, the importance of the series becomes more apparent. More recent work by writers like Kerswell and Nowell focuses on the *Friday the 13th* series' significance as a business model. This appears to be the start of an analytical tradition that touches upon both the popularity and significance of these movies. Throughout my research, I have encountered other writers who engage in textual analysis of the *Friday the 13th* series in order to discover the popular appeal and the pleasure they provide viewers. This sort of analysis is contributing more towards situating this franchise within the realm of serious academic focus within film studies, and demonstrating how these films contribute to the understanding of film.

I've tried to observe how the *Friday the 13th* series both appropriated—and ran contrary to—generic trends at certain points in its history. By doing so, we obtain a clearer understanding of the elements we respond to. This can lead to the potential for further study of historical and cultural reasons behind these responses. My approach is not mutually exclusive with sociocultural/political conversations.[4] For example, we can link the relatively poor reception of *Jason Goes to Hell* and *Jason X* to their extreme divergence from both traditional and popular contemporary stylistic trends. We can't blame their reception on a wane in the popularity of the genre, as other franchises were created and thrived during this period.

---

3. One reviewer of this manuscript rejected it based on this very argument. I don't disagree with arguments that, on the whole, the films in the franchise are products of a deeply reactionary, patriarchal, and colonial culture. However, Stephen Booth (1990) would argue that merely saying a work of art is a product of the culture that produced it is hardly a groundbreaking observation. I tend to stick with the more spineless position of enjoying the sort of analysis Booth creates, but I think there is value in considering social discourses.

4. See my own explanation of the long history of arguments between formalists and cultural theorists (Clayton 2015a).

The tendency to respond to contemporary trends sometimes results in complex aesthetic dynamics within these films. *The New Blood* is a muddle of alternating perspectives as it tells a story overtly about psychic phenomena and the supernatural. But it simultaneously incorporates a darker sensibility in both emotional affect and cinematographic palette. Caryn James's contemporary review in the *New York Times* and Richard Harrington's contemporary review in the *Washington Post* aim to convince the reader that the film attempts to incorporate elements of much better films and stories to keep the *Friday the 13th* series fresh. However, they argue that it fails to provide an experience that is significantly new or entertaining. The only problem is that to dismiss *The New Blood* as such misses valuable aesthetic complexity that may help to explain how the franchise retained its cultural significance up to that point (1988).

Furthermore, *Friday the 13th Part V: A New Beginning* at least proves a unique artefact in the history of the slasher subgenre. At best, it is a significant overlooked text due to the complexity and relative superiority of its aesthetic. I maintain that *A New Beginning* is noteworthy as an important film regardless of genre. Not only does *A New Beginning* make unique responses to contemporary and historical film trends, but it also manages to take unusual risks in response to its own franchise. However, I have only covered a small amount of its innovative approach and there is still more to be found.

The sum of these observations is very direct. Firstly, perspective is a significant part of the aesthetic creation of the cinematic experience. Secondly, the *Friday the 13th* franchise is a largely untapped resource that we can use to expand the understanding of film aesthetics and the last forty years of cinema history, particularly within the horror genre. While these might seem like simplistic observations, they at least demonstrate that these for-profit productions, created within tight generic strictures and responding to immediate aesthetic trends, *have* had an impact on cinema more broadly. It may seem bold to suggest that these movies have contributed to the way stories are told in "upscale," "serious" films, especially within Hollywood. It may even seem bold to suggest that these nasty little movies provide predictive goalposts for "high art" storytelling over the last four decades. However, this is my final argument, so strap on your seatbelts and wish me luck.

Friday the 13th at the Oscars

It's very easy to question the validity of awards ceremonies. What makes a *good* movie or even a *great* one is highly subjective. In my own discussion of value judgements, I tend to gauge comparative merits of movies against those that are valued by our (primarily Western) culture.⁵ It is still apparent that the Academy of Motion Picture Arts and Sciences' annual awards ceremony (the Oscars) is at least esteemed by the Hollywood professional community. According to Paul McDonald, "The value of the Academy Awards depends on collective belief in their value and recognition that the works or acts they celebrate are things of value" (231). This collective belief, and the Academy's supposed aim of recognizing superior works of filmic art and use of its brand to promote them, tell us a lot about what contemporary cultures valued. Receiving an Oscar often has a lasting impact on a movie's perception and legacy. We can certainly conclude that the films that are either nominated for, or win, the coveted Best Picture Oscar are deemed "worthy" of acclaim. Even if it is only for that brief moment in time.

Within the Hollywood film industry, we can see the significant influence of the slasher and its communication of perspective on the films recognized by the Hollywood elite. We can see how key films have employed techniques closely resembling structural elements of the slasher. This illustrates that this subgenre of critically derided films does not simply develop stylistically in an insular manner. The slasher manages to impact films deemed "respectable" through Oscar recognition, even if it usually comes after some delay.

First, the eye/camera dominates in terms of the way in which movies stylistically create perspective in a manner interlinked with the slasher. While this is not limited to the slasher, nor to horror as a whole, it frequently works to communicate dread and fear. This is apparent either through proximity fear or through experiencing the perspective of a victim. That said, the conjunction of unseen sound and editing during violent sequences also appears in these movies. One significant example of these elements appearing in Academy-recognized films occurred at the beginning of the second wave of slasher popularity.

Oliver Stone's *Platoon* (1986) is one of the earliest slasher contemporaries that won the Academy's biggest prize. The film received both the Best Picture and Best Director awards, among eight at the fifty-ninth edition of the awards ceremony. This is particularly significant, and useful, as it frequently conveys extreme violence as central to the movie's story. Two sequences prove useful, and are climactic scenes of violence. These sequences very closely model the aesthetics of slasher set pieces. The first occurs during the raid on the village. Stone frames Chris, the main character played by Charlie Sheen, in an unsympathetic way. He screams in English at a disabled Vietnamese villager, who clearly does not understand what he is saying. Bunny—part of the faction

---

5. This is not to say that I don't think there's relevance to movies valued by other cultures, it is merely that I am personally better informed on what Western culture values cinematically.

that follows the antagonist, Sgt. Barnes—tries goading Chris into killing the villager. Instead, Chris shoots in front of the villager's one remaining foot, yelling at him to "dance, motherfucker!" before breaking down in tears. Bunny takes over, menacingly moving towards the villager. Bunny knocks him over, and in medium shot we see the villager, laying on the ground, hit once with the butt of Bunny's rifle in the face. There is then a close-up of Chris, with blood splattered on his face, wincing against the display.

We can argue that the following shot is an off-model eye/camera shot. The camera, seemingly looking up at Bunny from a short distance to the left of the villager, captures Bunny striking the villager repeatedly. We see this in low-angle, as Bunny thrusts the butt of the rifle from the top left of the frame diagonally to the bottom right (figure 5.1).

While we do not share the villager's point-of-view, we inhabit a perspective close to that of the victim without actually *being* the victim. The visual power dynamic is there, but the viscerality is blunted slightly from the off-model shot. At the same time, with the hut's construction, we can see the beams and slats above Bunny, the movement of the rifle matching the lines behind him, creating a compositional and visual dynamism that also helps to explain the choice of angle. The overall effect, however, is one that stops just short of slasher framing. This is also a particularly illustrative sequence in showing the combined effect of unseen sound and editing.

Bunny knocks over the villager, and strikes him through four shots cut in quick succession. First, Bunny knocks over the villager; then there is a hard cut to a woman trying to stop Bunny, who is quickly and easily thrown aside. This cuts to a very brief low-angle shot of Bunny raising and then bringing down the butt of the rifle out of frame, followed by a cut to a close-up of the villager lying on the ground as the rifle strikes him. We see this first hit and we hear a dull, wooden thud/knock. The duration of these four shots in total lasts four seconds, with the first shot using up two and a half seconds; the remaining 1.5 seconds is devoted to the following three shots.

There is then a cut to the close-up of Chris's face spattered with blood, and halfway through the shot, there is another dull thud/knock as Chris flinches. We see another cut back to the low-angle shot of Bunny as he continues to hit the villager two more times. On the second strike, there is a cut to a close-up of Sgt. O'Neill, looking shocked at the events, and there are no more blows heard after this cut. There is a cut back to Bunny in close-up. There has been no alteration in the timbre of the blows throughout the sequence, but it is here we discover the extent of the violence. Bunny says, "Holy shit, d'you see that fuckin' head come apart, man?" There is then a cut to Chris actively weeping as Bunny continues, "I've never seen brains like that before, man." While the

Figure 5.1. *Platoon*—An off-model eye/camera shot of Bunny's attack on a disabled villager. (Hemdale, 1986)

sequence isn't cut with the same sort of rhythm as previously analyzed, it still uses sound and editing, along with its visual dynamism, to create a visceral impact. The sequence also obscures the level of violence, using dialogue to convey this instead. This sequence also aims for brutal realism, unlike the other relevant part of the movie.

During the final battle, in which many people are killed, there is an ultimate face-off between Chris and Sgt. Barnes. Barnes is risking court martial because of Chris's whistleblowing. This sequence reaches its climax as Barnes kneels astride Chris, preparing to strike him with a hinged shovel. The ultimate blow, meant to kill Chris in a chaotic firefight, is interrupted by a bomb dropped by a military plane, which kills Barnes but not Chris. In the moment just before the explosion, we see a shot/reverse shot from both characters in eye/camera, in a sequence strikingly similar to a slasher set piece. Chris's eye/camera looks up at Barnes in medium shot as he raises the shovel, which cuts to Barnes's eye/camera as he looks down at Chris in medium shot, who in slow-motion reaches towards the camera, screaming "NOOO!" This cuts to the jet preparing to deliver the payload, and then back to Chris's off-model eye/camera.

This shot communicates the intensity of the moment by showing Barnes, not in medium shot, but in close-up. Shadows darken the edges of his face but his eyes glow, reflecting the surrounding fire, and making Barnes appear monstrous. Demonic, even, if you follow the symbolic logic of the story. This moment of altering perspectives between victim and aggressor, and, in turn, altering the eye/camera from direct to off-model in the case of Chris, is consistent with the eye/camera's usage at the time of release, contemporary with *Jason Lives!*

The following years saw the use of various types of eye/camera shots in suspenseful sequences, often using eye/camera coding. *Dances with Wolves*[6] (1990) uses direct eye/camera coding in a way closely resembling the end of *Jason Takes Manhattan*. We see Lt. Dunbar, asleep in his bunk and alone at the military post after first arriving. No music plays, but we hear movement. A moving shadow darkens his face briefly, before he rouses. He follows the sound of movement outside with his eyes, before pulling out his pistol and cocking it, preparing to shoot. The assumption is that he may be in danger from local natives who could take his appearance as a hostile gesture from white people, who frankly deserve suspicion here. Significantly, his isolation makes him vulnerable. There is a cut to a direct eye/camera shot outside the building, tracking left to right, then rounding the corner before reaching the door. This type of shot, bolstered by familiarity with its use in the recently declined slasher, suggests threat. It establishes a proximity fear—we know exactly how close this threat is to Dunbar. The punch line occurs when his horse, Cisco, appears in the doorway revealing the source of the eye/camera shot. Dunbar collapses back onto the bed, gesturing with his pistol before saying, "Bad horse. Bad horse." Here the eye/camera is used for more overtly comic effect than in the epilogue of *Jason Takes Manhattan*. In *Jason Takes Manhattan*, Toby the dog's eye/camera shot appears for the purposes of establishing a final suspenseful moment.

We can see a mimic eye/camera shot and a direct eye/camera shot in *Dead Poets Society* (1989).[7] The teenage boys, venturing out to their first meeting of the titular society, are framed in strongly gothic compositions. The school is largely in shadow and the boys are dressed in black-hooded cloaks, presumably in line with boarding school uniform regulation (one would hope). Their faces remain unseen, and the sequence is scored using synthesized keyboards, which sound not at all dissimilar to the work of Goblin for Argento's films *Suspiria* and *Deep Red*. As the students sneak out of the school, there is a seeming eye/camera shot, tracking forward, and looking up at the sculptured ceiling of the building's foyer. However, the camera tilts down to show the students exiting the doorway. The camera stops, as the students close the door behind them, leaving the camera inside. This indicates we are viewing a mimic eye/camera shot.

Later in the sequence, as the boys run through the woods to the cave where they have their meeting, the character of Steven Meeks stops and looks up. The

---

6. Nominated for a total of twelve Oscars, winning seven, including Best Picture and Best Director, at the sixty-third edition of the Academy Awards.

7. Nominated for four Oscars, including Best Film and Best Director, winning one—Best Original Screenplay—at the sixty-second edition of the Academy Awards.

music has stopped and it is dark, at night in a forest, and there is a continuity edit between Meeks looking up, and an extreme low-angle shot looking up, indicating a direct eye/camera shot. The image cuts back to Meeks, slowly walking through the woods, when one of the other boys leaps out of the darkness. The other boy shines a flashlight upwards on his face, grabs Meeks by the shoulder and pushes him down as the other boy screams, in a threatening way, "Aaagh, I'm a dead poet!" The change in the soundtrack's volume and tone provides a shock, as do the sudden movement in the frame and the appearance of a new light source. Furthermore, the establishment of an eye/camera shot suggests a cognitive link to slashers, along with the stylistic elements of the horror genre throughout the sequence. This helps to set up the scare, as well as aids the moment's integration into the sequence.

The opening of *Goodfellas* (1990)[8] is striking in its use of eye/camera here as well. The film begins with the protagonist, Henry, driving a car at night, with his friends and fellow gang members Tommy and Jimmy riding along. There is a loud bump and a series of nondescript noises and further bumps, sounding like something hitting the car. Henry, confused, says, "What the fuck is that?" and they mumble amongst each other, with Henry saying, "Did I hit something?" and "It's a flat?" Tommy, from the backseat, says, "What the fuck, you better pull over and see." There is a cut to the characters standing by the rear of the car. The red taillights illuminate the surrounding forest they have apparently pulled into. The car is still but idling, yet the bumping persists. They walk to the back of the car, stand in a row, and look at the closed trunk. There is a cut to the trunk, as the camera tracks toward it in what appears to be an eye/camera shot, indicating someone approaching it, anticipating something dangerous and threatening.

This turns out to be a mimic eye/camera however, as the next cut shows the men standing still. They look at each other, as the camera tracks in to Jimmy who is holding a shovel and Tommy, who removes a knife from a holster. There is then a pan right to Henry, who moves toward the trunk with keys, and we see him unlock it in a return to the mimic eye/camera shot, which now seems to be from Tommy's position. Henry opens the trunk, and within is a heavily bloodied man wrapped in a white sheet, saying, "No. No. No, don't," in a raspy voice that is revealed through a tilt down and push-in. There is then a cut back to Tommy, who still has not moved, but starts to after the cut, saying, "He's still alive." He then stabs the man, in frame, trying to kill him. There's a cut back to Jimmy, who moves toward them, as Tommy continues stabbing. The image cuts

---

8. Nominated for six Oscars, including Best Picture and Best Director, winning Best Supporting Actor for Joe Pesci, at the sixty-third edition of the Academy Awards.

back to Tommy stabbing the body, and the camera tracks backwards, showing Jimmy aiming and shooting the body in the trunk.

This sequence demonstrates a fascinating use of cognitive confusion through established generic expectations. The characters' clear unawareness of what the noise is at the start suggests that what is ultimately in the trunk is dangerous and mysterious. Before they open the trunk, we are in horror territory. The surrounding forest, the red lighting, the seeming fear from what could potentially be victims, all point toward horror coding. The opening of the trunk subverts this position of power, as the assumed potential victims are actually the aggressors, and Tommy's use of the knife aids in linking this to the slasher.

This is by no means comprehensive, but these are key examples of how the slasher film, particularly surrounding this period of extreme popularity and profitability, can and has affected aesthetics or the reading of aesthetics in more critically accepted fare. Note that these films were released during the second wave of slasher popularity—*Platoon* at its height, and the other three in its decline, being close contemporaries with *Jason Takes Manhattan*.[9] I could point to some films that used these techniques in interesting ways, such as *Pulp Fiction* and especially *Saving Private Ryan*, as discussed, but in the interest of time, let's move forward eleven years when a filmmaker known for making low-budget horror films gained widespread box-office success and institutional validation.

Peter Jackson began his feature filmmaking career with the aptly titled film *Bad Taste* (1987), about a man (played by Jackson himself) trying to stop alien fast-food franchisers from eating locals. He followed this with the highly irreverent Muppets send-up *Meet the Feebles* (1989), and the now iconic gross-out zombie film *Dead Alive* (1992). In 1994, Jackson changed tack with the surprisingly sensitive account of the background to a true crime with *Heavenly Creatures*. Yet he returned to horror, albeit more mainstream and comedically infused, with *The Frighteners* (1996), starring Michael J. Fox. With this background, it is quite fascinating that he was allowed the budget and creative good faith from New Line Cinema[10] to make the three films comprising the *Lord of the Rings* trilogy: *The Fellowship of the Ring* (2001),[11]

---

9. Fun fact: *Jason Takes Manhattan* was released seven weeks after the wide release of *Dead Poets Society*, both during the same summer season. It's entirely possible that they could have been shown in cinemas at the same time. I kind of want to see them presented as a double bill.

10. Approximately a $281 million budget for all three films (Mathijs 2006, 3).

11. Nominated for thirteen Oscars, including Best Picture and Best Director, at the seventy-fourth edition of the Academy Awards.

The Two Towers (2002),¹² and *The Return of the King* (2003),¹³ all parts of which were filmed simultaneously.

Isolating horror aesthetics within *The Lord of the Rings* trilogy proves an incredibly difficult task, as Jackson steeps all of his movies in them. We can link this to several causes. First, Peter Jackson's background in horror cinema, even if often tongue-in-cheek, lends itself quite well to these stories.

Secondly, the nature of intensified continuity has seen horror aesthetics almost seamlessly blended into the stylistic template of Hollywood filmmaking. This often appears in very subtle ways. Free-roaming cameras, particularly in the way that Jackson uses them, lend a significant amount of suspense and ambiguity as to the personality of the camera, and if, indeed, it is inhabiting the visual field of anyone in particular.¹⁴

Finally, the story itself envisions a fantastical apocalyptic battle between the essences of good and evil. Borrowing from horror iconography are the Ring Wraiths, black-cloaked and hooded figures riding black horses whose faces cannot be seen. This story and these characters point to the movies containing a stylistic design saturated in the aesthetics of horror, including slashers.

Detailing the extent of the use of slasher aesthetics in the trilogy would also take a significant amount of time and space. All three films are riddled with various iterations of the eye/camera. These movies use direct eye/camera

---

12. Nominated for six Oscars, including Best Picture at the seventy-fifth edition of the Academy Awards.

13. Nominated for eleven Oscars, including Best Picture and Best Director, and winning every award it was nominated for at the seventy-sixth edition of the Academy Awards.

14. Furthermore, at this point, Peter Jackson intensified contemporary intensified continuity. A useful counterpoint is *Harry Potter and the Sorerer's Stone* (2001). This movie was released within a month of *The Fellowship of the Ring*.ᵃ The intensified continuity of *The Fellowship of the Ring* is *more* intensified than that of *The Sorcerer's Stone*, particularly as regards the free-ranging camera and the editing together of shots with different focal lengths. According to cinemetrics.com,ᵇ *The Fellowship of the Ring* has an average shot length of 3.2 seconds, whereas *The Sorcerer's Stone* has an average shot length of 5.8 seconds, demonstrating that the latter likely uses longer takes, with less fast-paced editing.

ᵃ I was working at a cinema during my final year of study at UNCW in 2001. I clearly remember these two films appealing initially to different fandoms, and ultimately being adopted each by the other. It was kind of lovely to watch that phenomenon. It was also pretty busy time for the cinema. I had friends; I'd just fallen in love. The sociocultural background was very different altogether.

ᵇ This is admittedly an open source website and can't be trusted entirely, but it is useful for comparison.

Figure 5.2. *The Lord of the Rings: The Two Towers*—Monsters disembowel another monster (see bowel in upper center right) in an Academy Award-nominated film. (New Line Cinema / WingNut Films / The Saul Zaentz Company, 2002)

often during confrontations. During these fights, we often see alternating perspectives, particularly centering on (appropriately enough) the eye of Sauron. There is a particularly wonderful moment in *The Return of the King* in which Frodo stumbles into the lair of Shelob, the giant spider. He falls and looks around, as we see a dead bird, the skull of an unidentifiable creature, and a rotting human corpse suspended by webbing. This sequence seems to owe a very precise debt to the sequence of Pam falling into the grotesquely decorated living room (ironically) of Leatherface's house in *The Texas Chain Saw Massacre*. There are multiple uses of unseen sound and editing used to communicate violence—see, for example, the decapitation of the orc who is arguing for killing and eating Merry and Pippin early in *The Two Towers* (figure 5.2). Once he is decapitated, the orc who killed him says, "Looks like meat's back on the menu, boys," as the others proceed to disembowel and eat him—*quelle horreur!*

It is important to note, though it is inconclusive, that *The Two Towers* and *The Return of the King*, are rarities: two sequels nominated for Best Picture, with the latter winning the prize. It's not unprecedented, though. *The Godfather Part II* (1974) won Best Picture and Best Director,[15] and *The Godfather Part III* (1990)[16] was nominated for those awards as well. The significance of this is it provides a case study (as does *The Godfather Part III*) for considering the perspective of the viewer during the opening sequences. *The Godfather Part III* was released at a time when the slasher eschewed the film trailer/campfire

---

15. The film was nominated for eleven Oscars, three of which were supporting actors, at the forty-seventh edition of the Academy Awards.

16. The film was nominated for seven Oscars at the sixty-third edition of the Academy Awards.

story framing traditionally used to orient the viewer into the narrative. Remember, we can see this in the *Friday the 13th* movies until 1988 (with the clear exceptions of *A New Beginning* and *Jason Lives!* to very different effects).

The Godfather Part III provides a narrative excuse for using footage from previous films, used sparingly at the beginning. The film starts with the deserted Las Vegas estate of Michael Corleone, which was the primary setting of *The Godfather Part II*. This is accompanied by the theme music, and a voice-over of Michael reading a letter he is writing to his children. The letter states that Michael has moved to New York and he invites them to a "ceremony of papal honors given for my charitable work." There is a cut to a New York City skyline with the superimposed intertitle "New York City, 1979." The image dissolves to the interior of Michael's home and a close-up of his hand, writing the letter.

The voice-over continues, as there is a cut to Michael in medium shot stepping up to receive the honors at the ceremony. We see cuts to his children in attendance and the ceremony itself, seen from behind Michael. The shot cuts back to Michael in medium shot, which dissolves to footage from the previous film, before cutting back to the ceremony (figures 5.3–5.4). The flashback is a single sequence of Michael having his brother Fredo assassinated, indicating Michael's memory of the event. His guilt over this becomes a primary narrative point for the present film, and his aging and memory is an overarching theme.

At the end of the film, when his daughter Mary is shot and killed, there are several cuts to footage of Michael dancing with Mary from earlier in this film. There is also footage from the previous films in the series, including his dancing with his ex-wives from when he was married to them. However, Coppola grounds the viewer at the opening using footage from older films using only the one sequence involving Fredo. The rest of the opening does this using dialogue, the earlier voice-over from Michael, and cameo appearances from characters from the earlier films. It is also useful to note that this was not done with the earlier film, which opts to begin the story while only occasionally hinting at the events of *The Godfather* (1972).[17] *The Lord of the Rings* films orient the viewer in similar ways to these movies. However, these methods are somewhat confounding to the model provided by the slashers of the 1980s and even the 2000s. This is interesting in light of the fact that that all three films in the series were shot simultaneously.

The Two Towers begins similarly to *The Godfather Part III*, with location establishment (an aerial shot of mountains), moving into the Mines of Moria,

---

17. Berliner's article (2001) which was later developed into a chapter in *Hollywood Incoherent* (2010), is a fascinating discussion of the pleasures of the series' first sequel, its links to the originals, and occasionally dismissing the comparatively weaker structure of *The Godfather Part III*.

Figures 5.3 and 5.4. *The Godfather Part III*—A shot from *The Godfather Part II* showing the aftermath of Fredo's killing cuts to Michael remembering this event during a ceremony. (Paramount Pictures / A Coppola Company Production, 1974) (Paramount Pictures / Zoetrope Studios, 1990)

the location of a significant set piece in the first film, which is here revisited. After this aerial shot, we see footage from the first film, but of a single incident. The film shows the confrontation between Gandalf and the Balrog on the Bridge of Khazad-dûm, where Gandalf uses magic to make the bridge collapse under the Balrog so that it falls into a chasm underneath. However, as the Balrog falls, he drags Gandalf down as well, and with a final warning, Gandalf slips into the chasm.

Almost all of this footage is shown as it appears in *The Fellowship of the Ring*. However, in *Fellowship* Gandalf slips below the broken edge

Figure 5.5. *The Lord of the Rings: The Fellowship of the Ring* and *The Lord of the Rings: The Two Towers*—"Fly, you fools!" Gandalf warns in both films, using this same shot. (New Line Cinema / WingNut Films / The Saul Zaentz Company, 2001, 2002)

Figure 5.6. *The Lord of the Rings: The Fellowship of the Ring*—Only in *Fellowship* do we see Gandalf descend away from a stationary camera. Which cuts to: (New Line Cinema / WingNut Films / The Saul Zaentz Company, 2001)

of the bridge and disappears from the narrative. In the opening of *The Two Towers*, the camera follows him into the chasm, separating from the story we see in the first film. Here, we see the film beginning its narrative without establishing the foregoing narrative of the previous film to orient new viewers. Instead, *The Two Towers* treats the story in serialized fashion, picking up a new element of the story we have seen in the previous movie (figures 5.5–5.8). This is distinctly different from the establishment of the previous narrative history through dialogue in *Jason X*, released the same year. *The Two Towers* instead powers ahead with the narrative with few occasional references to what is past.

The Return of the King doesn't even make this type of slight reference to the previous films. Instead, the movie begins with the backstory of one of the

Figure 5.7. *The Lord of the Rings: The Fellowship of the Ring* and *The Lord of the Rings: The Two Towers*—In both films, we see this shot of Frodo reacting to Gandalf's fall. However, in *Fellowship*, this shot comes after the shot from figure 5.6, whereas in *The Two Towers*, it comes *prior to* figure 5.5. (New Line Cinema / WingNut Films / The Saul Zaentz Company, 2001, 2002)

Figure 5.8. *The Lord of the Rings: The Two Towers*—. . . but in the sequel, the camera follows Gandalf as he descends and continues fighting the Balrog. (New Line Cinema / WingNut Films / The Saul Zaentz Company, 2002)

significant characters, Gollum/Smeagol and his discovery of the ring. These events occur prior to the main narrative introduced in *The Fellowship of the Ring*,[18] so there is no need here to use footage from earlier films. Again, there is little reference to the previous narratives. This opening stands in contrast to the early sequences of *Freddy vs. Jason*, which was released the same year. *Freddy vs. Jason* establishes the previous narrative by introducing iconography and a generic set piece. We discover that the generic set piece, as discussed, is a dream sequence establishing character motivation and providing us with the thrust of the previous films (save *Jason Goes to Hell*).

---

18. That is, if you ignore the opening of *Fellowship* which goes back several generations.

We should remember that both Coppola and Jackson have very distinctive styles. These films do somewhat connect to and reference the manner in which serialized narratives and sequels establish previous information. However, there is a potential argument for later installments of *The Lord of the Rings* and *The Godfather* films working as the result of a unique *auteurist* vision, as opposed to a clear identifier of influence from horror and slasher sequels. The Academy doesn't exactly make a habit of nominating sequels, so there aren't many examples to draw from here. Establishing a clear link between slashers and critically respected sequels proves difficult, but there are some elements that help make these connections.

Friday the 13th (2009) has an interesting contemporary in Kathryn Bigelow's *The Hurt Locker* (2008).[19] I say "interesting" because *The Hurt Locker* shares a lot visually with the problematic eye/camera reading of *Friday the 13th* (2009). Much of the film, with the exception of some key sequences such as the death of Sgt. Thompson at the beginning, is shot using handheld cameras held at a relatable height. Furthermore, the violence that occurs within the story is often shown clearly, sometimes repeatedly and from different angles. This results in insignificant instances of unseen sound and editing used to convey this. Again, the results here are inconclusive, but it could be argued that horror aesthetics, slowly bleeding into the language of film, results in a style shared by violent movies. This shared style can appear in the slasher just as easily as in the war film, as they have developed parallel sensibilities, while different, key stylistics arise with the aim of developing suspense in these violent narratives. It could be that non-horror violent movies borrowed from the aesthetics of the slasher. After all, it is noteworthy that Hitchcock is a significant filmmaker in formulating suspenseful sequences, as well as slashers specifically. And Hitchcock, of course, was deeply influenced by German Expressionist film, which created a style strongly associated with horror.

That said, I'd very much like to conclude by going back a little. I'd like to take you to a time after the decline of the second wave of slashers, when a film so closely linked to the slasher subgenre won the Academy's highest honor. Jonathan Demme's *The Silence of the Lambs* (1991) won Oscars for Best Picture, Best Director, Best Actress, Best Actor, and Best Adapted Screenplay, from a total of eight nominations.[20] The film focuses on FBI agent trainee Clarice

---

19. The film was nominated for eleven Oscars at the eighty-second edition of the Academy Awards, winning six, including Best Picture and Best Director.

20. At the sixty-fourth edition of the Academy Awards. *The Silence of the Lambs* is also listed at number seventy-four on the American Film Institute's 2007 list of the 100 greatest American films (AFI 2007).

Starling, played by Jodie Foster. Starling receives the opportunity to create a profile of the infamous psychoanalyst-cannibal Hannibal Lecter, iconically played by Anthony Hopkins. This is ultimately a means of gaining Lecter's trust, which is normally difficult for authorities. Starling creates the profile in order to see if she can gather information on the possible identity of a serial killer known to the FBI as Buffalo Bill.

The relationship Starling develops with Lecter helps involve her closely in the case, which helps advance her career. Starling ultimately tracks down and kills Buffalo Bill, who turns out to be a man named Jame Gumb. Gumb is kidnapping women and killing them to make a suit of their skin. He does this to aid his desired transformation into a woman. In the meantime, Lecter, taking advantage of promises for relocation in exchange for his help, escapes by killing two guards and is free, anonymous amongst the crowd. There are, of course, clear superficial narrative links to *The Texas Chain Saw Massacre* with respect to both Hannibal's cannibalistic proclivities as well as Gumb's desire for wearing somebody's skin. This movie provides a clear, critically and industry-approved case study of a film bearing extensive intersections both narratively and aesthetically with the slasher.

The eye/camera is dominant throughout the movie, leaning more towards inhabiting the perspective of Clarice Starling. This is particularly noteworthy in the film, as there is a strong focus throughout on her character's vulnerability. This is highlighted through her roles as both a trainee agent working with professionals and very dangerous people, as well as a woman in a primarily male-dominated career. Throughout, Demme often frames conversations through her eye/camera. Reverse shots do not always inhabit the perspective of the person she is talking with, but they do regularly. An early conversation with the agent that brought her onto the case, Jack Crawford, demonstrates this (figures 5.9–5.10). Most conversations between Starling and Lecter do as well (figure 5.11), and we see a discussion with her roommate Ardelia Mapp in extreme close-up, reverse eye/camera shots (figure 5.12).

We can also see a strong preference towards direct eye/camera, particularly in these sequences. However, there is also occasional use of the off-model eye/camera shot, as in a sequence featuring a conversation between Lecter and Starling in the art museum where police temporarily hold him. This sequence uses tracking-in as well as interchanging medium shots with close-ups, although the characters address the camera at all times. There is also a sequence which involves Jame Gumb and his next victim, Catherine Martin, whom he has trapped in a well. He talks to her, as she realizes she's trapped. In this conversation, again, while the speakers address the camera within the conversation, the shots of the characters alternate in distance, between long

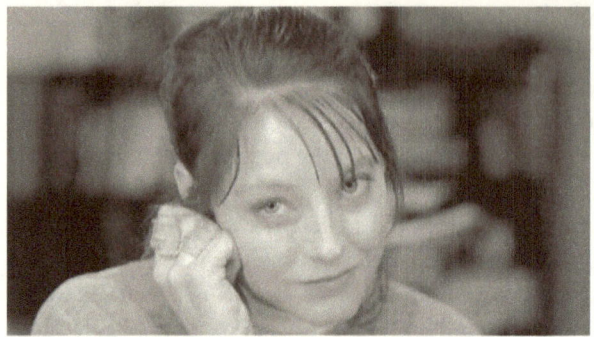

Figures 5.9, 5.10, 5.11, and 5.12. *The Silence of the Lambs*—Shots of Clarice Starling (5.9) in conversation with Jack Crawford (5.10), Hannibal Lecter (5.11), and Ardelia Mapp (5.12). (A Strong Heart/Demme Production /Orion Pictures, 1991)

shot, medium shot, and close-up. However, the movie still keeps the space dynamic of low-angle looking up at Gumb in the well, and high-angle looking down the well at Catherine.

At one point, Catherine turns around, with her back to Gumb, yet as she does this, there is a reverse shot to Gumb still looking at the camera. This provides a shot impossible for her to see with her back turned, but still engaging the viewer in a sort of eye/camera shot. We can also see, again, a frequent shift between the perspectives the eye/camera inhabits.

Furthermore, the eye/camera communicates perspective in a way closely tied to, and in some cases innovating from, the aesthetics of the slasher during the key sequences of stalking and violence. Jame Gumb's regular use of night-vision goggles, while in a sense somewhat similar to the use of victim-camera footage in *Jason Takes Manhattan*, looks ahead to later victim-camera sequences in films such as *House of Wax* (2005) and *[Rec]* (2007), as well as *[Rec]*'s Hollywood remake, *Quarantine* (2008) (figures 5.13–5.16). We see Gumb's use of the night-vision goggles early in the movie while he is first tracking Catherine, and later during the climactic set piece. At this point in the movie, Gumb lures Starling into the basement and turns the lights off so he has the advantage of sight over her.[21] The night-vision eye/camera is particularly effective as it immediately follows Starling's eye/camera, as she is tracking Gumb through the house. In both cases, we see the eye/camera of the stalker/pursuer, even if the initial eye/camera is also that of the protagonist. Once the lights go out, her vision is lost, and we then see the eye/camera of Gumb's goggles.

This is also of note because the camera movement in these shots is extremely smooth, without the usual shaky, handheld camera framing. We see the image framed with the twin, overlapping circle outlines typically indicating binoculars. The color is entirely green and black. We see Starling moving about the frame blindly, unable to see around her and desperately trying to catch a glimpse of Gumb. Starling moves about the different areas of the basement as the camera smoothly follows her. The proximity fear of this sequence is enhanced when we see Gumb's hand reach into frame. His hand almost touches Starling's hair (figure 5.12) and later her face as she reaches into the darkness, before receding out of frame again. This sequence reaches its climax as we see Gumb's hand raising a gun to the back of Starling's head. The sound of Gumb cocking of the gun alerts Starling both to his proximity and to his intent. This allows Starling time to move and fire back, using only the light emanating from the muzzle of the guns.

---

21. A theme many theorists of the slasher movie clearly attach great significance to.

Figure 5.13. *House of Wax* (2005)—Night-vision camera setting capturing a sex act featuring Paris Hilton, referencing some movie she was in prior to this. (Warner Bros / Village Roadshow Pictures / Dark Castle Entertainment, 2005)

Figure 5.14. *[REC]*—Night-vision with a fleeting glimpse of the zombie on the top floor. (Castelao Producciones / Filmax / Televisión Española [TVE] / Canal+ España / Instituto de la Cinematografia y de las Artes Audiovisuales [ICAA] / Instituto de Crédito Oficial [ICO] / ICF Institut Català de Finances / Generalitat de Catalunya—Institut Català de les Indústries Culturals [ICIC],

The graphic violence in the film is limited to one sequence, which uses both the eye/camera and unseen sound. This occurs during Lecter's escape from his cell in the art museum. Lecter, seated and handcuffed to the bars of the cell is secured for the safety of the guards who need to bring his food. We have already seen a safety pin secured in his hand, and are aware of his intent to escape. We see him begin to unlock his handcuffs as the guards move around the cell, setting down his food.

Figure 5.15. *Quarantine*—Top floor zombie, in night-vision, from a similar sequence as *[REC]*. (Andale Pictures / Screen Gems / Vertigo Entertainment, 2008)

Figure 5.16. *The Silence of the Lambs*—Gumb reaches out for Starling, watching with night-vision goggles as she stumbles in the dark. (A Strong Heart/Demme Production / Orion Pictures, 1991)

As one guard gets close to him, Lecter puts the handcuffs on the guard, and attaches the other end of the handcuffs to the bars of the cell. Lecter kicks the cell door shut, briefly preventing the escape of the other guard. He advances on this guard, which we see through the guard's eye camera. Lecter lunges at the camera from close-up into extreme close-up with his mouth open. He grabs the guard's head and leans in as though for a kiss. In the longest take in this section, we see behind the head of the guard, with one of Lecter's eyes visible as his head quickly nods and shakes. The backs of each person's head obscures what the sound reveals: the wet crunching and tearing sound of Lecter eating the guard's face. There is a cut to the other guard, who screams "Jesus Christ!" while witnessing the scene and struggling against the handcuffs.

Another cut reveals an over-the-shoulder shot from behind the guard. Lecter, still holding the guard's head, slams it against the cell's bars, which are just out of the left of the frame. The sound of Lecter eating the guard's face could reasonably be from either perspective, as the source is equidistant from both characters. However, the loud banging of the guard's head against the bars, as Lecter hurts him, draws the viewer closer to the victim's perspective. While the editing does not enhance these cases of unseen sound, the unseen sound still aids in our reading of perspective.

The victim's perspective remains as Lecter, his face covered in blood, advances on the second guard, who is kneeling on the ground. Lecter has attached the handcuffs to the cell bars low to the floor. We see what seems to be a direct eye/camera shot as Lecter approaches him, in low-angle, looking at the camera. Lecter lifts the guard's truncheon, in a balletic movement, before a cut to the panicked guard's face in close-up. The guard screams in fear and looks up and to the left of the frame. The image cuts back to Lecter looking at the camera, as he strikes the guard repeatedly. However, while we can hear the loud, wet, crunching strikes of the truncheon against the guard, the strikes have no effect on the camera, even though the guard's screams are cut short. The camera zooms in to Lecter's face in close-up. The score, loud and intense, overwhelms this part of the sequence. It is therefore difficult to analyze how the sound communicates perspective here. Visually, however, it clearly demonstrates the victim's perspective through an off-model eye/camera shot.

It may be difficult to establish definitively direct influence from the slasher to these movies recognized by the Hollywood establishment (except perhaps the films of Peter Jackson). However, it is evident that *The Silence of the Lambs* both adopts and develops slasher film aesthetics and narration. Furthermore, it is clear that these sequences in the other films *benefit* from an awareness of slasher film aesthetics. Filmmakers structured these sequences using elements, particularly eye/camera and unseen sound, to cognitively conjure an expectation of slasher aesthetics and horror stylization. This keeps these individual moments closely integrated into the films, especially if they are weaved into the film's stylistic pattern. Again this is particularly relevant to Jackson, a horror-filmmaker-turned-Oscar-winner.

And it is with this that I will leave you: a filmmaker, making low-budget, exploitative horror films, ultimately becomes a force in Hollywood by making critically acclaimed movies that set records at the box office, while changing

Figure 5.17. The disappointed author at the closed-for-the-season Profondo Rosso shop in Rome, Italy, on August 30, 2017. (Wickham Clayton, 2017)

his own individual style surprisingly little. Writers could say many things to separate generic slashers from these lauded films. This includes V. F. Perkins's favoring of narrative and stylistic harmony and cohesion. Or we could consider Berliner's more challenging concept of carefully designed incoherence, or some sort of perceived thematic or interpretative consistency or innovation.

But it is my claim, my argument, my fervent belief that the slasher film, a genre that owes an aesthetic debt to international cinema going back to gothic literature, lantern shows, and primitive cinema, has made its own contribution to cinema. The slasher continues to contribute to the stylistic development, the historical poetics, of Hollywood cinema. This development of Hollywood cinema has bled into the aesthetics of Hollywood respectability while still, incestuously enough, developing the stylistics of the slasher in parallel—which, in turn, throws elements out into the mainstream.

And if that sounds a bit ambitious, then I will at least stand firm on the belief that our understanding, reading, and experience of viewing any and all cinema can be made richer through dipping our toes into the predictable, dirty, nasty, fun little world of the slasher. I recommend giving *Friday the 13th* a try.

Appendix 1

Plot Summaries for the *Friday the 13th* Films

Friday the 13th (1980; dir. Cunningham)

Friday the 13th centers on the sinister events at a summer camp, called Camp Crystal Lake, in the forest by a lake. The story begins on a Friday the 13th of an unspecified month in 1950. Two young camp counselors are interrupted while "making love" and subsequently killed by an unseen stalker. Thirty years later, on a Friday the 13th in 1980, camp counselors just arriving in preparation for the summer events are killed one at a time, again, by an unseen assailant. The sole survivor, Alice, is eventually confronted by the killer who introduces herself as Mrs. Voorhees, a former cook at the camp. Mrs. Voorhees, who initially appears as a comforting maternal figure, reveals that she killed the two counselors in 1950 because her son, Jason, had drowned while they should have been watching him. She has since been hearing Jason's voice, which has instructed her to kill all of the counselors of Camp Crystal Lake. Alice confronts Mrs. Voorhees and decapitates her. She then gets into a canoe and pushes out into the lake before falling asleep. She awakes as the police arrive, and as she sits up to communicate with them, a deformed boy leaps out of the lake and pulls her under. Alice comes to in the hospital, and in talking with a policeman asks what happens to the boy, who she refers to as Jason. The policeman reveals that they saw no sign of the boy, and the film ends with Alice stating, "Then he's still out there."

Friday the 13th Part 2 (1981; dir. Miner)

Friday the 13th Part 2 begins at some point following the events of the first film. Alice, now living alone, still has nightmares about the events of the previous film. An unseen attacker enters her house and kills her. After this, another group of counselors gather at Camp Crystal Lake to prepare for the arrival of the campers. They are told the story of Mrs. Voorhees and Jason, but it is suggested it is only a legend, a superstition that ought not to be believed. After a day of preparation, half of the counselors go out drinking while the others remain at camp, and those who remain are murdered by a person with a bag covering his head, save for a hole cut out for one eye to see through. One of the counselors, Ginny, and the head counselor, Paul, return to find the remains of the victims before being attacked themselves by the assailant, whom Ginny correctly identifies as Jason. After a chase, Ginny discovers Jason's makeshift shack in the forest, which contains a shrine to his mother, on which Mrs. Voorhees's decapitated, rotting head is displayed. Ginny subdues Jason and runs away. In the final moments, as Ginny rests in her cabin, Jason, unhooded, bursts through the window and grabs her. The film ends with Ginny taken away in an ambulance.

Friday the 13th Part III 3-D (1982; dir. Miner)

The film centers on a teenage girl named Chris and a group of her friends visiting her family's vacation house near Crystal Lake. Chris, who was attacked by Jason two years before while visiting the same house, is returning to show herself that there is no reason to be afraid. However, Jason returns and starts killing everyone visiting her, and in the course of this he discovers and dons a hockey mask. She confronts Jason, hits him in the head with a hatchet, and gets into a canoe, echoing what happens to Alice at the end of *Friday the 13th*. She awakes in the morning to see Jason in the window of her house. He seems to disappear into thin air, before the corpse of Mrs. Voorhees leaps out of the water and drags Chris under. At the end, the police have arrived, and are taking Chris away to safety, while Jason still lies apparently dead from the hatchet wound.

Friday the 13th: The Final Chapter (1984; dir. Zito)

The Final Chapter begins with Jason's supposed corpse being taken to the morgue at a hospital, yet he comes back to life, attacking hospital staff before disappearing. The story then moves back in time to a house by Crystal Lake, where a young boy, Tommy Jarvis, lives with his mother and teenage sister. Concurrently a group of teenagers visit the cabin next door to spend the weekend. Gradually, Jason kills everyone between the two houses except for Tommy and his sister. In the climax, Tommy bravely attempts to create a sympathetic connection in Jason by reminding him of the child he used to be, before furiously striking Jason repeatedly with his own machete. Jason is now dead, and Tommy and his sister are taken to the hospital. The film ends, implying that Tommy has been psychologically damaged and has the potential to become violent himself.

Friday the 13th Part V: A New Beginning (1985; dir. Steinmann)

Tommy Jarvis arrives at a new psychoanalytic institution in order to help cure him, as he is apparently still disturbed from the events of the previous film. He has bad dreams, rarely talks, and is antisocial. An altercation at the institution between two other patients results in one of them being violently killed, and the paramedics come to retrieve the body of Joey, the dead patient. Following this, Jason-style murders begin occurring, and a man wearing a hockey mask is seen perpetrating these acts of violence. Although he is suspected, Tommy, it transpires, is innocent, and in the climax confronts the killer and dispatches him. It is revealed that the killer was Roy, one of the paramedics sent to recover the body of Joey. Roy is said to have secretly been Joey's father, and was driven mad by the knowledge of his son's death. At the conclusion, Tommy is shown wearing the hockey mask and wielding a knife, again implying his violent potential.

Jason Lives! Friday the 13th Part VI (1986; dir. McLoughlin)

Jason Lives! again centers on Tommy. In the opening sequence, Tommy and a friend from the current institution where he lives covertly escape to see the grave of Jason. Tommy wants to make sure that Jason is, in fact, dead, and he proceeds to exhume Jason's body. The body is indeed still in the grave, rotting, and in a fit of rage, Tommy repeatedly stabs Jason with a metal fencepost. Lightning strikes the post, and Jason returns to life, immediately killing Tommy's friend. Tommy attempts to warn the local sheriff, who believes Tommy is either insane or playing a prank. Meanwhile, the sheriff's daughter is a counselor at the recently reopened Camp Crystal Lake. Jason attacks and kills locals as well as the camp counselors. In the climax, Tommy attaches one end of a chain to a heavy rock and the other around Jason's neck, proceeding to sink him to the bottom of Crystal Lake. Although Jason appears to struggle and drown, the final shot shows Jason opening his eye.

Friday the 13th Part VII: The New Blood (1988; dir. Buechler)

The New Blood tells the story of Tina, a telekinetic teenage girl who is exploited by her therapist because of her abilities, a fact of which her well-meaning mother remains oblivious. Tina suffers from the guilt of knowing that she unintentionally caused the death of her father at their cabin by Crystal Lake, when, using her mind, she caused the pier on which he was standing to collapse. Her therapist has taken Tina and her mother back out to the cabin under the guise of encouraging her to make peace with this part of her past, while secretly desiring to use her emotional fragility to cause greater telekinetic feats. At the same time, a group of teenagers visit a nearby cabin for the weekend. Tina, trying to bring her father back to life through telekinesis, accidentally resurrects Jason, who begins killing the people in the area. The film's climax comes with a confrontation between Tina and Jason, during which Tina's father comes back from the dead to reattach the chain around Jason's neck.

Friday the 13th Part VIII: Jason Takes Manhattan (1989; dir. Hedden)

Jason Takes Manhattan begins with a boat floating on Crystal Lake near Jason's corpse. The anchor of the boat catches a nearby power cable and the surge of electricity into the water brings Jason back to life. Meanwhile, a group of high school teenagers board a boat to go on a school trip to New York City. One of the group, a girl named Rennie, had an encounter with a young Jason when she was first learning to swim. Since this point, she has had supernatural visions of him, sometimes foretelling danger. Jason finds his way onto the boat and begins killing members of the group. The survivors make their way to New York City, with Jason in tow. Eventually, Rennie lures Jason into the sewers just before toxic waste is scheduled to flood through the pipeline. Rennie escapes as Jason is dissolved by the waste material.

Jason Goes to Hell: The Final Friday (1993; dir. Marcus)

The film begins with Jason being destroyed by heavy gunfire and missiles in a US Federal Bureau of Investigation sting operation. His remains are taken to the morgue, where the coroner impulsively eats Jason's still beating heart. He is then possessed by Jason's spirit and begins killing. Jason's spirit then passes from person to person via a large worm-like parasite that leaves and enters bodies (mostly) orally. Meanwhile, a bounty hunter named Creighton Duke publicly asserts that Jason isn't dead and will continue killing, offering money to stop him. Duke is aware of this spirit transference and claims that Jason can be restored to his true form if his spirit inhabits the body of a member of his family, and furthermore, asserts that the only thing which can truly kill him is a special dagger held by another member of his family. Living near Crystal Lake is a woman named Diana, whose daughter, Jessica, is coming to visit, bringing her newborn daughter, Stephanie. Diana, Jessica, and Stephanie are part of Jason's family tree, so Jason, possessing other vessels, pursues them with Duke in close pursuit. He is able to impart his knowledge of Jason to Steven, Stephanie's father who is estranged from Jessica, before Duke is himself killed by Jason. In the climax, Diana is killed, but the spirit of Jason is still able to enter her, resulting in a return to Jason's original form. The special dagger is discovered in Diana's basement, and Jessica uses it to kill Jason. Jason is then pulled underground by demonic hands, and the film ends with Jason's hockey mask being pulled underground by the hand of Freddy Krueger from the *A Nightmare on Elm Street* series.

Jason X (2002; dir. Isaac)

Ignoring the events of *Jason Goes to Hell*, *Jason X* begins in the year 2008, following the capture of Jason by authorities. He is placed in a research facility as previous attempts to enact capital punishment upon him have apparently proved unsuccessful. Researchers want to analyze Jason to see if they can discover information about body regeneration. One scientist, Rowan, believes he is dangerous, and that the only possibility of keeping society safe is to cryogenically freeze him. Jason escapes, kills several members of the research facility, and begins to pursue Rowan. She leads Jason into a cryogenic container and turns it on, just before Jason stabs her through the protective cover of the container. This results in both Jason and Rowan going into accidental cryogenic hibernation. In the year 2455, a group of science students from Earth Two are taken on an educational journey to Earth One, where they discover the frozen bodies of Rowan and Jason. Rowan is revived and healed through the use of micro-technology, while Jason is pronounced dead and moved to a different room for observation. Jason once more returns to life and begins killing students and members of the crew. The ship's android eventually confronts

Jason and destroys him using heavy weaponry, but Jason's body falls onto the micro-technology-based medical station, and his body is regenerated to a more powerful state than before. The few remaining crew members lure him outside the ship as it re-enters Earth Two's atmosphere, and Jason appears to catch fire. The closing of the film implies that this still may not have killed Jason.

Freddy vs. Jason (2003; dir. Yu)

The film begins with Freddy Krueger lamenting that he has been forgotten for too long, making him weak. He wants the people of Elm Street to fear him once again, so in order to do that, Freddy resurrects Jason to kill for him. This would cause people to remember Freddy, giving him strength again. Jason then begins to kill the people of Elm Street, mainly teenagers, while others begin to have nightmares of Freddy. As people gradually remember Freddy, he becomes increasingly more powerful until he is brought back to life. However, Freddy can no longer control Jason, leading to a fight between the two of them to determine who will continue to kill. The fight ends inside Crystal Lake, as Jason emerges carrying Freddy's severed head. The film ends, however, with Freddy's head looking at the camera and winking.

Friday the 13th (2009; dir. Nispel)

Friday the 13th (2009) begins much like the denouement of *Friday the 13th*, with a teenage girl confronted by Mrs. Voorhees, who says that the counselors should have been watching Jason when he drowned. The girl decapitates Mrs. Voorhees and she runs away. After this, a hand is shown picking up the locket that was previously around Mrs. Voorhees's neck. An unspecified amount of time after these events, a group of teenagers go camping around Crystal Lake only to be all apparently killed by Jason. Following this, a teenager named Clay arrives near Crystal Lake looking for his missing sister, Whitney, who was part of the group that was just killed. Clay encounters another group of teenagers traveling to their friend Trent's parents' lake house for the weekend. Jason begins to kill each member one at a time, while Clay continues searching for Whitney, who, it is eventually revealed, was kidnapped and being kept prisoner by Jason. Clay finds and rescues Whitney, with Jason in pursuit. Clay and Whitney are eventually trapped, so they confront and subdue Jason, finally throwing his body into the lake. In the final moments, Jason emerges from the water to attack them both.

Appendix 2

List and Description of Characters in the *Friday the 13th* Films

In alphabetical order, omitting titles (i.e., Mrs., Nurse, Sergeant, etc.)

Friday the 13th

Alice Hardy: The "Final Girl." There is either obvious romantic and sexual tension between her and the camp owner, Steve Christy, or sexual predation on his part. She kills Mrs. Voorhees, but is attacked by the boy Jason. She survives.

Annie: The cook who is killed en route to the camp. She admits to wanting to work with children. Annie dies having her throat slit with a hunting knife after being chased through the forest.

Bill: An attractive male counselor who proves adept at physically intensive tasks. His death is not seen, but his corpse is found suspended by several arrows to a door.

Brenda: A tall, attractive female counselor. She initiates a game of strip Monopoly with Alice and Bill. Brenda's death is not shown, but she is lured out to the archery range, and her body is later thrown through a window to frighten Alice.

Crazy Ralph: The local "prophet of doom." He warns the counselors that Camp Crystal Lake has a death curse.

Jack Burrel: Boyfriend of Marcie Cunningham. He is killed lying on a bed, an arrow penetrating his neck from underneath.

Marcie Cunningham: Girlfriend of Jack Burrel. She is killed by a hatchet in the girls' showers.

Ned Rubinstein: A thin male who frequently makes jokes and plays tricks on his fellow counselors. His death is not shown, but his body is seen on a bed, his throat having been cut.

Mrs. Pamela Voorhees: A cook at Camp Crystal Lake in 1950. Her son, Jason, drowns in the lake while two counselors were making love. She dispatches the two counselors, and then, imagining Jason's voice telling her to kill, systematically murders the counselors who are working at Camp Crystal Lake in 1980.

Steve Christy: Head counselor who has reopened and is renovating Camp Crystal Lake for use. He is presumably killed by being stabbed in the stomach.

Friday the 13th Part 2

Alice Hardy: Still alive after the previous film, she returns to her house to put her life back in order. Jason finds and kills her, stabbing her in the temple with an ice pick.

Crazy Ralph: Still tries to warn the counselors of potential danger, but is killed, strangled with barbed wire.

Ginny Field: The "Final Girl." She studies psychology, and is in a relationship with the head counselor, Paul Holt. She survives, but is taken away in an ambulance.

Jason Voorhees: Now an adult, and covering his head with a dirty sack with a single eye hole cut out, he finds and kills Alice and then returns to Camp Crystal Lake to kill the new counselors.

Jeff: Boyfriend of Sandra. He is stabbed with a spear along with Sandra while having sex.

Mark: Male counselor with an interest in sports. He has lost the use of his legs in a motorcycle accident. He is killed with a machete to his head just prior to a rendezvous with Vickie.

Paul Holt: Head counselor. He mysteriously disappears after Jason's final appearance.

Sandra: Girlfriend of Jeff. She, along with Jeff, is stabbed with a spear while having sex.

Scott: Attractive male counselor who makes inappropriate sexual advances on Terry. He is strung up to a tree by his feet and his throat is cut.

Ted: Close friend of Paul, Sandra, and Jeff. He frequently makes and tells jokes. Ted survives, and the last time he is seen, he is drunk in the local bar.

Terry: Attractive and sporty female counselor. She is frequently subject to the attention of Scott. Her death is not seen, but heavily implied.

Vicky: Young female counselor, who has a romantic interest in Mark. She is stabbed with a kitchen knife.

Deputy Winslow: Investigating trespassing in the nearby forest, he discovers Jason's house and is killed.

Friday the 13th Part III 3-D

Ali: Tall, bald gang member. He attacks Shelly and Vera with a chain, though they get away. Ali is bludgeoned with a wrench immediately after the deaths of Fox and Loco, but returns in the climax only to be killed by a machete.

Andy: Boyfriend of Debbie. He is cut in half by a machete while walking on his hands.

Chili: Romantically linked to Chuck. She is killed with a hot fire poker.

Chris Higgins: The "Final Girl." She has returned with some friends to her vacation house near Camp Crystal Lake where she was attacked by Jason. Chris is romantically linked with Rick. She survives and supposedly kills Jason, but it is implied that she is mentally disturbed by the events.

Chuck: Frequently smokes marijuana, he is romantically linked to Chili. He is killed by electrocution when Jason throws him into the fuse box.

Debbie: Pregnant girlfriend of Andy. She is killed with a kitchen knife in the back while lying in a hammock.

Edna: Wife of Harold. She is stabbed through the back of the head with a knitting needle.

Fox: Female gang member. She is stabbed through the neck with a pitchfork, and is suspended on a beam in the barn.

Harold: Store owner and husband of Edna. He is killed with a meat cleaver to his chest.

Jason: Attacks and kills most of the characters. He acquires Shelly's hockey mask after killing him.

Loco: Shorter male gang member. He is stabbed in the stomach with a pitchfork.

Rick: Local handyman and romantic interest of Chris. He is killed when Jason crushes his head.

Shelly: A prankster who is sad and lonely. He is rejected by his blind date, Vera. Shelly is killed by having his throat cut, and his body is discovered by Chili.

Vera: Brought along as a blind date for Shelly. She is killed by a harpoon shot through her eye.

Friday the 13th: The Final Chapter

Axel: Womanizing male orderly with a particular interest in Nurse Morgan. His throat is cut with a saw and his head twisted off.

Doug: Attractive male romantic interest of Sara. He is killed when his head is crushed against a wall, and stabbed through the throat with a spike.

Mrs. Jarvis: Mother of Trish and Tommy. Her death is not shown, but is heavily implied.

Jimmy: Shy, ineffectual young man who laments his poor sex life. His friend Ted calls him a "dead fuck." After having sex with one of the twins, Tina, he is killed with a meat cleaver, and his body is later used to block a doorway.

Nurse Morgan: Young female nurse who is subject to the attention of Axel, the orderly. She is stabbed with a scalpel.

Paul: Boyfriend of Samantha, but flirts heavily with Tina. He is killed with a spear gun aimed at his groin.

Rob Dier: A rugged young man who is searching for Jason under the pretense of hunting for a bear. He is killed with a garden claw and thrown through a window to scare Trish and Tommy.

Samantha: Girlfriend of Paul. She is killed while floating in a raft, impaled by a machete from underneath.

Sara: Shy young girl who has a romantic interest in Doug. She is killed by an axe thrown through a door.

Ted: An obnoxious womanizer who makes fun of his friend Jimmy's failed sexual conquests. He is stabbed in the back of the head through a small movie screen.

Terri: One of two identical twin girls. She refuses Ted's advances and leaves early. She is stabbed with a spear while unlocking her bike.

Tina: One of two identical twin girls. She makes romantic advances on Paul, who turns her down, so she then resorts to having sex with Jimmy. Tina is killed by being thrown from a window on the second level of the house onto a car.

Tommy Jarvis: A young boy who likes computer games and making monster masks and toys. He and his sister, Trish, are the central protagonists. Tommy kills Jason with a machete, and it is implied that he is mentally disturbed by the experience.

Trish Jarvis: The "Final Girl" and Tommy's older sister. She shows romantic interest in Rob. Trish survives along with Tommy.

Friday the 13th Part V: A New Beginning

Anita: Girlfriend of Demon. She is killed by having her throat cut.

Billy: Van driver who transfers Tommy to Pinehurst. He is killed before his date with Lana, struck in the back of the head with an axe.

Demon: Boyfriend of Anita and older brother of Reggie. He is impaled by a metal post through the back in an outhouse.

Duke: A paramedic who is killed by having his throat cut.

Eddie: Boyfriend of Tina and Pinehurst resident. His head is crushed with a leather strap tightened around a tree.

Ethel Hubbard: Local woman who objects to Pinehurst's proximity to her own home. She is killed with a meat cleaver to her face swung through a window.

George: Elderly cook for Pinehurst, grandfather of Reggie. His eyes are gouged out and he is thrown through a window to frighten Pam.

Jake: Resident of Pinehurst with a stutter. He has romantic inclinations towards Robin. Jake is killed when he is struck in the face with a cleaver.

Joey: A sweet but clumsy and annoying resident of Pinehurst. He is killed by Vic, who hits him in the back with an axe.

Junior: Brutish, dimwitted son of Ethel. He is decapitated by a machete while riding on his motorbike.

Lana: Attractive local waitress with plans to go on a date with Billy. She is hit in the chest with an axe.

Matthew Letter: Head doctor at Pinehurst. He is killed by having his throat cut.

Pam Roberts: The "Final Girl." She is a helper at the Pinehurst Youth Development Center where Tommy has been transferred. Pam survives, but is in danger from Tommy at the end of the film.

Pete: Friend of Vinnie who goes into the woods while Vinnie is repairing the car. His throat is cut with a machete.

Raymond: Hired hand for Ethel and Junior. He is stabbed in the stomach while watching Tina and Eddie having sex.

Reggie: A young boy, the grandson of the cook and younger brother of Demon. He survives along with Pam and Tommy.

Robin: Redheaded female resident of Pinehurst. She is the object of romantic interest from Jake. Robin is stabbed with a machete through her mattress from below.

Roy: Seeks revenge on Pinehurst residents in retribution for the murder of his son, Joey. He is the killer in the film, wearing a hockey mask and using similar methods of murder as Jason. He is killed when he is thrown from the top level of a barn onto a tractor harrow.

Tina: Girlfriend of Eddie. She is killed by garden shears through her eyes while lying nude in the forest.

Tommy Jarvis: Now a teenager, he has been transferred from a mental institution to Pinehurst. He rarely talks, but frequently sees Jason in his dreams and in hallucinations. He survives, but it is implied he has dangerous, violent potential.

Vic: A Pinehurst resident with anger management problems. He impulsively kills Joey with an axe.

Vinnie: A young man traveling with his friend Pete through the area. He tries to repair the car when it breaks down. Vinnie is killed when a road flare is shoved in his mouth.

Violet: A Pinehurst resident who is a friend of Robin and enjoys dancing. She is stabbed in the stomach with a machete.

Jason Lives! Friday the 13th Part VI

Cort: Male camp counselor and boyfriend of Nikki. He is killed by Jason while driving a recreational vehicle.

Darren: Traveling to camp with Lizabeth. Jason stabs him with a pole.

Jason: Returns to life, though is largely decomposed. He begins to kill people in the woods surrounding Crystal Lake including the new camp counselors. Jason is bested by Tommy and sunk to the bottom of Crystal Lake with a stone, but the closing shot reveals that he is still alive.

Katie: Confident female paintball-playing business executive. She is decapitated simultaneously with Stan and Larry.

Larry: Clumsy paintball-playing business executive who is decapitated simultaneously with Stan and Katie.

Lizabeth: Traveling to camp with Darren. Jason stabs her in the face with a pole.

Megan: Daughter of Sheriff Garris who displays romantic and sexual interest in Tommy. She survives, protecting the children of the camp.

Sheriff Michael Garris: Head law enforcement officer and father of Megan. He initially disbelieves Tommy's report of Jason's return to life. Sheriff Garris is killed when Jason breaks his back.

Nikki: Girlfriend of Cort. She is killed when Jason crushes her face against the caravan wall.

Paula: Female camp counselor whose death is not explicitly shown, but it is implied she is hacked apart by a machete.

Roy: Eager but ineffectual business executive playing paintball with his coworkers. He is killed by dismemberment.

Sissy: Female camp counselor who creates a card game called "Camp Blood." She is killed by having her head twisted off.

Stan: Obnoxious, mouthy male paintball-playing business executive who is decapitated simultaneously with Larry and Katie.

Officer Thornton: Works for Sheriff Garris. Jason kills him by throwing a knife at his head.

Tommy Jarvis: Escapes from the mental institution to make sure Jason is dead, but inadvertently resurrects him. He survives, having defeated Jason by sinking him to the bottom of Crystal Lake.

Friday the 13th Part VII: The New Blood

Amanda Shepard: Tina's mother. She has hired Dr. Crews and believes his false reports to her regarding Tina's progress. She is stabbed in the back by Jason.

Ben: Party attendee and boyfriend of Kate. Jason crushes his head.

Dr. Crews: An opportunistic doctor who, under the guise of trying to help Tina, tries to research her telekinetic abilities for his own professional benefit. Jason kills him using an electric saw.

Dan: Male camper, boyfriend of Judy. Jason shoves his hand through Dan's back and then snaps Dan's neck.

David: Attractive male partygoer who enjoys drinking and smoking marijuana. He is killed with a large kitchen knife after having sex with Robin.

Eddie: Writer of science fiction stories, party attendee, and romantically interested in Melissa. He is killed with a machete off-screen.

Jane: Girlfriend of Michael who organized his birthday party. She is killed with a tent spike through her neck.

Jason: Brought back to life by Tina, he begins to kill the locals. He is subdued by being pulled underwater by the resurrected John Shepard.

John Shepard: Tina's father, who drowned in Crystal Lake when Tina, as a young girl, telekinetically collapses the pier on which he was standing. In the end, he returns and drags Jason back into the lake.

Judy: Female camper, girlfriend of Dan. Jason picks her up in her sleeping bag and swings her into a tree.

Kate: Party attendee and girlfriend of Ben. Jason shoves a party horn into her eye.

Maddy: Shy, insecure party attendee with romantic interest in David. She is friends with Robin, but feels betrayed when Robin seduces David. Her throat is cut with a sickle.

Melissa: Attractive and cruel female attendee of Michael's party. Her unrequited interest in Nick is the impetus for her maltreatment of Tina. She is killed by an axe in her forehead.

Michael: The young man whose birthday is the cause of the teenagers having a party near Crystal Lake. He is the brother of Nick but is killed when Jason throws a tent spike into his back.

Nick: Brother of Michael and romantic interest of Tina. He survives along with Tina.

Robin: Confident and flirty friend of Maddy, with sexual and romantic interest in David. She is thrown from a window on the second level of the house.

Russell: Boyfriend of Sandra. He is hit in the face with an axe.

Sandra: Party attendee and girlfriend of Russell. In a sequence recreated from *Jaws* (1975), she is attacked and pulled underwater by Jason.

Tina Shepard: A telekinetic and the "Final Girl." She survives after fighting Jason.

Friday the 13th Part VIII: Jason Takes Manhattan

Mr. Carlson: First mate on Admiral Robertson's ship. He is harpooned in the back.

Charles McCulloch: School administrator and Rennie's uncle and guardian. He is drowned in a barrel of sewage.

Colleen Van Deusen: A high school teacher and school trip chaperone who has taken an interest in Rennie's potential and development. She is killed in an exploding car.

Eva: Smart student who allows herself to be manipulated by Tamara. She is strangled by Jason in the dance room.

J. J.: Aspiring guitarist and friend of Wayne. She is beaten to death with her guitar.

Jason: Resurrected by an electric current in the water caused by a severed power cable. He attacks and kills people from Crystal Lake on a boat to New York, and is eventually killed by a flood of toxic waste.

Jim: Boyfriend of Suzi, tells the background story of Jason. He is killed by a spear gun.

Julius: Aspiring boxer. He challenges Jason to a boxing match wherein his head is punched off.

Miles: Friend of Sean. He is killed when Jason throws him off the ship's mast.

Rennie Wickham: The "Final Girl" who encountered Jason while learning to swim, and now has a vague psychic connection. She, along with Sean, her romantic interest, lures Jason into the sewers where he is killed by a flood of toxic waste.

Admiral Robertson: Sean's father, who wants Sean to follow his own career path. Jason cuts his throat with a machete.

Sean Robertson: Son of Admiral Robertson and romantic interest of Rennie. He and Rennie best Jason and survive.

Suzi: Girlfriend of Jim. She is stabbed by a spear while hiding in a cargo hold.

Tamara: Attractive and cruel student and friend of Eva who frequently manipulates people and blackmails Charles. Jason stabs her in the shower with a sharp piece of glass from the mirror.

Toby: Rennie's dog.

Wayne: Aspiring filmmaker, friend of J. J., and enamored of Tamara. He is thrown into a control panel and electrocuted.

Jason Goes to Hell: The Final Friday

Alexis: Teenage camper, friend of Deborah and Luke. She is killed with a scalpel.

Coroner: Examines the remains of Jason after the FBI mission. While doing so, he is mesmerized by the still beating heart of Jason and eats it, becoming the first-person in the film to be possessed by Jason's spirit. The coroner passes the worm-spirit to Josh orally.

Creighton Duke: A sadistic and wily bounty hunter who has acquired the secret of destroying Jason. He is killed when Jason squeezes his body, crushing his back.

Dana Kimble: Mother of Jessica, grandmother of Stephanie and half-sister of Jason. She is killed in a struggle between the possessed Josh and Steven when a knife sharpener enters her back. However, in the climactic struggle, Jason's worm-spirit crawls into the vagina of her corpse, bringing Jason back to his original form, as she is part of his bloodline.

Deborah: Teenage camper, girlfriend of Luke. While having sex with Luke, she is stabbed through the back.

Edna: Girlfriend of Josh. She is killed by the possessed coroner by having her head crushed in a car door.

Jason: Still undead and killing people near Crystal Lake, he is lured into a trap by the FBI and his body is destroyed. His spirit, however, survives in the form of a giant demonic worm and is passed from person to person, usually orally, but can possess another person by entering any bodily orifice. Jason is killed by a relative, Jessica, holding a mystical dagger. According to legend, this is the only way his spirit can be destroyed.

Jessica Kimble: Estranged partner of Steven, mother of Stephanie, daughter of Dana, and distant relative of Jason. She sends Jason's spirit to Hell by stabbing him with a mystical dagger and survives.

Joey B.: Co-owner of the local diner and obese wife of Shelby. She is killed when her mouth is punched inwards by the possessed Robert.

Josh: Police officer who receives Jason's spirit from the coroner before passing it to Robert. Once the spirit passes to Robert, Josh's body melts.

Luke: Teenage camper, boyfriend of Deborah. He is killed, but it is unseen.

Officer Randy Parker: Local police officer and friend of Steven. He receives Jason's spirit from Robert, and is killed when his throat is cut with a machete and the spirit breaks out of his body through his neck.

Robert Campbell: Anchor of the "infotainment" show *American Case File* and boyfriend of Jessica. Jason's spirit is transferred into him by Josh, and later, is passed from Robert into Randy, and Robert, like Josh before him, likely dies when Jason's spirit leaves him, though this is not shown.

Officer Ryan: Police officer who helps Jessica at the station. She is killed by the possessed Robert when her head is crushed against a locker.

Shelby: Co-owner of the local diner and diminutive husband of Joey B. He is killed when the possessed Robert pushes his head into the deep fryer.

Sheriff Ed Landis: Local sheriff. Upon mistakenly suspecting that he might be possessed by the spirit of Jason, Jessica stabs him with the mystical dagger.

Stephanie Kimble: The infant daughter of Steven and Jessica. She survives.

Steven Freeman: Estranged partner of Jessica Kimble and father of Stephanie. He wants to reunite with Jessica, and upon discovering she is in danger, goes to great lengths to try to save her and Stephanie. Steven survives.

Vicki: Waitress at Joey B. and Shelby's diner. In trying to attack the possessed Robert, she is impaled on a skewer.

Ward: Teenage son of Joey B. and Shelby who works in the diner. He is attacked by Jason and killed when he is thrown against the diner doors.

Jason X

Adrienne: Professor Lowe's intern. Jason freezes her face in liquid nitrogen, then shatters it against a table.

Azrael: A very clumsy and not particularly bright student, who makes friends with the security team, particularly Dallas. He is killed with a machete after a virtual reality game.

Sergeant Brodski: A security officer aboard the spaceship, Grendel. He doggedly pursues Jason, and sacrifices himself in order to destroy Jason by also burning up in Earth Two's atmosphere upon re-entry.

Condor: A security officer with a preference for martial arts. He is pushed off of a platform and impaled by a large drill.

Crutch: Grendel's engineer. He is electrocuted when his head is smashed against a control panel.

Dallas: Large, muscular security officer. He is killed after playing a virtual reality game with Azrael by having his head bashed against a wall.

Geko: Female security officer who discovers the bodies of Condor and Sven. Her death is not seen, but it is implied she is killed with a machete.

Janessa: A smart, attractive student who is having an affair with Professor Lowe, presumably for good grades. She is killed when she is sucked through a grating surrounding a small breach in the ship's hull.

Jason: Captured and held in Crystal Lake Research Facility, with an acknowledged ability for cellular regeneration. He is frozen by Rowan and reawakened by Professor Lowe, proceeding to kill as many people as possible before being attacked and subjected to advanced regeneration. Jason then becomes Uber-Jason, a stronger and more powerful version of himself. He is potentially killed when he travels through the atmosphere of Earth Two.

Kay-Em 14: Android maintained by Tsunaron who resembles a tall, attractive female. She destroys the original Jason's body with heavy firepower just before he is regenerated and attacks her. Kay-Em 14 is still functional, although all that remains is her head.

Kinsa: A student and girlfriend of Stoney. Mentally broken after seeing Stoney killed by a surgical machete, she dies in trying to use an escape shuttle, which she crashes back into the ship, Grendel.

Fat Lou: Grendel's pilot. He is killed with a surgical machete.

Professor Lowe: Science professor who organizes a field trip to Earth One for his students. He is having an affair with Janessa, and he consults with his financial backer to discover how valuable Jason's remains are. He is decapitated by a machete.

Rowan: The "Final Girl." She is a researcher at Crystal Lake Research Facility who becomes cryogenically frozen and reawakened in the future along with Jason. She survives.

Stoney: Boyfriend of Kinsa. He is killed with a surgical machete.

Sven: Blonde male security officer. Jason breaks his neck.

Tsunaron: A student with an aptitude for electronics, as demonstrated by his maintenance of Kay-Em 14. He survives.

VR Teen Girls: Two holograms created to resemble attractive females at Camp Crystal Lake. Jason traps them in their sleeping bags and bashes them into a tree and each other.

Waylander: A student with an aptitude for engineering. He is killed when he blows up a section of the Grendel containing both himself and Jason.

Dr. Wimmer: Scientist at Crystal Lake Research Facility who undermines Rowan's authority and is determined to study Jason's regenerative abilities. He is stabbed in the back with a pole.

Freddy vs. Jason

Bill Freeburg: A student at the local school who enjoys smoking marijuana. He becomes possessed by Freddy, and is cut in half with a machete.

Blake: Friend of Trey who is intended as a blind date for Lori. He is killed with a machete.

Dr. Campbell: Father of Lori who originally had Will committed, and might have killed his wife. He survives.

Charlie Linderman: Socially awkward and bookish, he is the eventual romantic interest of Kia. He is killed by being thrown into a sharp metal wall fixture.

Freddy Krueger: A child killer who attacks people in their dreams, but needs belief, fear, and memory to make him strong. He resurrects Jason to kill for him until his own strength comes back, but is forced to fight Jason after he proves to be Freddy's competition in killing. He is decapitated by Jason, but survives.

Gibb: Friend of Lori and Kia and girlfriend of Trey who frequently drinks and smokes. She is impaled with a pipe by Jason.

Jason: Resurrected by Freddy using the memory of his mother, and is forced into a fight with Freddy. He survives.

Kia Waterson: Close friend of Lori, and eventual romantic interest of Linderman. She is stabbed with a machete and thrown into a tree.

Lori Campbell: The "Final Girl." Believing her boyfriend, Will, had left her, she later discovers he was institutionalized. Lori is the first person to have nightmares about Freddy. She survives, along with Will.

Mark: Friend of Will who was institutionalized at the same time. His older brother was killed by Freddy. Mark is killed in his sleep by being set on fire, and slashed with Freddy's razor glove.

Trey: Domineering boyfriend of Gibb. He is repeatedly stabbed with a machete and folded in half backwards.

Will Rollins: Institutionalized, along with his friend Mark, during a previous wave of attacks by Freddy. He has been trying to reunite with Lori. He survives along with Lori.

Friday the 13th (2009)

Amanda: Among the first group of teenagers, and girlfriend of Richie, she is tied up in her sleeping bag and suspended over a campfire until she is roasted to death.

Bree: Attractive female in the second group of teenagers. She is the object of attraction for multiple males in the group, including Chewie and Trent. Trent eventually has sex with Bree, and afterwards, Jason kills her by stabbing her with a set of antlers mounted to the wall and then throwing her from a window on the second story of the house.

Chelsea: Among the second group of teenagers and girlfriend of Nolan, she hides in the water under a small wooden pier. Jason stabs her in the head with his machete.

Chewie: Among the second group of teenagers, he is a close friend of Lawrence. He loves to drink and smoke marijuana, but is clumsy and laments his inability to find someone with whom to have sex. Chewie is killed when he is stabbed in the throat with a screwdriver.

Clay Miller: An attractive young man, and eventual romantic interest of Jenna, he is searching for his missing sister, Whitney. Clay survives, but is in peril at the close of the film.

Donnie: A local mechanic and farm worker who also sells marijuana. Jason cuts his throat with a machete.

Jason Voorhees: Son of Pamela who witnessed his mother's murder, and kills anyone who comes near what he considers his territory. Clay and Whitney supposedly kill him and dump his body in the lake, but he returns in the final shot to attack them.

Jenna: In the second group of teenagers, girlfriend of Trent, but eventual romantic interest of Clay. She is killed with a machete.

Lawrence: In the second group of teenagers, and friend of Chewie, he is chased after finding Jason and Chewie in the shed. Jason throws an axe into Lawrence's back.

Mike: Among the first group of teenagers and boyfriend of Whitney, his death is not seen, but he is slashed multiple times by a machete and pulled underground through the floorboards of a house by Jason.

Nolan: Among the second group of teenagers and boyfriend of Chelsea, he is killed when Jason shoots an arrow through his head as he is driving the boat from which Chelsea is waterskiing topless.

Pamela Voorhees: Mother of Jason who seeks vengeance for her son's supposed death. She is decapitated in the opening of the film.

Richie: Among the first group of teenagers, and boyfriend of Amanda, he gets his leg caught in a steel bear trap and is hit in the head with a machete.

Trent: The arrogant and cruel son of wealthy parents who invites his friends to his parents' lavish house near Crystal Lake. He is Jenna's boyfriend, but eventually has sex with Bree. He is stabbed through the back with a spike on the back of a truck.

Wade: Among the first group of teenagers, he is knowledgeable on local folklore and is eager to find a nearby growth of marijuana plants. He is killed with a machete.

Whitney Miller: Among the first group of teenagers, and sister of Clay and girlfriend of Mike, she is kidnapped by Jason, but is rescued by Clay and survives, though she is in peril at the close of the film.

Works Cited

AFI.com (2007). "100 Years . . . 100 Movies—10th Anniversary Edition," https://www.afi.com/100years/movies10.aspx (last accessed June 21, 2019).
Altman, Rick (1999). *Film/Genre*. London: BFI Publishing.
Balázs, Béla (1985). "Theory of the Film: Sound." In Elisabeth Weis and John Belton, eds., *Film Sound: Theory and Practice*, 116–25. New York: Columbia University Press.
Belton, John (1985). "Technology and Aesthetics of Film Sound." In Elisabeth Weis and John Belton, eds., *Film Sound: Theory and Practice* (1985), 63–72. New York: Columbia University Press.
Berliner, Todd (2010). *Hollywood Incoherent*. Austin: University of Texas Press.
Berliner, Todd (2001). "The Pleasures of Disappointment: Sequels and *The Godfather, Part II*." *Journal of Film and Video* 53:2–3 (2001): 107–123.
Berliner Todd (2005). "Visual Absurdity in *Raging Bull*." In Kevin J. Hayes, ed., *Martin Scorsese's* Raging Bull (Cambridge Film Handbooks), 41–68. Cambridge: Cambridge University Press.
Booth, Stephen (1990). "The Function of Criticism at the Present Time and All Others." *Shakespeare Quarterly* 41:2 (1990): 262–68.
Bordwell, David (2006). *The Way Hollywood Tells It: Story and Style in Modern Movies*. London: University of California Press
Bordwell, David, and Kristin Thompson (1985). "Fundamental Aesthetics of Sound in the Cinema." In Elisabeth Weis and John Belton, eds., *Film Sound: Theory and Practice*, 181–99. New York: Columbia University Press.
Box Office Mojo (1998). *Psycho*, http://www.boxofficemojo.com/movies/?id=psycho98.htm (last accessed February 1, 2012).
Bracke, Peter M. (2005). *Crystal Lake Memories: The Complete History of Friday the 13th*. London: Titan Books.
Branigan, Edward (1984). *Point of View in the Cinema: A Theory of Narration and Subjectivity in Classical Film*. Berlin: Mouton.
Budra, Paul (1998). "Recurrent Monsters: Why Freddy, Michael, and Jason Keep Coming Back." In Paul Budra and Betty A. Schellenberg, eds., *Part Two: Reflections on the Sequel*, 189–99. Toronto: University of Toronto Press.

Buscombe, Edward (1986). "The Idea of Genre in the American Cinema." In Barry Keith Grant, ed., *Film Reader III*. Austin: University of Texas Press.

Cherry, B. (2009). *Horror*, 12–26. London: Routledge.

Chion, Michel (1994). *Audio-Vision: Sound on Screen*. Translated from French by Claudia Gorbman, ed. New York: Columbia University Press.

Chion, Michel (1982). *The Voice in Cinema*. Translated from French by Claudia Gorbman, ed. New York: Columbia University Press

Cinemetrics (2014). "*Harry Potter and the Sorcerer's Stone* (2001)," http://www.cinemetrics.lv/movie.php?movie_ID=16707 (last accessed July 16, 2018).

Cinemetrics (2018) "*The Lord of the Rings: The Fellowship of the Ring* (2001)," http://www.cinemetrics.lv/movie.php?movie_ID=22940 (last accessed July 16, 2018).

Clair, René (1929). "The Art of Sound" (extract) in Elisabeth Weis and John Belton, eds., *Film Sound: Theory and Practice*, 92–95. New York: Columbia University Press.

Clayton, Wickham (2003). "Another Cynical Stab at Scaring" (film review of *Freddy vs. Jason*), *Danville Register and Bee*, August 21, 2003: 2C.

Clayton III, George Wickham (2013). "Bearing Witness to a Whole Bunch of Murders: The Aesthetics of Perspective in the *Friday the 13th* Films." PhD thesis, Roehampton University, London, UK, https://pure.roehampton.ac.uk/portal/files/442080/George_Wickham_Clayton_final_thesis.pdf (last accessed June 21, 2019).

Clayton, Wickham (2015a). "Introduction: The Collection Awakes." In Wickham Clayton, ed., *Style and Form in the Hollywood Slasher Film*, 1–14. Houndsmills, Basingstoke: Palgrave Macmillan.

Clayton, Wickham (2015b). "Undermining the Moneygrubbers, or: How I Learned to Stop Worrying and Love *Friday the 13th Part V*." In Wickham Clayton, ed., *Style and Form in the Hollywood Slasher Film*, 37–50. Houndsmills, Basingstoke: Palgrave Macmillan.

Clover, Carol J. (1992). *Men, Women and Chain Saws: Gender in the Modern Horror Film*. Princeton: Princeton University Press.

Conrich, Ian (2010). "The *Friday the 13th* Films and the Cultural Function of a Modern Grand Guignol." In Ian Conrich, ed., *Horror Zone* (2010), 173–88. London, I. B. Tauris.

Conrich, Ian (2000). "Seducing the Subject: Freddy Krueger, Popular Culture and the *Nightmare on Elm Street* Films." In Alain Silver and James Ursini, eds., *Horror Film Reader* (2000), 222–35. New York: Limelight Editions.

Crane, Jonathan Lake (1994). *Terror and Everyday Life: Singular Moments in the History of the Horror Film*. Thousand Oaks, CA: Sage Publications.

Dika, Vera (1990). *Games of Terror:* Halloween, Friday the 13th *and the Films of the Stalker Cycle*. London: Associated University Presses.

Dika, Vera (2003). *Recycled Culture in Contemporary Art and Film: The Uses of Nostalgia*. Cambridge: Cambridge University Press.

Donnelly, K. J. (2009). "Saw Heard: Musical Sound Design in Contemporary Cinema." In Warren Buckland, ed., *Film Theory and Contemporary Hollywood Movies*, 103–123. Abingdon: Routledge.

Ebert, Roger (2009). "*Friday the 13th*" (review), https://www.rogerebert.com/reviews/friday-the-13th-2009 (last accessed June 16, 2018).

Edelstein, David (2006). "Now Playing at Your Local Multiplex: Torture Porn." *New York*, http://nymag.com/movies/features/15622/ (last accessed June 1, 2018).

Fischer, Lucy, and Marcia Landy (1982). "*Eyes of Laura Mars*: A Binocular Critique." In Gregory A. Waller, ed., *American Horrors: Essays on the Modern American Horror Film*, 62–78. Urbana: University of Illinois Press.

Frampton, Daniel (2006). *Filmosophy*. London: Wallflower Press.

Fuchs, Michael (2010). "A Horrific Welcome to the Desert of the Real: Simulacra, Simulations and Postmodern Horror." In Petra Eckhard, Michael Fuchs, and Walter W. Hölbling, eds. *Landscapes of Postmodernity: Concepts and Paradigms of Critical Theory*, 71–90. London: Transaction Publishers.
Grant, Barry Keith (2007). *Film Genre: From Iconography to Ideology*. Chippenham: Antony Rowe.
Grove, David (2005). *Making Friday the 13th: The Legend of Camp Blood*. Surrey: Fab Press.
Hall, Sheldon (2002). "Tall Revenue Features: The Genealogy of the Modern Blockbuster." In Steve Neale, ed., *Genre and Contemporary Hollywood*, 11–26. London: BFI Publishing.
Harrington, Richard (1988). "*Friday the 13th Part VII: The New Blood*" (review), *Washington Post*, May 14, 1988.
Heffernan, Kevin (2004). *Ghouls, Gimmicks, and Gold: Horror Films and the American Movie Business, 1953–1968*. Durham, NC: Duke University Press.
Humphries, Reynold (1991). *The American Horror Film: An Introduction*. Edinburgh: Edinburgh University Press.
James, Caryn (1988). "*Friday the 13th Part VII—The New Blood*," *New York Times*, May 15, 1988.
Jameson, Fredric (1984). "Postmodernism, or the Cultural Logic of Late Capitalism," *New Left Review*, 146 (1984): 53–92.
Jones, Steve (2013). *Torture Porn: Popular Horror After Saw*. Houndsmills, Basingstoke: Palgrave Macmillan.
Kerswell, J. A. (2010). *Teenage Wasteland: The Slasher Movie Uncut*. London: New Holland Publishers.
King, Stephen (1974). *Carrie*. New York: Doubleday.
King, Stephen (1981). *Danse Macabre*, Warner Books: London.
Koven, Mikel (2006). *La Dolce Morte: Vernacular Cinema and the Italian Giallo Film*. London: Scarecrow Press.
Koven, Mikel (2008). *Film, Folklore, and Urban Legends*. Plymouth: Scarecrow Press.
Leitch, Thomas (2007). *Film Adaptations and its Discontents: From* Gone with the Wind *to* The Passion of the Christ. Baltimore: Johns Hopkins University Press.
Martin, Bob (1980). "*Friday the 13th*: A Day for Terror" in *Fangoria*, 6 (June): 14–16, 64.
Mathijs, Ernest (2006). "Popular Culture in Global Context: The *Lord of the Rings* Phenomenon." In Ernest Mathijs, ed., *The Lord of the Rings: Popular Culture in Global Context*, 1–19. London: Wallflower Press.
McDonald, Paul (2013). *Hollywood Stardom*. Oxford: Wiley-Blackwell.
Mittell, Jason (2009). "Previously On: Prime Time Serials and the Mechanics of Memory," *Just TV*, http://justtv.wordpress.com/2009/07/03/previously-on-prime-time-serials-and-the-mechanics-of-memory/ (last accessed July 4, 2018).
Morris, Jeremy (2010). "The Justification of Torture-Horror: Retribution and Sadism in *Saw*, *Hostel*, and *The Devil's Rejects*." In Thomas Fahy, ed., *The Philosophy of Horror*, 42–56. Lexington: University Press of Kentucky.
Muir, John Kenneth (1998). *Wes Craven: The Art of Horror*. Jefferson, NC: McFarland and Company.
Neale, Stephen (1980). *Genre*. London: BFI Publishing.
Newman, Kim (2011). *Nightmare Movies: Horror On Screen Since the 1960s*. London: Bloomsbury.
Nowell, Richard (2011). *Blood Money: A History of the First Teen Slasher Film Cycle*. London: Continuum.
Pally, M. (1984). "Double Trouble." In L. F. Knapp, ed., *Brian De Palma Interviews*, 92–107. Jackson: University Press of Mississippi.
Perkins, V. F. (1972). *Film as Film*. London: Penguin Books.
Psycho (1998). "Behind the Scenes," http://www.psychomovie.com/production/productionwhy.html (website expired April 9, 2018).

Pulleine, T. (1980). "Review of *Friday the 13th Part 2*." *Monthly Film Bulletin*, 47: 558 (July): 138.
Ray, Robert B. (1985). *A Certain Tendency of the Hollywood Cinema, 1930–1980*. Princeton: Princeton University Press.
Reichardt, Sarah (2011). "Music, Madness and Modernity in Karl Freund's *Mad Love* (1935)." *Horror Studies*, 2:1: 3–14
Rockoff, Adam (2002). *Going to Pieces: The Rise and Fall of the Slasher Film, 1978–1986*. Jefferson, NC: McFarland and Company.
Shaviro, Steven (1993). *The Cinematic Body*, London: University of Minnesota Press.
Shklovsky, Viktor (1970). *Bowstring: On the Dissimilarity of the Similar*. Translated from the Russian by S. Avagyan. London: Dalkey Archive Press.
Sipos, Thomas M. (2010). *Horror Film Aesthetics: Creating the Visual Language of Fear*. Jefferson, NC: McFarland & Company.
Sontag, Susan (1964). "Against Interpretation." In Sontag, *Against Interpretation and Other Essays*, 3–14. London: Penguin Group.
Sprague, Mike (2018). "*Friday the 13th* Remake Producers Heartbroken about Abandoned Sequel," *Dread Central*, March 25, 2018, https://www.dreadcentral.com/news/269814/friday-the-13th-remake-producers-heartbroken-about-abandoned-sequel/ (last accessed March 27, 2018).
Stilwell, Robynn J. (2005). "Sound and Empathy: Subjectivity, Gender and the Cinematic Soundscape." In Jacqueline Furby and Karen Randell, eds., *Screen Methods: Comparative Readings in Film Studies*, 48–58. London: Wallflower Press.
Thompson, Kristin (1988). *Breaking the Glass Armour: Neoformalist Film Analysis*. Princeton, NJ, Princeton University Press.
Thompson, Roy (1993). *Grammar of the Edit*. Oxford: Focal Press.
Tudor, Andrew (2002). "Why Horror?: The Peculiar Pleasures of a Popular Genre." In Mark Jancovich, ed., *Horror, The Film Reader*, 47–56. London: Routledge.
Verevis, Constantine (2006). *Film Remakes*. Edinburgh: Edinburgh University Press.
Vertov, Dziga (1922). "Kinoks: A Revolution." In Annette Michelson, ed., *Kino-Eye: The Writings of Dziga Vertov* (1984), translated from the Russian by Kevin O'Brien, 11–20. London: University of California Press.
Wharton, Sarah (2011). "Evil is Not Enough: The Re-Imagining of Michael Myers," presented at the 56th Annual British Association of American Studies Conference, University of Central Lancashire, April 16, 2011.
Wierzbicki, James (2010). "Lost in Translation?: Ghost Music in Recent Japanese Kaidan Films and Their Hollywood Remakes." *Horror Studies*, 1:2: 193–206.
Wood, Robin (1989). *Hitchcock's Films Revisited*. London: Faber and Faber.
Wood, Robin (1986). *Hollywood from Vietnam to Reagan*. New York: Columbia University Press.
Wood, Robin (2003). *Hollywood from Vietnam to Reagan . . . and Beyond*. New York: Columbia University Press.
Zanger, Anant. (2006) *Film Remakes as Ritual and Disguise: From Carmen to Ripley*. Amsterdam: Amsterdam University Press.

Music

Jackson, Michael (1982). "Thriller," *Thriller* LP. USA: Epic.
Night Ranger (1983). "Sister Christian," *Midnight Madness* LP. USA: MCA.

Video Games

Atlus (1989). *Friday the 13th*. Nintendo Entertainment System. New York: LJN.
Illfonic (2017) *Friday the 13th: The Game*. Microsoft Windows, Play Station 4, Xbox One. Lexington, KY: Gun Media.

TV Shows

Grace and Frankie (2015–Present). Netflix, Prod. Co. Okay Goodnight / Skydance Television.

Films

Alien. Dir. Ridley Scott, Prod. Gordon Carroll / David Giler / Walter Hill, Prod. Co. Brandywine Productions / Twentieth Century-Fox Productions, 1979, USA / UK. Main Cast: Tom Skerritt (Dallas), Sigourney Weaver (Ripley), Veronica Cartwright (Lambert), Harry Dean Stanton (Brett).

Aliens. Dir. James Cameron, Prod. Gale Anne Hurd, Prod. Co. Twentieth Century-Fox Film Corporation / Brandywine Productions / SLM Production Group, 1986, USA / UK. Main Cast: Sigourney Weaver (Ellen Ripley), Carrie Henn (Newt), Michael Biehn (Corporal Dwayne Hicks), Paul Reiser (Carter Burke).

American Sniper. Dir. Clint Eastwood, Prod. Zakariz Alaoui / Bradley Cooper / Clint Eastwood / Chris Kyle / Andrew Lazar / Robert Lorenz / Jessica Meier / Peter Morgan / Kristina Rivera, Prod. Co. Warner Bros. / Village Roadshow / RatPac-Dune Entertainment / Mad Chance / 22 & Indiana / Malpaso / Zak, 2014, USA. Main Cast: Bradley Cooper (Chris Kyle), Kyle Gallner (Goat-Winston), Cole Konis (Young Chris Kyle), Ben Reed (Wayne Kyle).

And Then There Were None. Dir. René Clair, Prod. René Clair, Prod. Co. Popular Pictures Inc., 1945, USA. Main Cast: Barry Fitzgerald (Judge Francis J. Quinncannon), Walter Huston (Dr. Edward G. Armstrong), Louis Hayward (Philip Lombard), Roland Young (Detective William Henry Blore).

As Seen Through a Telescope. Dir. George Albert Smith, Prod. George Albert Smith, Prod. Co. G. A. S. Films, 1900, UK. No credited cast.

AVP: Alien vs. Predator. Dir. Paul W. S. Anderson, Prod. Gordon Carroll / John Davis / David Giler / Walter Hill, Prod. Co. Twentieth Century Fox Film Corporation / Davis Entertainment / Brandywine Productions / Charenton Productions Limited / Impact Pictures / Inside Track 2 LLP / Zweite Babelsberg Film GmbH, 2004, USA / Germany / Czech Republic / UK. Main Cast: Sanaa Lathan (Alexa Woods), Raoul Bova (Sebastian de Rosa), Lance Henriksen (Charles Bishop Weyland), Ewen Bremner (Graeme Miller).

Bad Taste. Dir. Peter Jackson, Prod. Peter Jackson, Prod. Co., WingNut Films / New Zealand Film Commission, 1987, New Zealand. Main Cast: Peter Jackson (Derek / Robert), Terry Potter (Ozzy / 3rd Class Alien), Pete O'Herne (Barry / 3rd Class Alien), Mike Minett (Frank / 3rd Class Alien).

Beetlejuice. Dir. Tim Burton, Prod. Michael Bender / Richard Hashimoto / Larry Wilson, Prod. Co. The Geffen Company, 1988, USA. Main Cast: Alec Baldwin (Adam Maitland), Geena Davis (Barbara Maitland), Michael Keaton (Beetlejuice), Winona Ryder (Lydia Deetz).

Bird with the Crystal Plumage, The (L'uccello Dalle Piume di Cristallo). Dir. Dario Argento, Prod. Salvatore Argento, Prod. Co. Central Cinema Company Film / Glazier / Seda Spettacoli, 1970, Italy / West Germany. Main Cast: Tony Musante (Sam Dalmas), Suzy Kendall (Julia), Enrico Maria Salerno (Inspector Morosini), Eva Renzi (Monica Ranieri).

Black Christmas. Dir. Bob Clark, Prod. Bob Clark, Prod. Co. Film Funding / Vision IV / Canadian Film Development Corporation / Famous Players, 1974, Canada. Main Cast: Olivia Hussey (Jess), Keir Dullea (Peter), Margot Kidder (Barb), John Saxon (Lt. Fuller).

Black Christmas. Dir. Glen Morgan, Prod. Marty Adelstein / Steven Hoban / Glen Morgan / Dawn Parouse / Victor Solnicki / James Wong, Prod. Co. Dimension Films / 2929 Productions / Adelstein-Parouse Productions / Hard Eight Pictures / Hoban Segal Productions / Victor Solnicki Productions, 2006, USA / Canada. Main Cast: Katie Cassidy (Kelli Presley), Michelle Trachtenberg (Melissa), Mary Elizabeth Winstead (Heather Fitzgerald), Lacey Chabert (Dana).

Blair Witch Project, The. Dir. Daniel Myrick / Eduardo Sánchez, Prod. Robin Cowie / Gregg Hale, Prod. Co. Haxan Films, 1999, USA. Main Cast: Heather Donahue (Heather Donahue), Joshua Leonard (Josh Leonard), Michael Williams (Mike Williams).

Body Heat. Dir. Lawrence Kasdan, Prod. Fred T. Gallo, Prod. Co. The Ladd Company, 1981, USA. Main Cast: William Hurt (Ned Racine), Kathleen Turner (Matty Walker), Richard Crenna (Edmund Walker), Ted Danson (Peter Lowenstein).

Bride of Chucky. Dir. Ronny Yu, Prod. Grace Gilroy / David Kirschner, Prod. Co. Midwinter Productions Inc. / Universal Pictures, 1998, Canada / USA. Main Cast: Jennifer Tilly (Tiffany), Brad Dourif (Chucky), Katherine Heigel (Jade), Nick Stabile (Jesse).

Broadway Melody, The. Dir. Harry Beaumont, Prod. None credited, Prod. Co. Metro-Goldwyn-Mayer, 1929, USA. Main Cast: Charles King (Eddie Kearns), Anita Page (Queenie Mahoney), Bessie Love (Hank Mahoney).

Burning, The. Dir. Tony Maylam, Prod. Harvey Weinstein, Prod. Co. Miramax Films / The Cropsy Venture, 1981, USA / Canada. Main Cast: Brian Matthews (Todd), Leah Ayres (Michelle), Brian Backer (Alfred), Larry Joshua (Glazer).

Candyman. Dir. Bernard Rose, Prod. Steve Golin / Alan Poul / Sigurjon Sighvatsson, Prod. Co. PolyGram Filmed Entertainment / Propaganda Films, 1992, USA. Main Cast: Virginia Madsen (Helen Lyle), Tony Todd (The Candyman), Xander Berkeley (Trevor Lyle), Kasi Lemmons (Bernie Walsh).

Cannibal Holocaust. Dir. Ruggero Deodato, Prod. Franco Di Nunzio, Franco Palaggi, Prod. Co. F. D. Cinematografica, 1980, Italy. Main Cast: Robert Kerman (Harold Monroe), Francesca Ciardi (Faye Daniels), Perry Pirkanen (Jack Anders), Luca Giorgio Barbareschi (Mark Tomaso).

Carrie. Dir. Brian De Palma, Prod. Paul Monash, Prod. Co. United Artists, 1976, USA. Main Cast: Sissy Spacek (Carrie White), Piper Laurie (Margaret White), Amy Irving (Sue Snell), William Katt (Tommy Ross).

Chien Andalou, Un. Dir. Luis Bunuel, Prod. Luis Bunuel, Prod. Co. N/A, 1929, France. Main Cast: Simonne Mareuil (Young Girl), Pierre Batchef (Man).

Chinatown. Dir. Roman Polanski, Prod. Robert Evans, Prod. Co. Paramount Pictures / Penthouse / Long Road Productions, 1974, USA. Main Cast: Jack Nicholson (Jake Gittes), Faye Dunaway (Evelyn Mulwray), John Huston (Noah Cross), Perry Lopez (Escobar).

Cloverfield. Dir. Matt Reeves, Prod. J. J. Abrams / Bryan Burk, Prod. Co. Paramount Pictures / Bad Robot, 2008, USA. Main Cast: Lizzy Caplan (Marlena Diamond), Jessica Lucas (Lily Ford), T. J. Miller (Hud Platt), Michael Stahl-David (Rob Hawkins).

Critters. Dir. Stephen Herek, Prod. Rupert Harvey, Prod. Co. New Line Cinema / Sho Films / Smart Egg Pictures, 1986, USA. Main Cast: Dee Wallace Stone (Helen Brown), M. Emmett Walsh (Harv), Billy Green Bush (Jay Brown), Scott Grimes (Brad Brown).

Dances with Wolves. Dir. Kevin Costner, Prod. Kevin Costner / Jim Wilson, Prod. Co. Tig Productions /Majestic Films International, 1990, USA / UK. Main Cast: Kevin Costner (Lieutenant Dunbar), Mary McDonnell (Stands with A Fist), Graham Greene (Kicking Bird), Rodney A. Grant (Wind in his Hair).

Dawn of the Dead. Dir. George A. Romero, Prod. Richard P. Rubinstein, Prod. Co. Laurel Group, 1978, Italy / USA. Main Cast: David Emge (Stephen), Ken Foree (Peter), Scott H. Reiniger (Roger), Gaylen Ross (Francine).

Dead Alive. Dir. Peter Jackson, Prod. Jim Booth, Prod. Co. WingNut Films / The New Zealand Film Commission / Avalon/NFU Studios, 1992, New Zealand. Main Cast: Timothy Balme (Lionel Cosgrove), Diana Peñalver (Paquita Maria Sanchez), Elizabeth Moody (Vera Cosgrove), Ian Watkin (Uncle Les).

Dead Poets Society. Dir. Peter Weir, Prod. Steven Haft / Paul Junger Witt / Tony Thomas, Prod. Co. Touchstone Pictures / Silver Screen Partners IV / A Steven Haft Production / Witt-Thomas Productions, 1989, USA. Main Cast: Robin Williams (John Keating), Robert Sean Leonard (Neil Perry), Ethan Hawke (Todd Anderson), Josh Charles (Knox Overstreet).

Deep Red (*Profondo Rosso*). Dir. Dario Argento, Prod. Salvatore Argento, Prod. Co. Rizzoli Film / Seda Spettacoli, 1975, Italy. Main Cast: David Hemmings (Marcus Daly), Daria Nicolodi (Gianna Brezzi), Gabriele Lavia (Carlo), Macha Méril (Helga Ulmann).

Die Hard. Dir. John McTiernan, Prod. Lawrence Gordon / Joel Silver, Prod. Co. Twentieth Century Fox Film Corporation / Gordon Company / Lawrence Gordon Productions / Silver Pictures, 1988, USA. Main Cast: Bruce Willis (Officer John McClane), Bonnie Bedelia (Holly Gennaro McClane), Reginald Veljohnson (Sgt. Al Powell), Paul Gleason (Deputy Police Chief Dwayne T. Robinson).

Do You Like Hitchcock? (*Ti Piace Hitchcock?*). Dir. Dario Argento, Prod. Carlo Bixio / Joan Antoni Gonzáles / Fabrizio Zappi, Prod. Co. Film Commission Torino-Piemonte / Genesis Motion Pictures / Institut Del Cinema Català / Opera Film Produzione / Rai Trade / Televisió de Catalunya, 2005, Italy / Spain. Main Cast: Elio Germano (Giulio), Chiara Conti (Federica), Elisabetta Rocchetti (Sasha), Cristina Brondo (Arianna).

Dr. Jekyll and Mr. Hyde. Dir. Rouben Mamoulian, Prod. None credited, Prod. Co. Paramount Publix Corporation, 1931, USA. Main Cast: Fredric March (Dr. Henry Jekyll/Mr. Hyde), Miriam Hopkins (Ivy Pearson), Rose Hobart (Muriel Carew), Holmes Herbert (Dr. Lanyon).

Dracula. Dir. Tod Browning, Prod. Tod Browning / Carl Laemmle Jr., Prod. Co. Universal Pictures Corporation, 1931, USA. Main Cast: Bela Lugosi (Count Dracula), Helen Chandler (Mina), David Manners (John Harker), Dwight Frye (Renfield).

Dressed to Kill. Dir. Brian De Palma, Prod. George Litto, Prod. Co. Filmways Pictures Inc. / Cinema77 / Film Group / Warwick Associates, 1980, USA. Main Cast: Michael Caine (Doctor Robert Elliott), Angie Dickinson (Kate Miller), Nancy Allen (Liz Blake), Keith Gordon (Peter Miller).

Evil Dead, The. Dir. Sam Raimi, Prod. Robert Tapert, Prod. Co. Renaissance Pictures. 1981, USA. Main Cast: Bruce Campbell (Ash Williams), Ellen Sandweiss (Cheryl), Hal Delrich (Scott), Betsy Baker (Linda).

Evil Dead 2. Dir. Sam Raimi, Prod. Robert G. Tapert, Prod. Co. DeLaurentiis Entertainment Group / Renaissance Pictures, 1987, USA. Main Cast: Bruce Campbell (Ash Williams), Sarah Berry (Annie Knowby), Dan Hicks (Jake), Kassie Wesley (Bobby Joe).

Eyes of Laura Mars. Dir. Irvin Kershner, Prod. Jon Peters, Prod. Co. Columbia Pictures Corporation, 1978, USA. Main Cast: Faye Dunaway (Laura Mars), Tommy Lee Jones (John Neville), Brad Dourif (Tommy Ludlow), Rene Auberjonois (Donald Phelps).

Eyes Wide Shut. Dir. Stanley Kubrick, Prod. Stanley Kubrick, Prod. Co. Hobby Films / Pole Star / Stanley Kubrick Productions / Warner Bros. Pictures, 1999, UK / USA. Main Cast: Tom Cruise (Bill Harford), Nicole Kidman (Alice Harford), Madison Eginton (Helena Harford), Sydney Pollack (Victor Ziegler).

Fade to Black. Dir. Vernon Zimmerman, Prod. George G. Braunstein / Ron Hamady, Prod. Co. Leisure Investment Company / Movie Ventures, 1980, USA. Main Cast: Dennis Christopher (Eric Binford), Tim Thomerson (Jerry Moriarty), Gwynne Gilford (Officer Anne Oshenbull), Normann Burton (Marty Berger).

Final Destination 5 3-D. Dir. Steven Quale, Prod. Craig Perry / Warren Zide, Prod. Co. New Line Cinema / Practical Pictures / Zide Pictures / Jellystone Films, 2011, USA. Main Cast: Nicholas D'Agosto (Sam Lawton), Emma Bell (Molly Harper), Miles Fisher (Peter Friedkin), Ellen Wroe (Candice Hooper).

Fly, The. Dir. David Cronenberg, Prod. Stuart Cornfeld, Prod. Co. Brooksfilms, 1986, USA. Main Cast: Jeff Goldblum (Seth Brundle), Geena Davis (Veronica Quaife), John Getz (Stathis Borans), Joy Boushel (Tawny).

Fly II, The. Dir. Chris Walas, Prod. Steven-Charles Jaffe, Prod. Co. Brooksfilms, 1989, USA. Main Cast: Eric Stotlz (Martin), Daphne Zuniga (Beth), Lee Richardson (Bartok), John Getz (Stathis).

Formula 51. Dir. Ronny Yu, Prod. Jonathan Debin / Andras Hamori / Malcolm Kohll / Seaton Mclean / David Pupkewitz, Prod. Co. Alliance Atlantis / Focus Films / Fifty First Films / National Lottery / Artists Production Group / Canadian Film or Video Production Tax Credit / Film Council / The Film Consortium, 2001, UK / Canada. Main Cast: Samuel L. Jackson (Elmo McElroy), Emily Mortimer (Dakota Parker), Meat Loaf (The Lizard), Robert Carlyle (Felix DeSouza).

400 Blows, The (*Les Quatre Cents Coups*). Dir. François Truffaut, Prod. None credited, Prod. Co. Les Films du Carrosse / Sédif Productions, 1959, France. Main Cast: Jean-Pierre Léaud (Antoine Doinel), Claire Maurier (Gilberte Doinel-le mere d'Antoine), Albert Rémy (Julien Doinel), Guy Decomble ("Petite Feuille," the French teacher).

Frankenstein. Dir. James Whale, Prod. Carl Laemmle, Jr. / E. M. Asher, Prod. Co. Universal Pictures, 1931, USA. Main Cast: Colin Clive (Henry Frankenstein), Mae Clark (Elizabeth), John Boles (Victor Moritz), ? [Boris Karloff] (The Monster).

Frankenstein. Dir. Marcus Nispel, Prod. Marcus Nispel, Prod. Co. Flame TV / Flame Ventures / L. I. F. T. Production / USA Cable Network, 2004, USA. Main Cast: Parker Posey (Detective Carson O'Conner), Vincent Perez (Deucalion), Thomas Kretschmann (Victor Helios), Adam Goldberg (Detective Michael Sloane).

Freddy vs. Jason. Dir. Ronny Yu, Prod. Sean S. Cunningham, Prod. Co. New Line Cinema / Cecchi Gori Group Tiger Cinematografica / Avery Pix / Sean S. Cunningham Films / WTC Productions / Yannix Technology Corporation, 2003, Canada / USA / Italy. Main Cast: Robert Englund (Freddy Krueger), Ken Kirzinger (Jason), Monica Keena (Lori Campbell), Jason Ritter (Will Rollins).

Freddy's Dead: The Final Nightmare. Dir. Rachel Talalay, Prod. Robert Shaye / Aron Warner, Prod. Co. New Line Cinema / Nicolas Entertainment, 1991, USA. Main Cast: Robert Englund (Freddy Krueger), Lisa Zane (Maggie Burroughs), Shon Greenblatt (John Doe), Lezlie Deane (Tracy).

Friday the 13th. Dir. Sean S. Cunningham, Prod. Sean S. Cunningham, Prod. Co. Paramount Pictures / Georgetown Productions Inc. / Sean S. Cunningham Films, 1980, USA. Main

Cast: Betsy Palmer (Mrs. Pamela Voorhees), Adrienne King (Alice Hardy), Jeannine Taylor (Marcie Cunningham), Robbie Morgan (Annie).

Friday the 13th. Dir. Marcus Nispel, Prod. Michael Bay / Sean S. Cunningham / Andrew Form / Brad Fuller, Prod. Co. New Line Cinema / Paramount Pictures / Platinum Dunes / Crystal Lake Entertainment, 2009, USA. Main Cast: Jared Padalecki (Clay Miller), Danielle Panabaker (Jenna), Amanda Righetti (Whitney Miller), Travis Van Winkle (Trent).

Friday the 13th Part 2. Dir. Steve Miner, Prod. Steve Miner, Prod. Co. Georgetown Productions Inc., 1981, USA. Main Cast: Amy Steel (Ginny Field), John Furey (Paul Holt), Adrienne King (Alice Hary), Kirsten Baker (Terry).

Friday the 13th Part III. Dir. Steve Miner, Prod. Frank Mancuso Jr., Prod. Co. Paramount Pictures / Georgetown Productions Inc. / Jason Productions, 1982, USA. Main Cast: Dana Kimmell (Chris Higgins), Paul Kratka (Rick), Tracie Savage (Debbie), Jeffrey Rogers (Andy).

Friday the 13th Part III 3-D. Dir. Steve Miner, Prod. Frank Mancuso Jr., Prod. Co. Paramount Pictures / Georgetown Productions Inc. / Jason Productions, 1982, USA. Main Cast: Dana Kimmell (Chris Higgins), Paul Kratka (Rick), Tracie Savage (Debbie), Jeffrey Rogers (Andy).

Friday the 13th: The Final Chapter. Dir. Joseph Zito, Prod. Frank Mancuso Jr., Prod. Co. Paramount Pictures, Georgetown Productions Inc., 1984, USA. Main Cast: Kimberly Beck (Trish Jarvis), Peter Barton (Doug), Corey Feldman (Tommy Jarvis), E. Erich Anderson (Rob Dyer).

Friday the 13th Part V: A New Beginning. Dir. Danny Steinmann, Prod. Timothy Silver, Prod. Co. Georgetown Productions Inc. / Paramount Pictures / Terror Inc., 1985, USA. Main Cast: Melanie Kinnaman (Pam Roberts), John Shepard (Tommy Jarvis), Shavar Ross (Reggie), Richard Young (Matthew Letter).

Friday the 13th Part VII: The New Blood. Dir. John Carl Buechler, Prod. Iain Paterson, Prod. Co. Friday Four Films / Paramount Pictures, 1988, USA. Main Cast: Lar Park-Lincoln (Tina Shepard), Terry Kiser (Dr. Crews), Kane Hodder (Jason Voorhees), Susan Blu (Mrs. Amanda Shepard).

Friday The 13th Part VIII: Jason Takes Manhattan. Dir. Rob Hedden, Prod. Randolph Cheveldave, Prod. Co. Paramount Pictures / Horror Inc., 1989, USA. Main Cast: Kane Hodder (Jason Voorhees), Jensen Daggett (Rennie Wickham), Peter Mark Richman (Charles McCulloch), Scott Reeves (Sean Robertson).

Frighteners, The. Dir. Peter Jackson, Prod. Peter Jackson / Jamie Selkirk / Tim Sanders, Prod. Co., Universal Pictures / WingNut Films, 1996, New Zealand / USA. Main Cast: Michael J. Fox (Frank Bannister), Trini Alvarado (Dr. Lucy Lynskey), Peter Dobson (Ray Lynskey), John Astin (The Judge).

Gate, The. Dir. Tibor Takács, Prod. John Kemeny, Prod. Co. New Century Entertainment Corporation / The Vista Organization Ltd. / Alliance Entertainment / Gate Productions, 1986, Canada / USA. Main Cast: Stephen Dorff (Glen), Christa Denton (Al), Louis Tripp (Terry Chandler), Kelly Rowan (Lori Lee).

Girl Who Knew Too Much, The (*La Ragazza Che Sapeva Troppo*). Dir. Mario Bava, Prod. Massimo De Rita, Prod. Co. Galatea Film / Coronet S. R. L., 1963, Italy. Main Cast: Letícia Román (Nora Davis), John Saxon (Dr. Marcello Bassi), Valentina Cortese (Laura Craven-Torrani), Titti Tomaino (Inspector).

Godfather, The. Dir. Francis Ford Coppola, Prod. Albert S. Ruddy, Prod. Co. Paramount Pictures / Alfran Productions, Inc., 1972, USA. Main Cast: Marlon Brando (Don Vito Corleone), Al Pacino (Michael Corleone), James Caan (Sonny Corleone), Robert Duvall (Tom Hagen).

Godfather Part II, The. Dir. Francis Ford Coppola, Prod. Francis Ford Coppola / Gray Frederickson / Fred Roos, Prod. Co. Paramount Pictures / A Coppola Company

Production, 1974, USA. Main Cast: Al Pacino (Michael), Robert Duvall (Tom Hagen), Diane Keaton (Kay), Robert De Niro (Vito Corleone).

Godfather Part III, The. Dir. Francis Ford Coppola, Prod. Francis Ford Coppola / Gray Frederickson / Charles Mulvehill / Fred Roos, Prod. Co. Paramount Pictures / Zoetrope Studios, 1990, USA. Main Cast: Al Pacino (Don Michael Corleone), Diane Keaton (Kay Adams Michelson), Talia Shire (Connie Corleone Rizzi), Andy Garcia (Vincent Mancini).

Goodfellas. Dir. Martin Scorsese, Prod. Irwin Winkler, Prod. Co. Irwin Winkler Production / Warner Bros. Pictures, 1990, USA. Main Cast: Robert De Niro (James Conway), Ray Liotta (Henry Hill), Joe Pesci (Tommy DeVito), Lorraine Bracco (Karen Hill).

Grandma's Reading Glass. Dir. George Albert Smith, Prod. George Albert Smith, Prod. Co. G. A. S. Films, 1900, UK. Main Cast: Harold Smith (Willy, the little grandson).

Gremlins. Dir. Joe Dante, Prod. Michael Finnell, Prod. Co. A Warner Communications Company / Amblin Entertainment, 1984, USA. Main Cast: Hoyt Axton (Randall Peltzer), Zach Galligan (Billy Peltzer), Phoebe Cates (Kate Beringer), Corey Feldman (Pete Fountaine).

Halloween. Dir. John Carpenter, Prod. Debra Hill, Prod. Co. Compass International Pictures / Falcon International Pictures, 1978, USA. Main Cast: Donald Pleasance (Dr. Sam Loomis), Jaime Lee Curtis (Laurie Strode), Nancy Loomis (Annie Brackett), P. J. Soles (Lynda van der Klok). With reference to the twenty-fifth anniversary edition: Divimax, Troy, MI: Anchor Bay, 2003,

Halloween. Dir. Rob Zombie, Prod. Malek Akkad / Andy Gould / Rob Zombie, Prod. Co. Dimension Films / Nightfall Productions / Spectacle Entertainment Group / Trancas International Films / The Weinstein Company, 2007, USA. Main Cast: Malcolm McDowell (Dr. Samuel Loomis), Scout Taylor-Compton (Laurie Strode), Tyler Mane (Michael Myers), Daeg Faerch (Michael Myers, age 10).

Halloween: The Curse of Michael Myers. Dir. Joe Chappelle, Prod. Paul Freeman, Prod. Co. Halloween VI Productions / Miramax Films / Nightfall, 1995, USA. Main Cast: Donald Pleasance (Dr. Sam Loomis), Paul Stephen Rudd (Tommy Doyle), Marianne Hagan (Kara Strode), Mitchell Ryan (Dr. Terence Wynn).

Halloween: Resurrection. Dir. Rick Rosenthal, Prod. Paul Freeman / Michael Leahy, Prod. Co. Dimension Films / Nightfall Productions / Trancas International Films, 2002, USA. Main Cast: Jamie Lee Curtis (Laurie Strode), Brad Loree (Michael Myers), Busta Rhymes (Freddie Harris), Bianca Kajlich (Sarah Moyer).

Halloween H20. Dir. Steve Miner, Prod. Paul Freeman, Prod. Co. Dimension Films / Nightfall Productions, 1998, USA. Main Cast: Jamie Lee Curtis (Laurie Strode/Keri Tate), Josh Hartnett (John Tate), Adam Arkin (Will Brennan), Michelle Williams (Molly Cartwell).

Halloween II. Dir. Rick Rosenthal, Prod. John Carpenter / Debra Hill, Prod. Co. DeLaurentiis / Universal Pictures, 1981, USA. Main Cast: Jamie Lee Curtis (Laurie Strode), Donald Pleasance (Sam Loomis), Charles Cyphers (Leigh Brackett), Jeffrey Kramer (Graham).

Halloween II. Dir. Rob Zombie, Prod. Malek Akkad / Andy Gould / Rob Zombie, Prod. Co. Dimension Films / Spectacle Entertainment Group / Trancas International Films, 2009, USA. Main Cast: Sheri Moon Zombie (Deborah Myers), Chase Vanek (Young Michael), Scout Taylor-Compton (Laurie Strode), Brad Dourif (Sheriff Lee Brackett).

Halloween 4: The Return of Michael Myers. Dir. Dwight H. Little, Prod. Paul Freeman, Prod. Co. Trancas International Films, 1988, USA. Main Cast: Donald Pleasance (Dr. Sam Loomis), Ellie Cornell (Rachel Carruthers), Danielle Harris (Jamie Lloyd), George P. Wilbur (Michael Myers).

Halloween 5: The Revenge of Michael Myers. Dir. Dominique Othenin-Girard, Prod. Ramsey Thomas, Prod. Co. Magnum Pictures Inc. / The Return of Myers / Trancas International

Films, 1989, USA. Main Cast: Donald Pleasance (Dr. Sam Loomis), Danielle Harris (Jamie Lloyd), Ellie Cornell (Rachel Carruthers), Beau Starr (Sheriff Ben Meeker).

Happy Birthday to Me. Dir. J. Lee Thompson, Prod. John Dunning / Andre Link, Prod. Co. Canadian Film Development Corporation / Columbia Pictures Corporation / Famous Players / The Birthday Film Company, 1981, Canada. Main Cast: Melissa Sue Anderson (Virginia Wainwright), Glenn Ford (Dr. David Faraday), Lawrence Dane (Hal Wainwright), Sharon Acker (Estelle Wainwright).

Harry Potter and the Philosopher's Stone. Dir. Chris Columbus, Prod. David Heyman / Tanya Seghatchian, Prod. Co. Warner Bros. / Heyday Films / 1492 Pictures, 2001, UK / USA. Main Cast: Daniel Radcliffe (Harry Potter), Emma Watson (Hermione Granger), Rupert Grint (Ron Weasley), Richard Harris (Professor Albus Dumbledore).

Heavenly Creatures. Dir. Peter Jackson, Prod. Jim Booth / Peter Jackson, Prod. Co. WingNut Films / Fontana Productions / New Zealand Film Commission, 1994, New Zealand / Germany. Main Cast: Melanie Lynskey (Pauline Parker), Kate Winslet (Juliet Hulme), Sarah Peirse (Honora Parker Rieper), Diana Kent (Hilda Hulme).

Hell Night. Dir. Tom DeSimone, Prod. Bruce Cohn Curtis / Mark L. Rosen / Irwin Yablans, Prod. Co. B. L. T. Productions / Media Home Entertainment, 1981, USA. Main Cast: Linda Blair (Marti Gaines), Vincent Van Patten (Seth), Peter Barton (Jeff Reed), Kevin Brophy (Peter Bennett).

Henry: Portrait of a Serial Killer. Dir. John McNaughton, Prod. Lisa Dedmond / Steven A. Jones / John McNaughton, Prod. Co. Maljack Productions, 1986, USA. Main Cast: Michael Rooker (Henry), Tom Towles (Otis), Tracy Arnold (Becky), David Katz (Henry's Boss).

Hills Have Eyes, The. Dir. Wes Craven, Prod. Peter Locke, Prod. Co. Blood Relations Co., 1977, USA. Main Cast: John Steadman (Fred), Janus Blythe (Ruby), Arthur King (Mercury), Russ Grieve (Big Bob Carter).

Hills Have Eyes, The. Dir. Alexandre Aja, Prod. Wes Craven / Peter Locke / Marianne Maddalena, Prod. Co. Craven-Maddalena Films / Dune Entertainment / Major Studio Partners, 2006, USA. Main Cast: Aaron Stanford (Doug Bukowski), Kathleen Quinlan (Ethel Carter), Vinessa Shaw (Lynn Carter), Emilie de Ravin (Brenda Carter).

Hills Have Eyes II, The. Dir. Martin Weisz, Prod. Wes Craven / Samy Layani / Peter Locke / Marianne Maddalena, Prod. Co. Fox Atomic / Craven-Maddalena Films / Dune Entertainment, 2007, USA. Main Cast: Michael McMillian (Napoleon), Jessica Stroup (Amber), Jacob Vargas (Crank), Flex Alexander (Sarge).

Hitcher, The. Dir. Dave Meyers, Prod. Michael Bay / Andrew Form / Brad Fuller / Alfred Haber / Charles Meeker, Prod. Co. Focus Features / Intrepid Pictures / Platinum Dunes, 2007, USA. Main Cast: Sean Bean (John Ryder), Sophia Bush (Grace Andrews), Zachary Knighton (Jim Halsey), Neal McDonough (Lt. Esteridge).

House. Dir. Steve Miner, Prod. Sean S. Cunningham, Prod. Co. New World Pictures, 1986, USA. Main Cast: William Katt (Roger Cobb), George Wendt (Harold Gorton), Richard Moll (Big Ben), Kay Lenz (Sandy Sinclair).

House of Wax. Dir. André DeToth, Prod. Bryan Foy, Prod. Co. Bryan Foy Pictures / Warner Bros. Pictures, 1953, USA. Main Cast: Vincent Price (Prof. Henry Jarrod), Frank Lovejoy (Lt. Tom Brennan), Phyllis Kirk (Sue Allen), Carolyn Jones (Cathy Gray).

House of Wax. Dir. Jaume Collet-Serra, Prod. Susan Levin / Richard Mirisch / Joel Silver / Robert Zemeckis, Prod. Co. Warner Bros / Village Roadshow Pictures / Dark Castle Entertainment, 2005, Australia / USA. Main Cast: Elisha Cuthbert (Carly Jones), Chad Michael Murray (Nick Jones), Brian Van Holt (Bo / Vincent), Paris Hilton (Paige Edwards).

Hurt Locker, The. Dir. Kathryn Bigelow, Prod. Kathryn Bigelow / Mark Boal / Nicholas Chartier / Donall McCusker / Greg Shapiro, Prod. Co. Voltage Pictures / Grosvenor Park Media / F.C.E.F. S.A. / First Light Production / Kingsgate Films / Summit Entertainment, 2008, USA. Main Cast: Jeremy Renner (Staff Sergeant William James), Anthony Mackie (Sergeant JT Sanborn), Brian Geraghty (Specialist Owen Eldridge), Guy Pearce (Sergeant Matt Thompson).

I Know What You Did Last Summer. Dir. Jim Gillespie, Prod. Stokely Chaffin / Erik Feig / Neal H. Moritz, Prod. Co. Columbia Pictures / Mandalay Entertainment / Summer Knowledge LLC, 1997, USA. Main Cast: Jennifer Love Hewitt (Julie James), Freddie Prinze Jr. (Ray Bronson), Sarah Michelle Gellar (Helen Shivers), Ryan Phillippe (Barry William Cox).

I Still Know What You Did Last Summer. Dir. Danny Cannon, Prod. William S. Beasley / Stokely Chaffin / Erik Feig / Neal H. Moritz, Prod. Co. Mandalay Entertainment / Summer Knowledge LLC, 1998, USA. Main Cast: Jennifer Love Hewitt (Julie James), Freddie Prinze Jr. (Ray Bronson), Brandy (Karla Wilson), Mekhi Phifer (Tyrell).

Invisible Man, The. Dir. James Whale, Prod. Carl Laemmle Jr., Prod. Co. Universal Pictures, 1933, USA. Main Cast: Claude Rains (The Invisible Man), Gloria Stuart (Flora Cranley), William Harrigan (Dr. Arthur Kemp), Henry Travers (Dr. Cranley).

Jason Goes to Hell: The Final Friday. Dir. Adam Marcus, Prod. Sean S. Cunningham, Prod. Co. New Line Cinema / Sean S. Cunningham Films, 1993, USA. Main Cast: John D. LeMay (Steven Freeman), Kari Keegan (Jessica Kimble), Kane Hodder (Jason Voorhees), Steven Williams (Creighton Duke).

Jason Lives! Friday the 13th Part VI. Dir. Tom McLoughlin, Prod. Don Behrns, Prod. Co. Paramount Pictures / Terror Films Inc., 1986, USA. Main Cast: Thom Mathews (Tommy Jarvis), Jennifer Cooke (Megan Garris), David Kagen (Sheriff Michael Garris), Renee Jones (Sissy Baker).

Jason X. Dir. James Isaac, Prod. Noel Cunningham, Prod. Co. Crystal Lake Entertainment / Friday X Productions / New Line Cinema, 2002, USA. Main Cast: Kane Hodder (Jason Voorhees/Uber-Jason), Lexa Doig (Rowan), Jonathan Potts (Professor Lowe), Lisa Ryder (Kay-Em 14). With reference to the New Line Platinum DVD release: Los Angeles, 2004.

Jaws. Dir. Steven Spielberg, Prod. David Brown / Richard D. Zanuck, Prod. Co. Zanuck/Brown, 1975, USA. Main Cast: Roy Scheider (Brody), Robert Shaw (Quint), Richard Dreyfuss (Hooper), Lorraine Gray (Ellen Brody).

Jigsaw. Dirs. Michael Spierig / Peter Spierig, Prod. Mark Burg / Kym Crepin / Gregg Hoffman / Ketura Kestin / Oren Koules, Prod. Co. Serendipity Productions / Twisted Pictures / A Bigger Boat, 2017, USA / Canada. Main Cast: Matt Passmore (Logan Nelson), Tobin Bell (Jigsaw / John Kramer), Callum Keith Rennie (Detective Halloran), Hannah Emily Anderson (Eleanor Bonneville), Clé Bennett (Detective Keith Hunt).

Joy Ride. Dir. John Dahl, Prod. J. J. Abrams / Chris Moore, Prod. Co. Regency Enterprises / Epsilon Motion Pictures / New Regency Pictures / Bad Robot / LivePlanet, 2001, USA. Main Cast: Steve Zahn (Fuller Thomas), Paul Walker (Lewis Thomas), Leelee Sobieski (Venna), Jessica Bowman (Charlotte).

Lady in the Lake. Dir. Robert Montgomery, Prod. George Haight, Prod. Co. Metro-Goldwyn-Mayer, 1947, USA. Main Cast: Robert Montgomery (Phillip Marlowe), Audrey Totter (Adrienne Fromsett), Lloyd Nolan (Lt. DeGarmot), Tom Tully (Capt. Kane).

Last House on the Left, The. Dir. Wes Craven, Prod. Sean S. Cunningham / Katherine D'Amato, Prod. Co. Lobster Enterprises / Sean S. Cunningham Films / The Night Co., 1972, USA. Main Cast: Sandra Cassell (Mari Collingwood), Lucy Grantham (Phyllis Stone), David A. Hess (Krug Stillo), Fred Lincoln (Fred "Weasel" Podowski).

Last Laugh, The (Der Letzte Mann). Dir. F. W. Murnau, Prod. Erich Pommer, Prod. Co. Universum Film, 1924, Germany. Main Cast: Emil Jannings (Hotel Porter), Maly Delschaft (His Niece), Max Hiller (Her Bridegroom), Emilie Kurz (Bridegroom's Aunt).

Leprechaun. Dir. Mark Jones, Prod. Jeffrey B. Mallian, Prod. Co. Trimark Pictures, 1993, USA. Main Cast: Warwick Davis (Leprechaun), Jennifer Aniston (Tori Reding), Ken Olandt (Nathan Murphy), Mark Holton (Ozzie).

Lord of the Rings, The: The Fellowship of the Ring. Dir. Peter Jackson, Prod. Peter Jackson / Barrie M. Osborne / Tim Sanders / Fran Walsh / Rick Porras / Jamie Selkirk, Prod. Co. New Line Cinema / WingNut Films / The Saul Zaentz Company, 2001, New Zealand / USA. Main Cast: Elijah Wood (Frodo), Ian McKellan (Gandalf), Sean Astin (Sam), Viggo Mortensen (Aragorn).

Lord of the Rings, The: The Return of the King. Dir. Peter Jackson, Prod. Peter Jackson / Barrie M. Osborne / Fran Walsh / Rick Porras / Jamie Selkirk, Prod. Co. New Line Cinema / WingNut Films / The Saul Zaentz Company, 2003, New Zealand / USA. Main Cast: Elijah Wood (Frodo), Ian McKellan (Gandalf), Sean Astin (Sam), Viggo Mortensen (Aragorn).

Lord of the Rings, The: The Two Towers. Dir. Peter Jackson, Prod. Peter Jackson / Barrie M. Osborne / Fran Walsh / Rick Porras / Jamie Selkirk, Prod. Co. New Line Cinema / WingNut Films / The Saul Zaentz Company, 2002, New Zealand / USA. Main Cast: Elijah Wood (Frodo), Ian McKellan (Gandalf), Sean Astin (Sam), Viggo Mortensen (Aragorn).

Mad Love (The Hands of Orlac). Dir. Karl Freund, Prod. John W. Considine Jr., Prod. Co. Metro-Goldwyn-Mayer, 1935, USA. Main Cast: Peter Lorre (Doctor Gogol), Frances Drake (Yvonne Orlac), Colin Clive (Stephen Orlac), Ted Healy (Reagan, the American Reporter).

Maniac. Dir. William Lustig, Prod. Andrew Garroni / William Lustig, Prod. Co. Magnum Motion Pictures Inc., 1980, USA. Main Cast: Joe Spinell (Frank Zito), Caroline Munro (Anna D'Antoni), Gail Lawrence (Rita), Kelly Piper (Nurse).

Maniac Cop 3: Badge of Silence. Dir. William Lustig, Prod. Michael Leahy / Joel Soisson, Prod. Co. NEO Motion Pictures / First Look Pictures / Overseas FilmGroup, 1993, USA. Main Cast: Robert Davi (Det. Sean McKinney), Robert Z'Dar (Matt Cordell), Caitlin Dulany (Dr. Susan Fowler), Gretchen Becker (Katie Sullivan).

Meet the Feebles. Dir. Peter Jackson, Prod. Jim Booth / Peter Jackson, Prod. Co. WingNut Films, 1989, New Zealand. Main Cast: Danny Mulheron (Heidi the Hippo), Donna Akersten (Samantha the Cat / The Sheep), Stuart Devenie (Sebastian / Dr. Quack / Daisy the Cow / Sandy the Chicken), Mark Hadlow (Heidi / Robert / Barry the Bulldog).

Minority Report. Dir. Steven Spielberg, Prod. Jan De Bont / Bonnie Curtis / Gerald R. Molen / Walter F. Parkes, Prod. Co., Twentieth Century Fox / DreamWorks Pictures / Cruise/Wagner / Blue Tulip Productions / Ronald Shusett / Gary Goldman, 2002, USA. Main Cast: Tom Cruise (Chief John Anderton), Max von Sydow (Director Lamar Burgess), Steve Harris (Jad), Neal McDonough (Fletcher).

Munich. Dir. Steven Spielberg, Prod. Kathleen Kennedy / Barry Mendel / Steven Spielberg / Colin Wilson, Prod. Co. DreamWorks SKG / Universal Pictures / Amblin Entertainment / The Kennedy/Marshall Company / Barry Mendel Productions / Alliance Atlantis Communications / Peninsula Films, 2006, USA / Canada / France. Main Cast: Eric Bana (Avner), Daniel Craig (Steve), Ciarán Hinds (Carl), Mathieu Kassovitz (Robert).

My Bloody Valentine. Dir. George Mihalka, Prod. John Dunning / Andre Link / Stephen Miller, Prod. Co. Canadian Film Development Corporation / Famous Players / Paramount Pictures / Secret Films, 1981, Canada. Main Cast: Paul Kelman (T. J. Hanniger), Lori Hallier (Sarah), Neil Affleck (Axel Palmer), Keith Knight (Hollis).

My Bloody Valentine 3-D. Dir. Patrick Lussier, Prod. Jack L. Murray, Prod. Co. Lionsgate, 2009, USA. Main Cast: Jensen Ackles (Tom Hanniger), Jaime King (Sarah Palmer), Kerr Smith (Axel Palmer), Betsy Rue (Irene).

Nightmare on Elm Street, A. Dir. Wes Craven, Prod. Robert Shaye, Prod. Co. New Line Cinema / Media Home Entertainment / Smart Egg Pictures / The Elm Street Venture, 1984, USA. Main Cast: John Saxon (Lt. Donald Thompson), Ronee Blakley (Marge Thompson), Heather Langenkamp (Nancy Thompson), Amanda Wyss (Tina Gray).

Nightmare on Elm Street, A. Dir. Samuel Bayer, Prod. Michael Bay / Andrew Form / Bradley Fuller, Prod. Co. New Line Cinema / Platinum Dunes, 2010, USA. Main Cast: Jackie Earle Haley (Freddy Krueger), Kyle Gallner (Quentin Smith), Rooney Mara (Nancy Holbrook), Katie Cassidy (Kris Fowles).

Nightmare on Elm Street Part 2, A: Freddy's Revenge. Dir. Jack Sholder, Prod. Robert Shaye, Prod. Co. New Line Cinema / Heron Communications / Smart Egg Pictures / Second Elm Street Venture, 1985, USA. Main Cast: Mark Patton (Jesse Walsh), Kim Myers (Lisa Webber), Robert Rusler (Ron Grady), Clu Gulager (Ken Walsh).

Nightmare on Elm Street Part 4, A: The Dream Master. Dir. Renny Harlin, Prod. Robert Shaye / Rachel Talalay, Prod. Co. New Line Cinema / Heron Communications / Smart Egg Pictures, 1988, USA. Main Cast: Lisa Wilcox (Alice Johnson), Andras Jones (Rick Johnson), Danny Hassel (Dan Jordan), Rodney Eastman (Joey Crusel).

Nightmare on Elm Street Part 5, A: The Dream Child. Dir. Stephen Hopkins, Prod. Rupert Harvey / Robert Shaye, Prod. Co. New Line Cinema / Heron Communications / Smart Egg Pictures / The Fourth New Line-Heron Joint Venture, 1989, USA. Main Cast: Robert Englund (Freddy Krueger/Featured Maniac), Lisa Wilcox (Alice Johnson), Kelly Jo Minter (Yvonne), Danny Hassel (Dan Jordan).

North by Northwest. Dir. Alfred Hitchcock, Prod. None credited, Prod. Co. Metro-Goldwyn-Mayer, 1959, USA. Main Cast: Cary Grant (Roger O. Thornhill), Eva Marie Saint (Eve Kendall), James Mason (Phillip Vandamm), Jessie Royce Landis (Clara Thornhill).

Nosferatu (*Nosferatu, Eine Symphonie des Grauens*). Dir. F. W. Murnau, Prod. Enrico Dieckmann / Albin Grau, Prod. Co. Jofa-Atelier Berlin-Johannisthal / Prana-Film GmbH, 1922, Germany. Main Cast: Max Schreck (Graf Orlok/Nosferatu), Gustav v. Wagenheim (Hutter), Greta Schroeder (Ellen Hutter), Alexander Granach (Knock).

Notorious. Dir. Alfred Hitchcock, Prod. None credited, Prod. Co. RKO Radio Pictures, 1946, USA. Main Cast: Cary Grant (Devlin), Ingrid Bergman (Alicia Huberman), Claude Rains (Alexander Sebastian), Louis Calhern (Paul Prescott).

Opera. Dir. Dario Argento, Prod. Dario Argento, Prod. Co. ADC Films, Cecchi Gori Group Tiger Cinematografica, 1987, Italy. Main Cast: Cristina Marsillach (Betty), Ian Charleson (Marco), Urbano Barberini (Inspector Alan Santini), Daria Nicolodi (Mira).

Peeping Tom. Dir. Michael Powell, Prod. None credited, Prod. Co. Michael Powell (Theatre), 1960, UK. Main Cast: Carl Boehm (Mark Lewis), Moira Shearer (Vivian), Anna Massey (Helen Stephens), Maxine Audley (Mrs. Stephens).

Pieces (*Mil Gritos Tiene La Noche*). Dir. Juan Piquer Simón, Prod. Dick Randall, Prod. Co. Almena Films / Film Ventures International / Fort Films / Montoro Productions Ltd., 1982, Spain / USA / Puerto Rico. Main Cast: Christopher George (Lt. Bracken), Linda Day (Mary Riggs), Frank Braña (Sgt. Holden), Edmund Purdom (The Dean).

Platoon. Dir. Oliver Stone, Prod. Arnold Kopelson / A. Kitman Ho, Prod. Co. Hemdale, 1986, UK / USA. Main Cast: Charlie Sheen (Chris), Tom Berenger (Sgt. Barnes), Willem Dafoe (Sgt. Elias), Kevin Dillon (Bunny).

Poltergeist. Dir. Tobe Hooper, Prod. Frank Marshall / Steven Spielberg, Prod. Co. Metro-Goldwyn-Mayer / SLM Production Group, 1982, USA. Main Cast: Craig T. Nelson (Steve Freeling), JoBeth Williams (Diane Freeling), Beatrice Straight (Dr. Lesh), Dominique Dunne (Dana Freeling).

Poltergeist II: The Other Side. Dir. Brian Gibson, Prod. Michael Grais / Mark Victor, Prod. Co. Metro-Goldwyn-Mayer, 1986, USA. Main Cast: JoBeth Williams (Diane Freeling), Craig T. Nelson (Steve Freeling), Heather O'Rourke (Carol Anne Freeling), Oliver Robbins (Robbie Freeling).

Prom Night. Dir. Paul Lynch, Prod. Peter Simpson, Prod. Co. Quadrant Trust Company / Simcom Limited, 1980, Canada. Main Cast: Leslie Nielsen (Mr. Hammond), Jamie Lee Curtis (Kim), Casey Stevens (Nick), Eddie Benton (Wendy).

Prom Night. Dir. Nelson McCormick, Prod. Toby Jaffe / Neal H. Moritz, Prod. Co. Alliance Films / Newmarket Films / Original Film, 2008, USA / Canada. Main Cast: Brittany Snow (Donna Keppel), Scott Porter (Bobby), Jessica Stroup (Claire), Dana Davis (Lisa Hines).

Psycho. Dir. Alfred Hitchcock, Prod. None credited, Prod. Co. Shamley Productions, 1960, USA. Main Cast: Anthony Perkins (Norman Bates), Vera Miles (Lila Crane), John Gavin (Sam Loomis), Janet Leigh (Marion Crane).

Psycho. Dir. Gus Van Sant, Prod. Brian Grazer / Gus Van Sant, Prod. Co. Universal Pictures / Imagine Entertainment, 1998, USA. Main Cast: Vince Vaughn (Norman Bates), Julianne Moore (Lila Crane), Viggo Mortensen (Samuel Loomis), Anne Heche (Marion Crane).

Psycho III. Dir. Anthony Perkins, Prod. Hilton A. Green, Prod. Co. Universal Pictures, 1986, USA. Main Cast: Anthony Perkins (Norman Bates), Diana Scarwid (Maureen Coyle), Jeff Fahey (Duane Duke), Roberta Maxwell (Tracy Venable).

Pulp Fiction. Dir. Quentin Tarantino, Prod. Lawrence Bender, Prod. Co. A Band Apart / Jersey Films / Miramax Films, 1994, USA. Main Cast: John Travolta (Vincent Vega), Samuel L. Jackson (Jules Winnfield), Tim Roth (Pumpkin/Ringo), Amanda Plummer (Honey Bunny / Yolanda).

Quarantine. Dir. John Erick Dowdle, Prod. Sergio Agüero / Doug Davison / Roy Lee, Prod. Co. Andale Pictures / Screen Gems / Vertigo Entertainment, 2008, USA. Main Cast: Jennifer Carpenter (Angela Vidal), Steve Harris (Scott Percival), Jay Hernandez (Jake), Johnathon Schaech (George Fletcher).

Raging Bull. Dir. Martin Scorsese, Prod. Robert Chartoff / Irwin Winkler, United Artists / A Robert Chartoff-IrwinWinkler Production, 1980, USA. Main Cast: Robert De Niro (Jake La Motta), Cathy Moriarty (Vickie La Motta), Joe Pesci (Joey), Frank Vincent (Salvy).

Saving Private Ryan. Dir. Steven Spielberg, Prod. Ian Bryce / Mark Gordon / Gary Levinsohn / Steven Spielberg, Prod. Co. Amblin Entertainment / DreamWorks SKG / Mark Gordon Production / Mutual Film Company / Paramount Pictures, 1998, USA. Main Cast: Tom Hanks (Capt. John H. Miller), Tom Sizemore (Sgt. Mike Horvath), Edward Burns (Pvt. Richard Reiben), Barry Pepper (Pvt. Daniel Jackson).

Saw. Dir. James Wan, Prod. Mark Burg / Gregg Hoffman / Oren Koules, Prod. Co. Evolution Entertainment / Saw Productions Inc. / Twisted Pictures, 2004, USA / Australia. Main Cast: Leigh Whannell (Adam Faulkner-Stanheight), Cary Elwes (Dr. Lawrence Gordon), Danny Glover (Detective David Tapp), Ken Leung (Detective Steven Sing).

Saw II. Dir. Darren Lynn Bousman, Prod. Mark Burg / Gregg Hoffman / Oren Koules, Prod. Co. Twisted Pictures / Evolution Entertainment / Got Films / Lions Gate Films / Saw 2 Productions, 2005, USA / Canada. Main Cast: Tobin Bell (Jigsaw/John Kramer), Shawnee Smith (Amanda Young), Donnie Wahlberg (Eric Matthews), Erik Knudsen (Daniel Matthews).

Saw III. Dir. Darren Lynn Bousman, Prod. Mark Burg / Gregg Hoffman / Oren Koules, Prod. Co. Twisted Pictures / Evolution Entertainment / Saw 2 Productions, 2006, USA / Canada. Main Cast: Tobin Bell (Jigsaw/John), Shawnee Smith (Amanda), Angus Macfadyen (Jeff), Bahar Soomekh (Lynn).

Saw IV. Dir. Darren Lynn Bousman, Prod. Mark Burg / Gregg Hoffman / Oren Koules, Prod. Co. Twisted Pictures, 2007, USA / Canada. Main Cast: Tobin Bell (Jigsaw/John Kramer), Costas Mandylor (Lt. Mark Hoffman), Scott Patterson (Agent Peter Strahm), Betsy Russell (Jill Tuck).

Saw V. Dir. David Hackl, Prod. Mark Burg / Gregg Hoffman / Oren Koules, Prod. Co. Twisted Pictures, 2008, USA / Canada. Main Cast: Tobin Bell (Jigsaw/John), Costas Mandylor (Mark Hoffman), Scott Patterson (Agent Strahm), Betsy Russell (Jill).

Saw VI. Dir. Kevin Greutert, Prod. Mark Burg / Oren Koules, Prod. Co. Twisted Pictures / A Bigger Boat / Saw VI Productions, 2009, Canada / USA / UK / Australia. Main Cast: Tobin Bell (Jigsaw/John), Costas Mandylor (Mark Hoffman), Mark Rolston (Dan Erickson), Betsy Russell (Jill Tuck).

Saw 3-D. Dir. Kevin Greutert, Prod. Mark Burg / Oren Koules, Prod. Co. Twisted Pictures / A Bigger Boat / Serendipity Productions, 2010, Canada / USA. Main Cast: Tobin Bell (Jigsaw/John Kramer), Costas Mandylor (Det. Mark Hoffman), Betsy Russell (Jill Tuck), Cary Elwes (Dr. Lawrence Gordon).

Scream. Dir. Wes Craven, Prod. Cathy Konrad / Cary Woods, Prod. Co. Dimension Films / Woods Entertainment, 1996, USA. Main Cast: Drew Barrymore (Casey), Neve Campbell (Sidney), Skeet Ulrich (Billy), Courteney Cox (Gale Weathers).

Scream 2. Dir. Wes Craven, Prod. Cathy Konrad / Marianne Maddalena, Prod. Co. Dimension Films / Konrad Pictures / Craven-Maddalena Films / Maven Entertainment / Miramax Films, 1997, USA. Main Cast: Neve Campbell (Sidney Prescott), Liev Schreiber (Cotton Weary), Courteney Cox (Gale Weathers), David Arquette (Dewey Riley).

Scream 3. Dir. Wes Craven, Prod. Cathy Konrad / Marianne Maddalena / Kevin Williamson, Prod. Co. Dimension Films / Konrad Pictures / Craven-Maddalena Films, 2000, USA. Main Cast: Neve Campbell (Sidney Prescott), Courteney Cox Arquette (Gale Weathers), Parker Posey (Jennifer Jolie), Emily Mortimer (Angelina Tyler).

Scream 4. Dir. Wes Craven, Prod. Wes Craven / Iya Labunka / Kevin Williamson, Prod. Co. Dimension Films / Corvus Corax / Outerbanks Entertainment / The Weinstein Company, 2011, USA. Main Cast: Neve Campbell (Sidney Prescott), Courteney Cox (Gale Weathers-Riley), David Arquette (Dewey Riley), Emma Roberts (Jill Roberts).

Silence of the Lambs, The. Dir. Jonathan Demme, Prod. Ron Bozman / Edward Saxon / Kenneth Utt, Prod. Co. A Strong Heart/Demme Production / Orion Pictures, 1991, USA. Main Cast: Jodie Foster (Clarice Starling), Scott Glenn (Jack Crawford), Anthony Hopkins (Dr. Hannibal Lecter), Ted Levine (Jame Gumb).

Slumber Party Massacre, The. Dir. Amy Jones, Prod. Amy Jones, Prod. Co. New World Pictures, 1982, USA. Main Cast: Michele Michaels (Trish Devereaux), Robin Stille (Val Bates), Michael Villela (Russ Thorn), Debra Deliso (Kim Clarke).

Sorority House Massacre. Dir. Carol Frank, Prod. Ron Diamond, Prod. Co. Concorde Pictures, 1986, USA. Main Cast: Angela O'Neill (Beth), Wendy Martel (Linda), Pamela Ross (Sara), Nicole Rio (Tracy).

Stepfather, The. Dir. Joseph Ruben, Prod. Jay Benson, Prod. Co. ITC Productions, 1987, UK / USA. Main Cast: Terry O'Quinn (Jerry Blake), Jill Schoelen (Stephanie), Shelley Hack (Susan), Charles Lanyer (Dr. Bondurant).

Suspiria. Dir. Dario Argento, Prod. Claudio Argento, Prod. Co. Seda Spettacoli, 1977, Italy. Main Cast: Jessica Harper (Suzy Bannion), Stefania Casini (Sara), Flavio Bucci (Daniel), Miguel Bosé (Mark).

Tenebrae. Dir. Dario Argento, Prod. Claudio Argento, Prod. Co. Sigma Cinematografica Roma, 1982, Italy. Main Cast: Anthony Franciosa (Peter Neal), Christian Borromeo (Gianni), Mirella D'Angelo (Tilde), Veronica Lario (Jane McKerrow).

Terror Train. Dir. Roger Spottiswoode, Prod. Harold Greenberg, Prod. Co. Astral Bellevue Pathé / Sandy Howard Productions / Triple T Productions, 1980, Canada / USA. Main Cast: Ben Johnson (Carne), Jamie Lee Curtis (Alana Maxwell), Hart Bochner (Doc Manley), David Copperfield (Ken the Magician).

Texas Chain Saw Massacre, The. Dir. Tobe Hooper, Prod. Tobe Hooper, Prod. Co. Vortex, 1974, USA. Main Cast: Marilyn Burns (Sally Hardesty), Allen Danziger (Jerry), Paul A. Partain (Franklin Hardesty), William Vail (Kirk).

Texas Chainsaw Massacre, The. Dir. Marcus Nispel, Prod. Michael Bay / Mike Fleiss, Prod. Co. New Line Cinema / Focus Features / Radar Pictures / Platinum Dunes / Next Entertainment / Chainsaw Productions LLC, 2003, USA. Main Cast: Jessica Biel (Erin), Jonathan Tucker (Morgan), Erica Leerhsen (Pepper), Mike Vogel (Andy).

Texas Chainsaw Massacre, The: The Beginning. Dir. Jonathan Liebesman, Prod. Michael Bay / Mike Fleiss / Andrew Form / Brad Fuller / Kim Henkel / Tobe Hooper, Prod. Co. New Line Cinema / Platinum Dunes / Next Entertainment / Vortex/Henkel/Hooper / Texas Chainsaw Productions, 2006, USA. Main Cast: Jordana Brewster (Chrissie), Taylor Handley (Dean), Diora Baird (Bailey), Matt Bomer (Eric).

Texas Chainsaw Massacre 2, The. Dir. Tobe Hooper, Prod. Yoram Globus / Menahem Golan, Prod. Co. Cannon Films, 1986, USA. Main Cast: Dennis Hopper (Lieutenant "Lefty" Enright), Caroline Williams (Vanita "Stretch" Brock), Jim Siedow (Drayton Sawyer, the Cook), Bill Moseley ("Chop-Top" Sawyer).

Thing, The. Dir. John Carpenter, Prod. David Foster / Lawrence Turman, Prod. Co. Universal Pictures / Turman-Foster Company, 1982, USA. Main Cast: Kurt Russell (R. J. MacReady), A. Wilford Brimley (Dr. Blair), T. K. Carter (Nauls), David Clennon (Palmer).

Toolbox Murders, The. Dir. Dennis Donnelly, Prod. Tony DiDio, Prod. Co. Cal-Am Productions / Tony DiDio Productions, 1978, USA. Main Cast: Cameron Mitchell (Vance Kingsley), Pamelyn Ferdin (Laurie Ballard), Wesley Eure (Kent Kingsley), Nicolas Beauvy (Joey Ballard).

Trauma. Dir. Dario Argento, Prod. Dario Argento, Prod. Co. ADC Films / Overseas FilmGroup, 1993, Italy / USA. Main Cast: Christopher Rydell (David Parsons), Asia Argento (Aura Petrescu), Piper Laurie (Adriana Petrescu), Frederic Forrest (Dr. Judd).

Triumph of the Will (Triumph Des Willens). Dir. Leni Riefenstahl, Prod. Leni Riefenstahl, Prod. Co. Leni Riefenstahl-Produktion / NSDAP Reichspropagandaleitung Hauptabt. Film, 1935, Germany. Main Cast: Adolf Hitler (Himself).

Troll. Dir. John Carl Buechler, Prod. Albert Band, Prod. Co. Empire Pictures / Altar Productions, 1986, USA / Italy. Main Cast: Noah Hathaway (Harry Potter Jr.), Michael Moriarty (Harry Potter Sr.), Shelley Hack (Anne Potter), Jenny Beck (Wendy Anne Potter).

Twitch of the Death Nerve (A Bay of Blood) (Reazione a Catena). Dir. Mario Bava, Prod. Giuseppe Zaccariello, Prod Co. Nuova Linea Cinematografica, 1971, Italy. Main Cast: Claudine Auger (Renata), Luigi Pistilli (Albert), Claudio Volonté (Simon), Anna M. Rosati (Laura).

Urban Legend. Dir. Jamie Blanks, Prod. Gina Matthews / Michael McDonnell / Neal H. Moritz, Prod. Co. Canal+ Droits Audiovisuels / Original Film / Phoenix Pictures, 1998, USA /

France. Main Cast: Jared Leto (Paul Gardener), Alicia Witt (Natalie Simon), Rebecca Gayheart (Brenda Bates), Michael Rosenbaum (Parker Riley).

Urban Legends: Final Cut. Dir. John Ottman, Prod. Gina Matthews / Neal H. Moritz / Richard Luke Rothschild, Prod. Co. Original Film /Phoenix Pictures, 2000, USA. Main Cast: Jennifer Morrison (Amy Mayfield), Matthew Davis (Travis Stark/Trevor Stark), Hart Bochner (Professor Solomon), Loretta Devine (Reese Wilson).

Valentine. Dir. Jamie Blanks, Prod. Dylan Sellers, Prod. Co. Warner Bros. Pictures / Village Roadshow Pictures / NPV Entertainment / Cupid Productions, 2001, USA. Main Cast: Denise Richards (Paige Prescott), David Boreanaz (Adam Carr), Marley Shelton (Kate Davies), Jessica Capshaw (Dorothy Wheeler).

Vertigo. Dir. Alfred Hitchcock, Prod. None credited, Prod. Co. Paramount Pictures / Alfred J. Hitchcock Productions, 1958, USA. Main Cast: James Stewart (John "Scottie" Ferguson), Kim Novak (Madeleine Elster/Judy Barton), Barbara Bel Geddes (Midge Wood), Tom Helmore (Gavin Elster).

Wes Craven's New Nightmare. Dir. Wes Craven, Prod. Marianne Maddalena, Prod. Co. New Line Cinema, 1994, USA. Robert Englund (Himself/Freddy Krueger), Heather Langenkamp (Herself/ N ancy Thompson), Miko Hughes (Dylan Porter), David Newsom (Chase Porter).

When a Stranger Calls. Dir. Fred Walton, Prod. Doug Chapin / Steve Feke, Prod. Co. Columbia Pictures Corporation / Melvin Simon Productions, 1979, USA. Main Cast: Carol Kane (Jill Johnson), Rutanya Alda (Mrs. Mandrakis), Carmen Argenziano (Dr. Mandrakis), Kirsten Larkin (Mandy).

When a Stranger Calls Back, Dir. Fred Walton, Prod. Tom Rowe, Prod. Co. Krost/Chapin Productions / MTE Inc. / Pacific Motion Pictures / Privilege Productions / The Producers Entertainment Group Ltd., 1993, USA. Main Cast: Carol Kane (Jill Johnson), Charles Durning (John Clifford), Jill Schoelen (Julia Jenz), Gene Lythgow (William Landis).

Wolf Man, The. Dir. George Waggner, Prod. George Waggner, Prod. Co. Universal Pictures Company Inc., 1941, USA. Main Cast: Lon Chaney (The Wolf Man), Claude Rains (Sir. John Talbot), Ralph Bellamy (Col. Montford), Warren William (Dr. Lloyd).

Yankee Doodle Dandy. Dir. Michael Curtiz, Prod. William Cagney, Prod. Co. Warner Bros., 1942, USA. Main Cast: James Cagney (George M. Cohan), Joan Leslie (Mary), Walter Huston (Jerry Cohan), Richard Whorf (Sam Harris).

[Rec]. Dir. Jaume Balagueró / Paco Plaza, Prod. Julio Fernández, Prod. Co. Castelao Producciones / Filmax / Televisión Española (TVE) / Canal+ España / Instituto de la Cinematografía y de las Artes Audiovisuales (ICAA) / Instituto de Crédito Oficial (ICO) / ICF Institut Català de Finances / Generalitat de Catalunya - Institut Català de les Indústries Culturals (ICIC), 2007, Spain. Main Cast: Manuela Velasco (Ángela Vidal), Ferran Terraza (Manu), Jorge-Yamam Serrano (Policía Joven), Pablo Rosso (Pablo).

Index

Academy Awards (Academy of Motion Picture Arts and Sciences), 157–58, 161–65, 170, 176
American Film Institute, 170n20
Alien, 111
Aliens, 33
Altman, Rick, 121
American Sniper, 154
And Then There Were None, 20, 22, 47
As Seen Through a Telescope, 14, 20, 22
AVP: Alien vs. Predator, 40

Bad Taste, 163
Balázs, Béla, 93
Beetlejuice, 132
Belton, John, 86, 96
Berliner, Todd, 3, 86n2
Bird with the Crystal Plumage, The, 21, 37
Black Christmas (1974), 23, 24, 31, 34n18, 42, 46, 47
Black Christmas (2006), 41–42
Blair Witch Project, The, 24–26, 40, 58
Body Heat, 148
Booth, Stephen, 156n3
Bordwell, David, 74; and Kristin Thompson, x, 102
Box Office Mojo, 41n30
Bracke, Peter M., 31n13, 33n16, 40, 45, 53, 87, 88, 113n14, 123
Branigan, Edward, 8

Bride of Chucky, 74
Broadway Melody, The, 85
Budra, Paul, 122–23
Buechler, John Carl, 72–73, 182
Burning, The, 31, 39, 89n6, 147
Buscombe, Edward, 81

Candyman, 37
Cannibal Holocaust, 25, 58
Carrie, 33n17
Cherry, Brigid, 121n4
Chien Andalou, Un, 88n5
Chinatown, 148
Chion, Michel, 7, 84–86, 96
Cinemetrics, 164nn14a–b
Clair, René, 85
Clayton, Wickham, 33n15, 138, 142n14, 143, 156n4, 177
Clover, Carol J., 12, 27–28, 46–47, 156
Cloverfield, 25–26
Conrich, Ian, 35, 83–84, 120, 128–29
Crane, Jonathan Lake, 84
Critters, 33
Cunningham, Sean S., 30–31, 45–46, 48, 49, 50–51, 79, 88, 89n6, 94–95, 123–24

Dances with Wolves, 161
Dawn of the Dead, 31–32, 46, 89
Dead Alive, 163
Dead Poets Society, 161–62, 163n9

Index

Deep Red, 37, 89–90, 161, 177
De Palma, Brian, 19, 31
Die Hard, 132
Dika, Vera, 12n4, 28, 46, 48, 76, 81, 123, 125, 148–49, 156
Do You Like Hitchcock? (*Ti Piace Hitchcock?*), 31
Donnelly, K. J., 84–85, 87–88
Dracula, 19, 122
Dressed to Kill, 31
Dr. Jekyll and Mr. Hyde, 19

Ebert, Roger, 43
Edelstein, David, 43n32
Evil Dead, The, 34, 125
Evil Dead 2, 34, 125
Eyes of Laura Mars, 23–24, 28, 31, 34
Eyes Wide Shut, 6–8

Fade to Black, 77
Final Destination 5 3-D, 49n2
Fischer, Lucy, and Marcia Landy, 28
Fly, The, 33
Fly II, The, 132
formalism, x–xi, 5, 11, 28, 125, 152, 155, 156n4
Formula 51, 74
400 Blows, The (*Les Quatre Cents Coups*), 115
Frampton, Daniel, 9
Frankenstein (1931), 33, 122
Frankenstein (2004), 64
Freddy vs. Jason, 29, 30, 40, 73–76, 79, 80, 112–13, 128n8, 138–41, 149, 169, 184, 196
Freddy's Dead: The Final Nightmare, 35–36
Friday the 13th (1980), ix, 3, 10n3, 12n4, 28, 29, 30–32, 34, 45–51, 52, 65, 66, 67n11, 71, 76, 80n28, 81, 85, 87–97, 115–16, 121–22, 123–28, 129, 131, 135, 149, 150, 154, 155, 179, 185–86
Friday the 13th (1989 game), xii, 154
Friday the 13th (2009), 29, 42, 43, 62–64, 79, 107–8, 128n8, 138n12, 146–51, 170, 184, 197–98
Friday the 13th: The Final Chapter, 29–30, 32, 36, 52, 66–67, 70–71, 98–100, 103–4, 116–17, 128n8, 129–31, 132, 133, 135, 141, 142–43, 145–46, 148, 180–81, 188
Friday the 13th: The Game, xii, 61, 63, 154
Friday the 13th Part 2, 29, 30, 32, 51–52, 53–54, 65–66, 76–77, 80–81, 101, 125–28, 129–33, 148–49, 180, 186–87
Friday the 13th Part III, 29nn12, 36, 128n8
Friday the 13th Part III 3-D, 29, 32, 36, 53–56, 58, 66, 76–77, 99n10, 102–3, 128–30, 133, 141, 143, 180, 187–88
Friday the 13th Part V: A New Beginning, 30, 33, 67–68, 70–72, 78, 80, 113–17, 128n8, 142–46, 155, 157, 166, 181, 189–90
Friday the 13th Part VII: The New Blood, 30, 33–35, 36n23, 42, 72–73, 77–78, 80, 105–7, 117, 128n8, 131–33, 135, 138–39, 141, 157, 182, 191–92
Friday the 13th Part VIII: Jason Takes Manhattan, 30, 35, 36, 56–59, 77–78, 80, 109, 111, 117, 128n8, 133–35, 141, 161, 163, 173, 182, 192–93
Frighteners, The, 163
Fuchs, Michael, 38n26

Gate, The, 132
German expressionism, 9, 14–19
Girl Who Knew Too Much, The (*La Ragazza Che Sapeva Troppo*), 21, 31
Godfather, The, 165–66
Godfather Part II, The, 165–67
Godfather Part III, The, 165–67
Goodfellas, 162–63
Grace and Frankie, xi
Grandma's Reading Glass, 14
Grant, Barry Keith, 80–81
Gremlins, 142
Grove, David, 45, 88n4, 123–24

Hall, Sheldon, 122
Halloween (1978), 12n4, 21–22, 24, 26, 28, 30–33, 35, 45–46, 48, 52, 71n17, 76, 77n23, 79, 88–89, 92n7, 122, 123, 125, 138
Halloween (2007), 41–42, 148
Halloween: Resurrection, 40–41, 119
Halloween: The Curse of Michael Myers, 37–38
Halloween H20, 39
Halloween II (1981), 31–32, 35, 39
Halloween II (2009), 42
Halloween 4: The Return of Michael Myers, 35
Halloween 5: The Revenge of Michael Myers, 35, 119
Happy Birthday to Me, 24, 31–32, 76
Harrington, Richard, 157

Harry Potter and the Philosopher's Stone, 120, 164
Heavenly Creatures, 163
Hedden, Rob, 110, 182
Heffernan, Kevin, 45–46, 53, 122n6
Hell Night, 24, 31–32, 76
Henry: Portrait of a Serial Killer, 34, 58
Hills Have Eyes, The (1977), 42
Hills Have Eyes, The (2006), 41–42
Hills Have Eyes II, The, 42
historical poetics, 5–6, 177
Hitchcock, Alfred, 11, 19–20, 27, 31, 170
Hitcher, The, 41–42
House, 33
House of Wax (1953), 53
House of Wax (2005), 173–74
Howling, The, 122
Humphries, Reynold, 26, 49–50, 65
Hurt Locker, The, 170

I Know What You Did Last Summer, 39
I Still Know What You Did Last Summer, 39
Invisible Man, The, 84
Isaac, Jim, 138, 183

James, Caryn, 33n17, 157
Jameson, Fredric, 138, 148–49
Jason Goes to Hell: The Final Friday, 28–29, 30, 34, 36–37, 38, 59–60, 62, 72, 78, 80n28, 110–11, 112, 117, 122n6, 125, 128n8, 135–37, 141, 142, 156, 169, 182–83, 193–94
Jason Lives! Friday the 13th Part VI, 30, 33, 67–70, 77–78, 104–6, 107, 108–9, 116–17, 128n8, 132, 133, 135, 144–46, 160, 166, 181–82, 190–91
Jason X, 28–29, 30, 40, 42, 60–62, 72, 76, 78–79, 80, 111–12, 122n6, 125n9, 128n8, 137–39, 140, 142, 156, 168, 183–84, 194–96
Jaws, 192
Jigsaw, 84
Jones, Steve, 43n32
Joy Ride, 39

Kerswell, J. A., 36, 40n27, 156
King, Stephen, 33n17, 129–30
Koven, Mikel, 21n8, 89n6, 130
Kurz, Ron, 125

Lady in the Lake, 19
Last House on the Left, The, 46
Last Laugh, The, 19
Leitch, Thomas, 138
Leprechaun, 37
Lord of the Rings, The: The Fellowship of the Ring, 163–69
Lord of the Rings, The: The Return of the King, 163–69
Lord of the Rings, The: The Two Towers, 163–69

Mad Love, 88
Maniac, 24
Maniac Cop 3: Badge of Silence, 37
Marcus, Adam, 182
Martin, Bob, 48, 124
Mathijs, Ernest, 163n9
McDonald, Paul, 158
McLoughlin, Tom, 69–70, 181
Meet the Feebles, 163
metanarrativity, 38–41, 138, 141
Miller, Victor, 30–31, 45, 125
Miner, Steve, 32, 33, 45, 53–56, 66, 76–77, 102–3, 125, 180
Minority Report, 150n18
Mittell, Jason, 120
Morris, Jeremy, 43n33
Muir, John Kenneth, 38n25
Munich, 150n18
My Bloody Valentine, 22, 24, 76, 77n23, 89n6
My Bloody Valentine 3-D, 41–42

Neale, Stephen, 81, 121
neoformalism. *See* formalism
Newman, Kim, 156
Nightmare on Elm Street, A (1984), 11, 29–30, 32–42, 120, 122, 138–41, 183
Nightmare on Elm Street, A (2010), 41–42
Nightmare on Elm Street Part 2, A: Freddy's Revenge, 33–34
Nightmare on Elm Street Part 4, A: The Dream Master, 34
Nightmare on Elm Street Part 5, A: The Dream Child, 36
Nispel, Marcus, 64, 79, 107, 184
North by Northwest, 19–20

Nosferatu (*Nosferatu, Eine Symphonie des Grauens*), 14–19
nostalgia, 148–51
Notorious, 19–20
Nowell, Richard, 31n13, 122n6, 124–25, 156

Oscars. *See* Academy Awards
Opera, 37

Pally, Marcia, 19
Peeping Tom, 58
Perkins, V. F., 177
Pieces, 32
Platoon, 158–60, 163
Poltergeist, 32, 120n3
Poltergeist II: The Other Side, 33
postmodern(ism). *See* metanarrativity
Prom Night (1980), 31–32, 89n6
Prom Night (2008), 41–42
Psycho (1960), 10–11, 20–21, 31, 39, 46, 47, 88
Psycho (1998), 41
Psycho III, 132
Pulleine, Tom, 125
Pulp Fiction, 103n12, 163

Quarantine, 173, 175

Raging Bull, 86
Ray, Robert B., 121–22
[Rec], 173–75
Reichardt, Sarah, 88
Rockoff, Adam, 37

sadism, 26–27, 50, 51, 80, 123n8, 193
Saving Private Ryan, 150n18, 163
Savini, Tom, 31–32, 89
Saw, 84, 87–88
Saw II, 84
Saw III, 84
Saw 3-D, 84
Saw IV, 84
Saw V, 84
Saw VI, 84
Scream, 38–40, 138
Scream 2, 38–39
Scream 3, 39–40

self-reflexivity/self-referentiality. *See* metanarrativity
Shaviro, Steven, 4–5, 94n8
Shklovsky, Viktor, 5
Silence of the Lambs, The, 170–76
Sipos, Thomas M., 53
"Sister Christian," 150–51
Slumber Party Massacre, The, 10, 32
Sontag, Susan, 5–6
Sorority House Massacre, 33, 34
sound effects, 86–89, 91–93, 96, 99, 104, 108, 111
Sprague, Mike, 29
Stepfather, The, 34
Steinmann, Danny, 181
Stilwell, Robynn J., 84
Suspiria, 89, 102, 161

Tenebrae, 37
Terror Train, 10, 31, 39, 76, 89n6
Texas Chain Saw Massacre, The, 23, 31, 89–91, 147n17, 165, 171
Texas Chainsaw Massacre, The, 41, 42, 64, 147n17
Texas Chainsaw Massacre, The: The Beginning, 42
Texas Chainsaw Massacre 2, The, 33, 34
Thing, The, 32
Thompson, Kristin, 5
Thompson, Roy, 85
"Thriller," 32n14
Toolbox Murders, The, 31
trailers (film), 126, 131–33, 147n16, 165–66
Trauma, 37
Triumph of the Will (*Triumph Des Willens*), 154
Troll, 33
Tudor, Andrew, 122
Twitch of the Death Nerve, 22–23, 30, 46–47, 123–24

Urban Legend, 39
Urban Legends: Final Cut, 39, 40

Valentine, 39
Verevis, Constantine, 125, 146–47, 148

Vertigo, 19
Vertov, Dziga, 12n5, 154
video game, xii, 61–63, 154
viscerality, 4–5, 53, 54, 56, 62, 64, 70, 74, 78, 80, 83–84, 94, 96–97, 99–100, 107, 117, 124, 159
visual effects, 31–32, 40, 53, 56, 117

Wes Craven's New Nightmare, 38
Wharton, Sarah, 41–42, 148
When a Stranger Calls, 34, 37, 77n23
When a Stranger Calls Back, 37
Wierzbicki, James, 87–88
Wolf Man, The, 19
Wood, Robin, 12n4, 26–27, 28, 47, 49–50, 156

Yankee Doodle Dandy, 154
Yu, Ronny, 74–75, 79, 139, 140, 184

Zanger, Anant, 119–20
Zito, Joseph, 99, 180

About the author

Photo credit: 2016, James Taylor-Mémé

Wickham Clayton is a lecturer in film production at the University for the Creative Arts in Farnham, UK. He is coeditor of *Screening Twilight: Critical Approaches to a Cinematic Phenomenon* and editor of *Style and Form in the Hollywood Slasher Film* and *The Bible Onscreen in the New Millennium: New Heart and New Spirit*. This is the first book he's written by himself.

www.ingramcontent.com/pod-product-compliance
Lightning Source LLC
Chambersburg PA
CBHW030621230426
43661CB00053B/2092